EXPLORING THE
UNIX
SYSTEM

HAYDEN BOOKS UNIX® System Library

Topics in C Programming
Stephen G. Kochan and Patrick H. Wood

UNIX® Networking
Stephen G. Kochan and Patrick H. Wood, Editors

UNIX® Shell Programming
Stephen G. Kochan and Patrick H. Wood

UNIX® System Security
Patrick H. Wood and Stephen G. Kochan

UNIX® Text Processing
Dale Dougherty and Tim O'Reilly

Exploring the UNIX® System, Second Edition
Stephen G. Kochan and Patrick H. Wood

UNIX® System Administration
David Fiedler and Bruce H. Hunter

RELATED TITLES

Waite Group

The Waite Group's UNIX® Communications
Bart Anderson, Bryan Costales, Harry Henderson

The Waite Group's UNIX® Primer Plus
Mitchell Waite, Donald Martin, Stephen Prata

The Waite Group's UNIX® System V Primer, Revised Edition
Mitchell Waite, Donald Martin, Stephen Prata

The Waite Group's Tricks of the UNIX® Masters
Russell G. Sage

The Waite Group's UNIX® Papers
The Waite Group

The Waite Group's UNIX® System V Bible
Stephen Prata and Donald Martin

The Waite Group's Advanced UNIX®—A Programmer's Guide
Stephen Prata

The Waite Group's Inside XENIX®
Christopher L. Morgan

---

*For the retailer nearest you, or to order directly from the publisher,
call 800-428-SAMS. In Indiana, Alaska, and Hawaii call 317-298-5699.*

EXPLORING THE
UNIX
SYSTEM

STEPHEN G. KOCHAN AND PATRICK H. WOOD

Pipeline Associates, Inc.

HAYDEN BOOKS

A Division of Macmillan Computer Publishing

11711 North College, Carmel, Indiana 46032 USA

SECOND EDITION
FIFTH PRINTING — 1991

International Standard Book Number: 0-672-48447-1
Library of Congress Catalog Card Number: 89-60588

Acquisitions Editor: *Scott Arant*
Cover Art: *RTS Color Graphics*
Typesetting: *Pipeline Associates, Inc.*

This entire text was edited and processed under UNIX. The text was formatted using `troff`, with the assistance of `tbl` for the tables and MacDraw for the figures. The `troff` output was converted to PostScript using `devps`. The camera ready copy was printed on an Apple LaserWriter Plus, with no pasteup required.

Printed in the United States of America

Trademark Acknowledgements

Hayden Books
UNIX
Library

The UNIX System Library is an integrated series of books covering basic to advanced topics related to the UNIX system. The books are written under the direction of Stephen G. Kochan and Patrick H. Wood, who worked for several years teaching introductory and advanced UNIX courses, and who themselves have written many books on the C programming language and the UNIX system.

The first title in the UNIX series is *Exploring the UNIX System*. The text introduces the new user to the UNIX system, covering things such as logging on, working with the file system, editing files with the `vi` editor, writing simple shell programs, and formatting documents. Also included in this text are descriptions of how to use electronic mail and networks and how to administrate a UNIX system.

UNIX Shell Programming uses a clear, step-by-step approach to teach all the features of the shell and shows the reader how to write programs using many actual examples. Also covered are tools used by many shell programmers, such as `grep`, `sed`, `tr`, `cut`, and `sort`, and a detailed discussion on how to write regular expressions. The newer Korn shell is also covered in detail in the book.

UNIX Text Processing gives a comprehensive treatment of the many tools that are available for formatting documents under UNIX. The book shows how `troff` can be used to format simple documents like letters and also how to exploit its capabilities to format larger documents like manuals and books. The text shows how to use the popular `mm` and `ms` macro packages and how to write custom macro packages.

UNIX System Administration is an essential guide to administration for anyone who owns or operates a UNIX system. The text describes how to set up file systems, make backups, configure a system, connect peripheral devices, install and administrate UUCP, work with the line printer spooler, and write shell programs to help make the administration process more manageable.

UNIX System Security is the only text devoted specifically to this important topic. Security for users, programmers, and administrators is covered in detail, as is network security. Source code listings for many useful security-related programs are given at the end of the book.

UNIX System Networking contains practical discussions of several important UNIX networking systems including UUCP, TCP/IP, NFS, RFS, Streams, and LAN Manager/X. Each chapter is written by a noted expert in the field of UNIX networking.

To my wife, Leela
                    S.G.K.

To my mother
                    P.H.W.

C O N T E N T S

P R E F A C E

to the Revised Edition

Since the introduction of *Exploring the UNIX System* in 1984, the UNIX system has undergone many changes, some minor and some major. Standards committees have worked out most of the differences between the major UNIX variants, and several vendors of different UNIX versions (most notably, AT&T, Sun, The Santa Cruz Organization, and Microsoft) have agreed to reduce or eliminate the differences between their products. New networking support for UNIX has appeared over the past five years, and UNIX is now available for a variety of small, modestly-priced hardware platforms.

Most of these differences aren't noticeable to new users, since the basic commands on UNIX haven't changed much for over ten years; however, advanced users and system administrators have seen UNIX undergo profound changes. The changes in *Exploring the UNIX System, Revised Edition* are also subtle in some chapters and major in others.

Chapters 1 through 4 and 7 through 11 contain mostly minor, cosmetic changes; Chapters 5 and 6 discuss some features of newer versions of the Bourne shell and the Korn shell; and Chapter 12 has been changed to address new system software, file system organization, new networking software, and small UNIX systems. The Appendices have also changed. Back in 1984, there was a dearth of information on UNIX from sources outside academia; now there are so many places you can go for more information on UNIX that Appendix A lists only the most important or useful sources.

Since the first edition was written, the Hayden Books *UNIX System Library* and Hayden Books *C Library* grew to over ten books. Throughout this book, references for more information are made to the appropriate books in the series. All the books in both series are listed in Appendix A.

We would like to thank the following people for their help and suggestions: Sallie Johnson, Barbara Swingle, Irene Peterson, Anthony Iannino, Jo Anne Brown, John Kolb, Ed Lipinski, Charles Leiwant, John Musa, Dick Duane, Dick Fritz, and Mikie Wood. We would also like to thank the following people from Hayden Book Company: Douglas McCormick, Juliann Colvin, Maureen Connelly, and Jono Hardjo.

We would like to thank the following people for their help on the second edition: David Korn, Steven Levy, Phil Kennedy, Wendy Ford, and Scott Arant.

1

Introduction

The UNIX[†] operating system was pioneered by Ken Thompson and Dennis Ritchie at Bell Laboratories in the late 1960s. One of the primary goals in the design of this operating system was to create an environment that promoted efficient program development. Also important was that the operating system be small and memory efficient, also that it be easy to maintain.

Historically, operating systems were developed with a specific computer model in mind. For example, IBM's VM and CMS operating systems were designed for IBM's 360 and 370 computer line, Digital Research's CP/M for the Intel 8080, MS-DOS for the Intel 8086, and so on. Because each computer system has it own operating system, using a different computer entails undergoing an extensive relearning process. Simple procedures such as getting onto the system, copying a file, editing a file or even finding out the time are different from one to another. Application programs that you are accustomed to using may not even be available on a new system. Even your own programs may not run under another operating system without a significant amount of rework—or they may not run at all if they were developed in a programming language that's not supported under the new operating system.

And then along came the UNIX system. While the first UNIX system *was* developed with a particular computer system in mind (the DEC PDP-7), a version was developed shortly thereafter that could be easily transferred ("ported") to different computer systems. This was accomplished by designing the operating system without making many assumptions about the particular architecture of the computer and also by writing most of the operating system in the higher-level programming language C.

Today the UNIX system can be found running on a multitude of computer systems, ranging from small personal computers to large mainframe systems. This large diversity makes it easier on programmers and users: a programmer can expect the same programming tools and environment on any system that runs UNIX and can write programs to run *without modification* on any computer running UNIX; a user can learn one set of procedures and commands that can be

---

[†] UNIX is a trademark of AT&T Bell Laboratories.

used on any UNIX system.

This book proposes to teach you how to use the UNIX system—from typing in basic commands to administrating a small system.

The first thing you have to learn is just what an operating system is. After all, it doesn't do much good to learn about the UNIX "operating system" without knowing the meaning of these words. Chapter 2 serves this purpose by introducing you to operating systems and the types of functions they provide.

Since one of the most important features of the UNIX system is its *file system*, we decided to devote a separate chapter to it early in the book. Chapter 3 teaches the organization of the UNIX file system and the method that is used to identify files.

Chapter 4 is titled "Getting Started," and, as its name implies, teaches you how to get onto the computer, perform some simple functions, and then get off. You'll learn how to create, copy, rename, and remove files, and how to create your own file *directories* and work with them. This chapter also provides a short tutorial introduction to the text editor ed.

In Chapter 5, you are shown how to start putting the UNIX system to work for you. New commands are introduced, and two of the key concepts of the UNIX system, *I/O redirection* and *pipes*, are taught. By the end of this chapter you will have a good working knowledge of the UNIX system and an appreciation of its power.

Chapter 6 introduces the program that interprets everything you type in at the terminal: the *shell*. The shell also has its own built-in programming language. The primary purpose of this chapter is to introduce you to this language. You'll learn how you can effectively customize UNIX commands to your own liking, as well as develop your own commands.

Chapter 7 provides a tutorial introduction to the vi screen editor. This editor makes it easy to edit files on video terminals by allowing you to work with your files a "screenful" at a time.

Chapter 8 shows the usefulness of the UNIX system in an office environment. Among the topics covered are the *electronic mail* facilities and how to use the word processing packages to format documents.

Chapter 9 gives an overview of how to use the UNIX system for program development. The various tools and languages that are available for the programmer are described.

One of the most important aspects of any computer system is how secure it is. Until recently, however, this topic was not given much attention. Chapter 10 explains how you, the user, can ensure that no one tampers with your files or gains access to your account. This is done by giving you an overview of the security designed into the system and the commands you can use to make things more secure. As you will see, the UNIX system is by design a very secure system, but it needs your cooperation to guarantee this security.

In Chapter 11 the topic of communications is covered. This includes intrasystem as well as intersystem communications. As you'll see, the UNIX system provides many commands that make it simple to send data over a network.

The last chapter, Chapter 12, was written for new UNIX system owners and administrators. It explains how to start up a system, how to ensure security at the system level, how to add new users to the system, and so on. If you have just purchased a small UNIX system or are about to, then you should find this chapter particularly helpful.

We have included a complete command summary in Appendix C. Also included in the appendices are a list of references and some tables that you may find useful.

Since every reader will probably have different intended uses of the UNIX system, we have included Table 1-1. If you find a description of your interest in the first column, then in the second column you'll find a list of chapters you may want to read. Those chapters not listed in either column should be skimmed at the very least to get a good overview of the features and capabilities of the system. Of course, there's no harm to be served by thoroughly reading all chapters.

TABLE 1-1. How to read this book

If you're interested in	Then read these chapters	And optionally read chapters
Turning your system on	2,12 (first half)	
Word processing	3-5,7,8	6
Office automation	3-5,7,8	6
Program development	2-7,9	8,10,11
System administration	2-6,10-12	7-9
Running application programs	3-4	5,7,8
Don't know	2-5	Whatever interests you

If you have access to a UNIX system, you should try the examples at your terminal as you read through the text . And don't be afraid to experiment! The best way to learn about the UNIX system is by actually using it.

One last point about the philosophy of this book. It would be impossible to teach you every command and every option available in the UNIX system; such a treatment would fill several volumes. Our main goals here are to get you started, to give you a good overview of what's available, and primarily to teach the UNIX philosophy. This phlosophy preaches the doctrine that "small is beautiful." The UNIX user is provided with a vast assortment of commands that perform small, well-defined functions and the tools necessary to combine these commands to perform more sophisticated functions. If you are a programmer, then you will realize that this same principle forms the foundation of the structured programming discipline.

And now, welcome to the UNIX world!

What Is an Operating System?

An *operating system* is a collection of programs that coordinates the operation of computer hardware and software. It usually provides the functions depicted in Fig. 2-1.

Fig. 2-1. Operating system functions

Input/output

Input and output or (I/O) is essential to the operation of any computer. I/O allows the computer to store and retrieve data on disks or tapes, to interact with the users' terminals, and to print output on paper. Every operating system must provide some form of I/O.

Command interpreter

The command interpreter reads the commands a user types in at a terminal and changes, or *interprets*, them into instructions the computer can understand. Command interpreters vary widely from one operating system to another, but again, it's something that almost every one provides.

Data management

Data management allows the users to organize their data into logical groupings called *files*. Although not all operating systems provide data management, the few that don't are severely limited in their flexibility and usefulness.

Program development tools

Program development tools assist users in writing and maintaining programs. Compilers, assemblers, debuggers, and software maintenance systems fall into this category.

Time-sharing

Time-sharing is a way of allowing several people to run programs on different terminals at the same time. This feature is usually found only on larger operating systems.

Security

Security protects one user from another and the operating system from all users. Its main function is to make sure only authorized users access the computer and its data and that users do only things they are authorized to do. Most operating systems that don't have time-sharing have little or no security, since only one user is involved. Most large operating systems provide some measure of security, but the degree varies from one system to another.

Communication

Communication refers to the ability of one computer to communicate with other computers and terminals to transfer programs and/or data.

Accounting

Accounting keeps track of what each person has done on a computer in order to bill each one for the resources used. This is necessary on computers that have many users who must be charged for their use of the machine.

The UNIX operating system provides all of these functions.

♦ The UNIX Operating System ♦

The UNIX operating system can be broken down into three basic components: the *scheduler*, the *file system*, and the *shell*. In this chapter, we will discuss the scheduler in detail and touch lightly on the shell. Chapter 3 covers the file system, and Chapters 4 through 6 cover the shell more fully.

The UNIX Scheduler

The UNIX scheduler is a program that allows more than one person to use the computer at the same time. The scheduler shares computer resources among these users, allowing each a small *slice* of the computer's processor. As mentioned before, this concept is known as *time-sharing*.

For example, suppose three people want to run different programs, *a*, *b*, and *c*. The scheduler copies these three programs from the disk that stores programs into the computer's memory. In the UNIX system, these copies in memory are referred to as *processes*; in this way we make the distinction between a *program* that is kept in a file on the disk and a *process* that is in memory doing things.

The scheduler allows process *a* to run for a few hundreths (or less) of a second and do a little of the work it was designed to do. After this *time slice* is over, process *a* is temporarily stopped, or *suspended*, and process *b* is allowed to run. Later, when process *b*'s time slice is over process *c* gets its chance to run (see Fig. 2-2).

When each process has had a chance to run a while, the scheduler comes back to process *a*. It doesn't start *a* over at the beginning; instead, it starts *a* where it left off when it was suspended at the end of its time slice. In this way, the scheduler allows each process to work its way to completion, a little bit at a time.

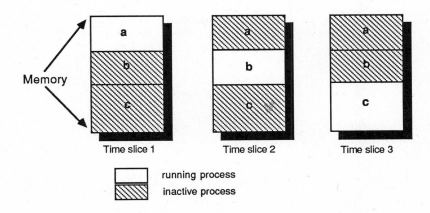

	running process	
	inactive process	

Fig. 2-2. Time slices

Most time-sharing systems allow many more than three processes to run at the same time; in fact, the UNIX scheduler can keep track of several hundred processes. It also allows each user to effectively run more than one process at a time.

Due to the high speed of computers, the overall effect of time-sharing is to give the users the impression they are all being served simultaneously, even though the scheduler actually serves them one at a time.

Swapping and Paging

This simple model of scheduling works fine at first, but sooner or later, all of the computer's memory gets filled with running processes. At this point, if a user wants to run a new program, the scheduler must find a way to fit it in.

This brings up the concept of *swapping*. When memory is full and a new program needs to be run, the scheduler takes a process in memory and copies it to a disk. The scheduler then places the new program in memory (creating a new process) and allows it to run. Later, the process copied to disk is swapped with one of the processes in memory. That is, the process in memory is copied to disk, and the process on the disk is copied back into memory.

For example, let's say there are three processes, *a, b,* and *c.* Now a request is made by a user to run program *d*:

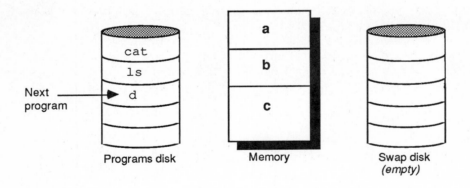

Fig. 2-3. New program *d*

Since there is no room left in memory for process *d*, process *a* is copied to the disk.

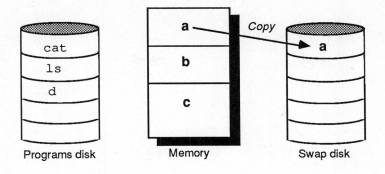

Fig. 2-4. Copy *a* to swap disk

After *a* is copied to the disk, a copy of *d* is then put in memory where *a* was.

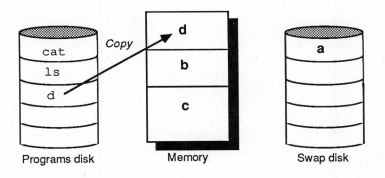

Fig. 2-5. Copy *d* to memory

After a few time slices, the scheduler will swap process *a* back into memory, usually exchanging it with the process that has been in memory the longest. Let's assume that *a* will be swapped with *b*. First, *b* must be copied to the disk.

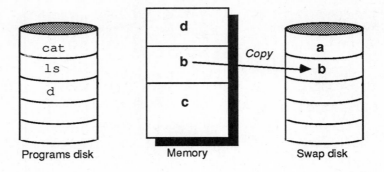

Fig. 2-6. Copy *b* to swap disk

Then *a* is copied back into memory.

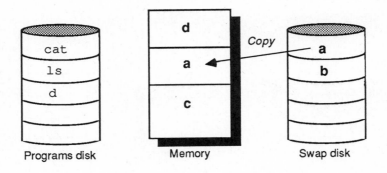

Fig. 2-7. Copy *a* to memory

This method of copying processes to and from disk and memory continues as long as there is not enough room for all of the processes to fit in memory at the same time. Of course, this example is very simple compared to the actual operation of the UNIX scheduler. It must handle hundreds of processes of all different sizes, of which only thirty or forty might fit into memory at one time.

These days, most UNIX systems employ a mechanism called *paging* instead of swapping. Paging is very similar to swapping, except only parts of a program (the *pages*) are copied to and from disk. Pages are fixed in size, usually 2,048 or 4,096 bytes. When memory is needed, a page is swapped to disk, freeing up that portion of memory. Later, when that page is needed by the program using it, it is swapped back into memory, possibly causing another page to be swapped out. Although more complex than swapping, paging is more efficient, as only small pieces of a program need be moved to disk when memory is required. Also, if a large program only uses a small amount of its memory most of the time, only the most-used portions spend any appreciable time occupying valuable main memory

The UNIX Shell

The shell is the UNIX system's command interpreter. It is a program that reads the lines you type in at a terminal and performs various operations depending on what you type in. The shell is the part of the UNIX system that sits between you and the "guts" of the system, forming a shell around the computer that is relatively consistent in its outward appearance. It attempts to convert your rantings and ravings into instructions that the computer can understand and act on.

Everyone on a UNIX system has his or her own copy of the shell program. So each user can do things without bothering or being bothered by other users. We'll talk more about the shell and the shell's environment in the next several chapters.

3

The UNIX File System

In this chapter you will learn about one of the most fundamental elements of the UNIX system–the *file system*.

◆ Files ◆

In its simplest form, a file system is a collection of *files* stored on a storage device, usually a *disk*. There are many different types of disks–floppy disks, hard disks, Winchester disks, and so on–and the most distinguishing qualities among them is the amount of information they can contain (their *storage capacity*) and the average amount of time it takes to retrieve information from them (their *access speed*).

As you can see from Fig. 3-1, there are two main types of storage on a computer system: *primary* and *secondary* storage.

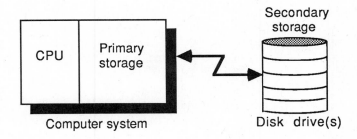

Fig. 3-1. Primary and secondary storage

Primary storage is the computer's memory. Secondary storage is the computer's disk. The computer can only execute programs or manipulate data that are in primary storage. Since the amount of secondary storage usually far exceeds the amount of primary storage on a particular system, programs and data are stored on the secondary storage device and are transferred to the computer's primary storage only as necessary. As mentioned in the previous chapter, this function is handled automatically by the operating system.

Whenever data is to be stored onto the disk from the primary storage, it is recorded onto a particular section of the disk, just as a song is recorded onto a particular section of a record. (But unlike a record, the information on the disk can later be recorded over if desired.) And just as a song has a title, so does a file. This title, called the *file name*, uniquely identifies particular information stored on the disk. You can have many files on the disk, just so long as they each have different names. You need be concerned only with the file's name. The operating system keeps track of all sorts of other information, such as who the file's owner is, when the file was last modified, precisely where on the disk it is located, and how large it is. This last piece of information is expressed in the number of *bytes* (or characters) of data contained in the file.

◆ File Directories ◆

File directories enable you to organize files in a logical and structured fashion. This type of organization has many analogies to everyday life; a recipe file is one of them. Recipe files are usually divided into catgories such as "Appetizers," "Entrees," and "Desserts." Under each category are stored all of the recipes of the particular type. So your recipe file might be organized as depicted in Fig. 3-2. Whenever you wanted to make a particular dessert, for example, you would simply turn to the recipe file and scan through the recipes filed under "Desserts." Or if you didn't know which dessert to make, you could simply thumb through all of the dessert recipes without having to sift through the appetizer and entree recipes. Obviously, a system of this type saves time since recipes are easier to find as well as to add. And if your recipe file were very large, you might even consider creating subcategories. For example, you might subcategorize "Entrees" into "Meat," "Poultry," and "Fish" recipes.

To make the analogy between the recipe file and the UNIX file system, think of the box that contains the recipes as the disk, the various categories and subcategories as file directories, and the recipes themselves as data files.

Suppose you had a set of files consisting of various memos, proposals, and letters. Further suppose that you had a set of files that were computer programs. It would seem logical to group this first set of files into a directory called `documents`, for example, and the latter set of files into a directory called `programs`. Such a directory organization is illustrated in Fig. 3-3.

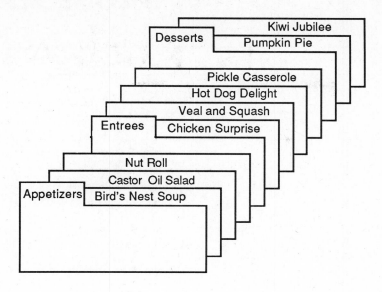

Fig. 3-2. Organization of a recipe file

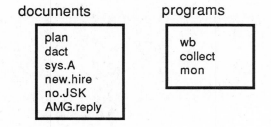

Fig. 3-3. Example directory structure

Here the files are divided into two categories: documents and programs. As mentioned, these categories are known as file directories under the UNIX system. So the file directory documents contains the files plan, dact, sys.A, new.hire, no.JSK, and AMG.reply. The directory programs contains the files wb, collect, and mon.

At some point you may decide to further categorize the files in a directory. This can be done by creating subdirectories and then placing each file into the appropriate subdirectory. For example, you might wish to create subdirectories called memos, proposals, and letters inside your documents directory. This is depicted in Fig. 3-4.

documents

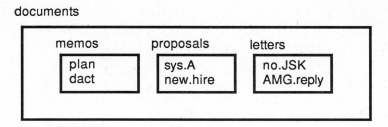

Fig. 3-4. Directories containing subdirectories

Here, the file directory named `documents` contains the subdirectories `memos`, `proposals`, and `letters`. These subdirectories in turn presumably contain files of the particular document type.

The file directory structure depicted in Fig. 3-4 is more precisely known as a *hierarchical* directory structure (since it is organized in levels) and is one of the most distinguishing qualities of the UNIX system. Perhaps the structure of the `documents` directory is clearer if conceptualized as in Fig. 3-5.

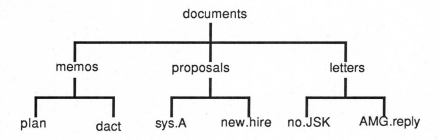

Fig. 3-5. Hierarchical directory structure

`documents` is at top of this directory hierarchy. It contains the subdirectories `memos`, and `letters`. Each of these subdirectories in turn contains two files: `memos` contains `plan` and `dact`; `proposals` contains `sys.A` and `new.hire`; and `letters` contains `no.JSK` and `AMG.reply`.

Let's now take a look at the directory structure with the `programs` directory included. As you will recall, the files `wb`, `collect`, and `mon` were placed in that directory. Figure 3-6 shows the overall directory structure.

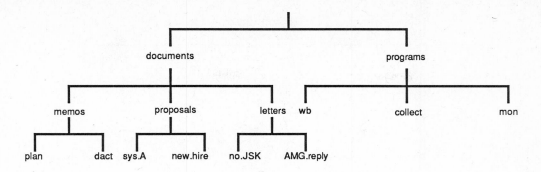

Fig. 3-6. Hierarchical directory structure

(We have illustrated the documents and programs directories as if they them-selves belong to a higher-level directory. As you shall see shortly, this is indeed most likely the case.) While each file in a given directory must have a unique name, files contained in different directories do not. So, for example, you could have a file in your programs directory called dact, even though there also exists a file by that name in the memos subdirectory.

The HOME Directory and Path Names

The UNIX system always associates each user of the system with a particular directory. When you log into the home system, you are placed automatically into a directory called your HOME directory. This directory was assigned to you by the system administrator when your account was created on the system.

On my system, my HOME directory is called steve. In fact, this directory is actually a subdirectory of a directory called al. Therefore, if I had the direc-tories documents and programs as illustrated in Fig. 3-6, my directory would actually look something like this:

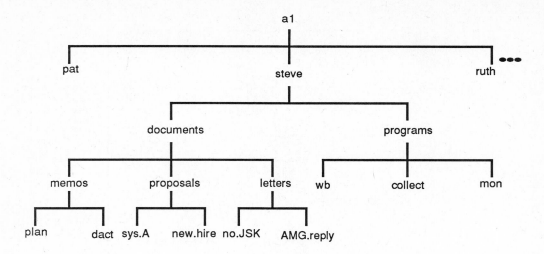

Fig. 3-7. File system a1

Since a1 is at the top of the directory structure, it is known as the root. The root directory and all associated subdirectories are collectively called a file system. Therefore, the file system depicted in Fig. 3-7 would be called a1.

Whenever you are "inside" a particular directory (called your *current working* directory), the files contained within that directory are immediately accessible. If you wish to access a file from another directory, then you can either first issue a command to "change" to the appropriate directory and then access the particular file, or you can specify the particular file by its *path name*.

A path name enables you to uniquely identify a particular file to the UNIX system. In the specification of a path name, successive directories along the path are separated by the slash character /. A path name that *begins* with a slash character is known as a *full* path name, since it specifies a complete path from the root. So, for example, the path name /a1/steve identifies the directory steve contained in the a1 file system. Similarly, the path name /a1/steve/documents references the directory documents as contained in the directory steve under the a1 file system. As a final example, the path name /a1/steve/documents/letters/AMG.reply identifies the file AMG.reply contained along the appropriate directory path.

In order to help reduce some of the typing that would otherwise be required, UNIX provides certain notational conveniences and also does not require that a full path name be specified. Path names that do not begin with a slash character are known as *relative* path names. The path is relative to your current working directory. For example, if I just logged into the system and was placed into my HOME directory /a1/steve, then I could directly reference the directory documents simply by typing documents. Similarly, the relative path name programs/mon could be typed to access the file mon contained inside my programs directory.

By convention, the directory name .. always references the directory that is one level higher. For example, after logging in and being placed into my HOME directory /a1/steve, the path name .. would reference the directory a1. And if I had issued the appropriate command to change my working directory to documents/letters, then the path name .. would reference the documents directory, ../.. would reference the directory steve, and ../proposals/new.hire would reference the file new.hire contained in the proposals directory. Note that in this case, as in most cases, there is usually more than one way to specify a path to a particular file. Usually, you'll want to use the one that requires the least amount of typing. The following table shows some examples of ways to reference the directory memos depending on your current directory.

TABLE 3-1. Path names to memos

Current directory	Path to memos
/a1	steve/documents/memos
/a1/steve	documents/memos
/a1/steve/documents	memos
/a1/steve/documents/letters	../memos
/a1/steve/programs	../documents/memos

Another notational convention is the single period ., which always refers to the current directory. You will see in later chapters of this book how this notation is used.

◆ File Types ◆

Since files can be used to contain all sorts of information, most operating systems usually associate a *type* with a file. For example, on many systems a file that contains human readable information (e.g. text information) is usually distinguished from a file that contains machine executable instructions. The UNIX system makes no such distinction on file types. In fact, under UNIX there are only three different types of files: *directory* files, *ordinary* files, and *special* files. You have already seen the directory file. An ordinary file is just that: any file on the system that contains data, text, program instructions, or just about anything else. As its name implies, a special file has a special meaning to the UNIX system, and typically is associated with some form of I/O. For the most part, you need not be concerned with these special files–at least not now. These files will be discussed in more detail in later sections of this book.

This concludes the brief introduction to the UNIX file system. In the next chapter you will put this new knowledge to work and you will see the many commands for working efficiently with files that the UNIX system provides.

4

Getting Started

◆ Logging In ◆

The first thing you must learn in order to use a UNIX system is how to *log in*. This is the process by which you identify yourself to the system. When the UNIX system is ready for you to log in, it prints:[†]

```
login:
```

You respond to this *prompt* (request for information) by typing in your *user id* and then pressing the RETURN key. Your user id uniquely identifies you to the system and usually is supplied by a person who administrates the system (known as a *system administrator*).

For this example, the user id pat will be used:

```
login: pat
```

Note that **pat** is in **boldface type**; throughout the book boldface represents what you type in and regular type represents what the UNIX system types back. Also note that, unlike other systems you may have used, the UNIX system distinguishes upper and lowercase letters. Therefore the user id **pat** is not the same as the user id **Pat** or the user id **pAT**. (In fact, if you type in your user id in all capital letters then the UNIX system will assume you are using a terminal that does not support lowercase letters. From that point on, all messages will be displayed by the system in uppercase. If this happens to you, simultaneously press the keys labeled CTRL and d and start over again.)

---

† If your system is connected to a "network", you may have to issue some special commands before getting the *login:* prompt. Ask your system administrator for help.

After typing in your user id to the `login:` prompt, the UNIX system responds with:

```
Password:
```

This means that you are now to enter your *password*. Your password is a sequence of letters and digits that is used to verify to the UNIX system that you are allowed to use this user id. Your particular password may be selected by the system administrator, or you may have the option to select your own password when you request a computer account on the system. In either case, since the password is the *only* way the system knows that you are authorized to use your user id, you should not reveal it to anyone.

When you type in your password, it won't get printed on the screen. This is to protect your password from others who may be around your terminal while you are logging in.

```
login: pat
Password: wizard2
```

The password *wizard2* is shown in italics and in smaller typeface to emphasize that it will *not* be shown on the terminal screen. After typing in your password followed by RETURN, the UNIX system may print various messages. Often the date is printed, along with a "message of the day" that contains information that is of interest (sometimes) to the users.

Once you have successfully logged in, you can begin your work. The UNIX system will indicate that it is ready to accept your commands by displaying a dollar sign ($) as the first character on the line. This character is your *prompt character*. It will *always* be displayed when the system is waiting for you to enter a command.

```
login: pat
Password: wizard2

Sat Oct 29 14:40:52 EDT 1988

*** The system will be shutdown at 19:00 for PM ***

$
```

If you misspell your password when typing it in, the UNIX system will not log you in but instead will respond with `Login incorrect` and will print `login:` again.

```
login: pat
Password: wizrd2
Login incorrect
login:
```

If this should happen to you don't worry; just type in your user id and password again. Chances are you'll get it right the second time around.

Some Simple Commands

Now you are ready to type in a *command*. A command tells the UNIX system to do something. For example, the command date tells the system to print the date and time:

```
$ date
Sat Oct 29 14:40:52 EDT 1988
$
```

As you can see, the date command prints the day of the week, month, day, time (24 hour clock, eastern daylight time), and year.

Try typing in date followed by a RETURN at your terminal. A similar response should be displayed.

Note now that *every* UNIX command must be ended with a RETURN. RETURN informs the system that you are finished typing things in and are ready for the UNIX system to do its thing. Unless it is stated otherwise, you can assume that every line typed in is ended with a RETURN.

The who command can be used to get information about all users who are currently logged into the system:

```
$ who
pat    tty29 Oct 29 14:40
ruth   tty37 Oct 29 10:54
steve tty25 Oct 29 15:52
$
```

Here there are three users logged in, pat, ruth, and steve. Along with each user id, is listed the *tty* number of that user and the day and time that each user logged in. The tty number is just a unique identification number the UNIX system gives to each terminal.

The who command also can be used to get information about yourself:

```
$ who am i
pat    tty29 Oct 29 14:40
$
```

Instead of printing information about all users, who am i prints only information about you. In the latter case, the am and i are *arguments* to the who command. Arguments tell a command to do something different from what it normally does. The am i arguments to who are *optional*. If they are supplied, then the who command performs the special function described above.

You will see later that most UNIX commands will do slightly different things depending on what arguments are supplied.

Let's now take a look at another command called echo. The echo command is a very simple and straightforward command; it prints (or *echoes*) at the terminal whatever else you happen to type on the line:

```
$ echo hello, world
hello,  world
$
```

Try experimenting with the echo command on your terminal. Here are a few examples to show how it works.

```
$ echo this is a test
this is a test
$ echo why not print out a longer line with echo?
why not print out a longer line with echo?
$ echo
                                        A blank line is displayed
$ echo one          two     three          four  five
one two three four five
$
```

You will notice from the last example that echo squeezes out extra blanks between words. That's because on a UNIX system, it's the words that are important; the blanks are merely there to separate the words. Generally, the UNIX system ignores extra blanks.

Correcting Typos

Sometimes when typing something in at the terminal you will make a mistake. If you type in whom instead of who, you'll get something that looks like this:

```
$ whom
whom:  not  found
$
```

The message whom: not found means that the UNIX system couldn't find the command whom. There is a way to counteract "finger-failure" or typos. The UNIX system allows you to back up over typing errors: each time you type in a *number sign* '#', also known as the *pound* or *sharp* sign, a previously typed character is erased. For example, let's say you typed whom and realized you had made a mistake. *Before* typing the RETURN, you can type a # to erase the m in whom:

```
$ whom#
pat    tty29 Oct   29  14:40
ruth   tty37 Oct   29  10:54
steve  tty25 Oct   29  15:52
$
```

To the UNIX system, whom# is equivalent to who. A more complicated example follows:

```
$ echo  this  are###is an exm#ampll#e of the erse##ase
this is an example of the erase
```

Table 4-1 shows some more examples.

TABLE 4-1. Erase character examples

What you type	What the UNIX system "sees"
dateee##	date
whpo##o	who
ddte###ate	date
ddte###atee#	date
whhoom####o	who
eccho###ho	echo
#echo	echo

It's possible to change your erase character to something else. In fact, if the # doesn't work on your system chances are it's already been changed for you. Try the key labeled BACKSPACE instead. If that still doesn't work, ask your system administrator to tell you what the erase character is. At the end of Chapter 5, you'll see how you can change the erase character.

You can also erase, or *kill*, an entire line. If a line is so hopelessly messed up that erasing characters is more trouble than simply starting over, you can type in an *at sign* (@). This causes everything typed before the @ to be ignored and starts you on a new line (but does *not* display a new prompt).

```
$ date@
who
pat    tty29 Oct 29 14:40
ruth   tty37 Oct 29 10:54
steve  tty25 Oct 29 15:52
$
```

The Delete Key

On some systems there may be a lot of people logged in at the same time (sometimes as many as forty or fifty), so when you do a who you can get a lot of lines of output at your terminal. To avoid looking at all of that output, which can be annoying if you're using a slow terminal, you can just press the Delete key (labeled DEL or RUBOUT on most terminals). This will stop (or interrupt) the who command and bring back the $ to your terminal without listing the rest of the who command's output. In general the DEL key can be used to interrupt any command and bring back the prompt. You can even use the DEL instead of the @ to wipe out an incorrect command line. The only difference here is that using the DEL key will cause a new $ to be displayed, and the @ won't.

◆ Logging Off ◆

Once you've finished using the system, you can log off by simultaneously pressing the key labeled CTRL (for control) and the letter d. This key sequence will be denoted hereafter as CTRL-d in the text. You will notice that nothing gets displayed at the terminal when this key sequence is typed. However, this command is in fact recognized by the system. After CTRL-d is typed (and pressing the RETURN key in this case is not necessary), the system responds as it did when you first logged in—with a new login: message:

```
$ CTRL-d
login:
```

The new login: message indicates that you are no longer logged into the system. At this point, the terminal is available for use by another user.

The following example shows a sample session with a UNIX system.

```
login: pat
Password: wizard2

Sat Oct 29 16:34:33 EDT 1988

*** The system will be shutdown at 19:00 for PM ***
```

```
$ who
pat    tty29 Oct 29 16:34
ruth   tty37 Oct 29 10:54
steve  tty25 Oct 29 15:52
$ datet#
Sat Oct 29 16:34:47 EDT 1988
$ date@
who am i
pat    tty29 Oct 29 16:34
$ CTRL-d
login:
```

◆ Working with Files ◆

The UNIX system provides many tools that enable you to work easily with files. Among these tools are commands that enable you to create new files, copy files, remove files, move files between directories, examine the contents of files, and so on. In this section you will learn how to use some of these commands.

Listing Files: the `ls` Command

Whenever you log into a UNIX system you are automatically placed inside a special directory known as your HOME directory. Typically, this directory will be a unique directory that was created for you at the time you were given an account on the system. To see if you have any files stored in your directory, you can type the `ls` command:

```
$ ls
```

If your account has been newly created, then chances are that no files are stored in your directory. In such a case, you should just get back another prompt:

```
$ ls
$
```

The UNIX system is typically very terse in response to commands. (As you shall see later in this book, there is a reason for this.) Therefore, if no files are currently stored in your directory, the system does not display a message such as `No Files`, but instead simply displays *nothing*.

If there *are* some files in your directory, then the names of these files will be displayed, typically one per line, when the `ls` command is issued:

```
$ ls
READ_ME
rje
$
```

This output indicates that two files called `READ_ME` and `rje` are contained in the current directory.

In the sample command sessions that follow, assume that there are *no* files present in the HOME directory.

Creating and Examining Files

Let's create a file on the system. Call the file `names` and store the five names Susan, Jeff, Henry, Allan, and Ken inside the file. In order to create this file, type the following lines at your terminal, *exactly as they are shown*.

```
$ cat > names
Susan
Jeff
Henry
Allan
Ken
CTRL-d              CTRL and d keys pressed simultaneously
$
```

This sequence creates a file called `names` containing the five indicated names. Don't worry about the actual command used to create the file—it will be discussed shortly. Just in case you're wondering, a file name can be composed of just about any character directly available from the keyboard (and even some that aren't) provided the total number of characters contained in the name is not greater than 14.[†] If more than 14 characters are specified, the UNIX system simply ignores the extra characters. The following are all examples of valid file names:

```
print_data
Jul16.1955
123
a.out
X
```

---

† For AT&T UNIX System V Release 4 or later and Berkeley UNIX 4.2 or later, file names can be up to 255 characters in length.

Now that you have created a file, you can use the `ls` command to verify that the file does in fact exist:

```
$ ls
names
$
```

As you can see, the system lists the file `names` in response to the `ls` command. This tells you that contained inside your current directory is a single file called `names`. You can examine the *contents* of this file by using the `cat` command. The argument to the `cat` command is the name of the file whose contents you wish to examine.

```
$ cat names
Susan
Jeff
Henry
Allan
Ken
$
```

The command `cat names` results in the display of the five names at the terminal, thus verifying the contents of the `names` file.

Sorting the Contents of a File: the `sort` Command

Now that you have a file stored in your directory, you can begin to perform some basic operations on the file. For example, you can easily *sort* the contents of the file into alphabetical order using a command called `sort`. As with the `cat` command, the name of the file to be sorted must be specified:

```
$ sort names
Allan
Henry
Jeff
Ken
Susan
$
```

The sort command sorts the contents of the indicated file line by line and displays the result of the sort at the terminal. The original contents of the `names` file remains unchanged, as can be verified by executing the `cat` command once again:

```
$ cat names
Susan
Jeff
Henry
Allan
Ken
$
```

Counting the Number of Words in a File: the wc Command

Another command that gives some useful information about the contents of a file is the wc command. With this command, you can get a count of the total number of lines, words, and characters of information contained in a file. Once again, the name of the file is needed as the argument to the command:

```
$ wc names
    5       5      27       names
$
```

The wc command lists three numbers followed by the file name. The first number represents the number of lines contained in the file (5), the second the number of words contained in the file (in this case also 5), and the third the number of characters contained in the file (27). You will notice that a quick count of the characters contained in the five names Susan, Jeff, Henry, Allan, and Ken gives only 22 characters. That leaves you five characters short. Did the wc program goof? Hardly. The "missing" five characters are a result of the fact that at the end of each line of data in the file is stored a special "invisible" character called the *newline* character. This character is generated every time you press RETURN on your terminal keyboard. For example, when you typed the name Susan at the terminal and pressed the RETURN key, the characters 'S', 'u', 's', 'a', and 'n' followed immediately by the newline character were written into the file names. The same applied to each of the remaining four names that were entered.

Command Options

Suppose, you were interested in counting only the number of lines in a file. Well, you know that you can use the wc command to obtain this sort of information. Unfortunately, it seems as though if you want a count of the number of lines that you must also get a count of the number of characters and the number of words, since this is what the wc command reports. Is there any way to obtain just a count of the number of lines? The answer to this question is "yes," and the method involves the use of *command-line options*. Most UNIX commands allow the specification of options at the time that a command is executed. These options generally follow the same format:

−letter

That is, a command option is a minus sign followed immediately by a single letter. For example, in order to count just the number of lines contained in a file, the option −l (that's the letter l) is given to the wc command:

```
$ wc -l names
        5 names
$
```

This time you see that just the number of lines contained in the file is displayed. And as you might have guessed, to count just the number of characters in a file the −c option is specified:

```
$ wc -c names
       27 names
$
```

Finally, the command option −w can be used to count the number of words contained in the file:

```
$ wc -w names
        5 names
$
```

The sort command described earlier sorted the lines of data in a file in alphabetical order. But there is a wide assortment of options available with this command. For example, the −r option causes the sort to be performed in *reverse* order:

```
$ sort -r names
Susan
Ken
Jeff
Henry
Allan
$
```

Most UNIX commands are fussy about the ordering of options on the command line. That is, some commands require that the options be listed before the file name arguments. For example, the command sort names −r would be quite acceptable; however, the command wc names −l would not. Let's generalize by saying that *all* command options should *precede* file names on the command line.

Not only does the UNIX system provide a large number of commands, but each command typically has several different options. When a new command is introduced in this text, every option for that command will not be described. Teaching every option would not only double the size of this book, but would also leave you quite confused. It's much better for you to learn the basic function of the command first and then later explore its options as the need arises. In Section 1 of your *UNIX User's Manual* you will find each command listed with a description of all its options.

Making a Copy of a File: the cp Command

After you have worked with files for a short time, you will realize the need to be able to make a copy of a file. Once a copy of a file has been made, the original file can be modified without fear of loss of the original information. If the original information is ever required, then the file can simply be *restored* from the *backup* copy.

In order to make a copy of a file, the cp command is used. The first argument to the command is the name of the file to be copied (known as the *source file*), and the second argument is the name of the file to place the copy into (known as the *destination file*). You can make a copy of the file names and call it saved_names as follows:

```
$ cp names saved_names
$
```

Execution of this command causes the file named names to be copied into a file named saved_names. As with many UNIX commands, the fact that a command prompt was displayed after the cp command was typed indicates that the command was executed successfully. Of course, you can verify that the new file was in fact created by using the ls command:

```
$ ls
names
saved_names
$
```

And you can examine the contents of saved_names in the usual manner:

```
$ cat saved_names
Susan
Jeff
Henry
Allan
Ken
$
```

Renaming a File: the mv Command

You sometimes need to change the name of a file. This is accomplished easily with the mv command. The arguments to the mv command follow the same format as the cp command. The first argument is the name of the file to be renamed, and the second argument is the new name. So to change the name of the file saved_names to hold_it, for example, the following command would do the trick:

```
$ mv saved_names hold_it
$
```

Issuing the ls command will still result in the listing of two files, since you did not create a new file but simply renamed an old one:

```
$ ls
hold_it
names
$
```

It is worth noting that the ls command always lists your files in alphabetical order.

A word of caution when using the cp and mv commands: the UNIX system does not care whether the file specified as the second argument already exists. If it does, then in both cases the contents of the original file will be lost. So, for example, if a file called old_names exists, then executing the command cp names old_names would copy the file names to old_names, destroying the previous contents of old_names in the process. Similarly, the command mv names old_names would rename names to old_names, even if the file old_names existed prior to execution of the command. (There *is* a way to protect against this sort of thing, and you'll learn about it in Chapter 10.)

Removing a File: the rm Command

No system that enabled you to create files would be complete without a command that also allowed you to remove them. Under the UNIX system, this command is called rm. The argument to the rm command is simply the name of the file to be removed:

```
$ rm hold_it
$
```

This command removes the file `hold_it` from the current directory. The `ls` command will verify that the file has in fact been removed:

```
$ ls
names
$
```

As you can see you are now left with only one file in your directory: `names`.

You can remove more than one file at a time with the `rm` command by simply specifying all such files on the command line. For example, the following would remove the three files `wb`, `collect`, and `mon` from your current directory:

```
$ rm wb collect mon
$
```

While the `rm` command is conceptually one of the simplest UNIX commands, it should be noted that it is one of the most potentially dangerous. It is quite easy to accidentally remove *all* of your files with this command, which is why you must be careful when you use it.

Displaying and Printing Files

You have seen how the `cat` command is used to display a file at the terminal. So the command

```
cat names
```

would list the contents of `names`. This approach works fine for relatively small files. Most video terminals can display 24 lines of information, so if your file is larger than that and you try to `cat` it, all but the last 24 lines will "fly" right off the screen.

The UNIX system provides a program called `pg` that allows you to view your file a screenful at a time. The format of this command is simple enough:

pg file

where *file* is the name of the file you want to look at. The program automatically displays enough lines from the file to fill up your entire screen and then waits for you to type a key before continuing. This gives you as much time as you need to read the information on the screen. When you are ready to view the next "screenful," you simply press RETURN. After displaying the next screenful of data, the program once again waits for you to press RETURN. If you decide that you've seen enough, you can type in q instead to stop the display; otherwise, pressing RETURN will once again cause the next screenful to be displayed.

If you're not running UNIX System V Release 2 or later, then you won't have the `pg` program. However, chances are that you will have a program called `more` that performs the same function[†]. Unlike `pg`, `more` displays the next screenful from the file when you type a "space" and not RETURN. However, it too accepts a `q` as an indication that you've seen enough of the file.

If you want to get a hard copy printout of your file, you can use the `lp` command. This command takes as its argument the name of the file to be printed. So

```
lp names
```

will cause the file `names` to be printed on your line printer. Many installations have special commands that can be used to obtain fancy headings on the printout, or to print your files on other types of printers. You should ask someone about the usual commands that are used at your site to get hard copy printouts of files.

♦ Working with Directories ♦

Now that you are familiar with some of the basic file operations under the UNIX system, it is time to learn how to work with directories. You will recall from Chapter 3 that directories provide a convenient means of organizing files. You will also recall that the UNIX system has what is known as a hierarchical directory structure, meaning that a directory can itself contain directories.

Displaying Your Working Directory: the pwd Command

In order to learn how to work with directories, it is necessary to first learn about the `pwd` command. This command is used to help you "get your bearings" by telling you the name of your current working directory.

---

† This program is actually what's known as a "Berkeley enhancement" since it was added to the UNIX system by the University of California at Berkeley and is not included in the standard UNIX system.

Recall the directory structure from Chapter 3:

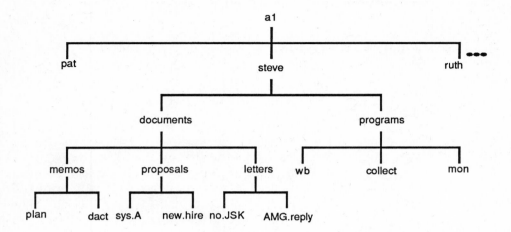

Fig. 4-1. File system a1

The special directory that you are placed in upon logging in to the system is called your HOME directory. You can assume from Fig. 4-1 that the HOME directory for the user steve is /a1/steve. Therefore, whenever steve logs into the system, he will *automatically* be placed inside this directory. To verify that this is the case, the pwd (print working directory) command can be issued:

```
$ pwd
/a1/steve
$
```

The output from the command verifies that steve's current working directory is /a1/steve.

Changing Directories: the cd Command

Now that you know how to find out where you are with the pwd command, let's go "exploring." A very useful command provided by the UNIX system enables you to easily change your current working directory. The command is cd (change directory) and it takes as its argument the name of the directory you wish to change to.

Let's assume that the user steve has just logged into the system and was placed inside his HOME directory, /a1/steve. This is depicted by the pointing finger in Fig. 4-2.

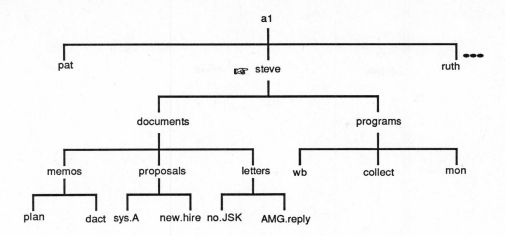

Fig. 4-2. Current working directory is steve

You know from Fig. 4-2 that there are two directories directly "below" steve's HOME directory: documents and programs. In fact, this can be verified at the terminal by issuing the ls command:

```
$ ls
documents
programs
$
```

The ls command lists the two directories documents and programs the same way it listed other files in previous examples. You will see shortly how we can use the ls command to help distinguish directory files from nondirectory files.

In order to make documents your current working directory, you issue the cd command, followed by the name of the directory to change to:

```
$ cd documents
$
```

As with most other commands, the UNIX system lets you know that the cd command executes successfully by "saying nothing." After executing the previous command, you will be placed inside the documents directory, as depicted in Fig. 4-3.

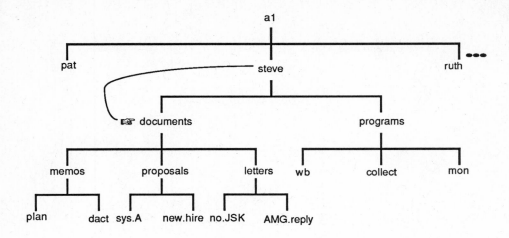

Fig. 4-3. `cd documents`

You can verify at the terminal that the working directory has been changed by issuing the `pwd` command:

```
$ pwd
/a1/steve/documents
$
```

and you can list the files contained in the current directory with the `ls` command:

```
$ ls
letters
memos
proposals
$
```

To continue the exploration, let's change now to the `memos` directory:

```
$ cd memos
$ pwd
/a1/steve/documents/memos
$ ls
dact
plan
$
```

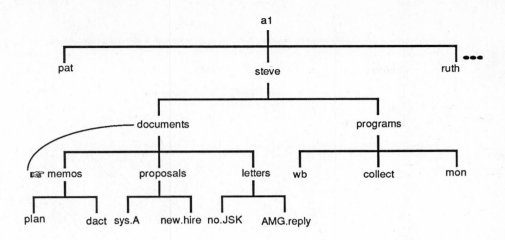

Fig. 4-4. `cd memos`

Now let's try something "illegal":

```
$ cd plan
plan: bad directory
$
```

As you can see, the UNIX system issues an error message when you try to change to a nonexistent directory. (You will recall that the file `plan` is a data file and *not* a directory.)

Now that you know how to work your way down a directory path, let's see how you can get back up. The easiest way to get one level up is to issue the command

```
cd ..
```

since by convention `..` always refers to the directory one level up.

```
$ pwd
/a1/steve/documents/memos
$ cd ..
$ pwd
/a1/steve/documents
$
```

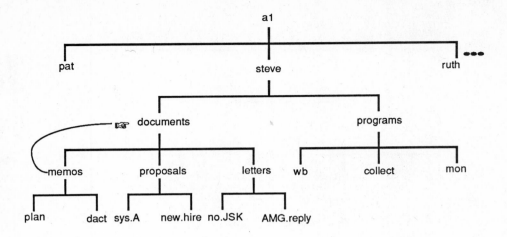

Fig. 4-5. `cd ..`

Issuing the `cd ..` command another time will bring you up one more level to the HOME directory:

```
$ cd ..
$ pwd
/a1/steve
$
```

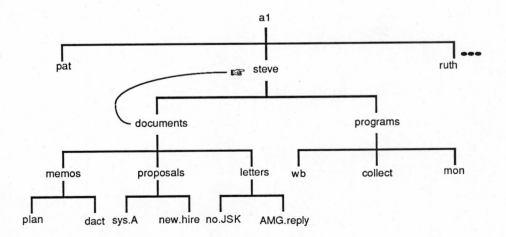

Fig. 4-6. `cd ..`

Suppose now that you wanted to go to the letters directory. Well, you know that you can get there by simply issuing two cd commands:

```
$ cd documents
$ cd letters
$ pwd
/a1/steve/documents/letters
$
```

Alternatively, you can get to the letters directory with a single cd command by specifying the relative path documents/letters:

```
$ cd documents/letters
$ pwd
/a1/steve/documents/letters
$
```

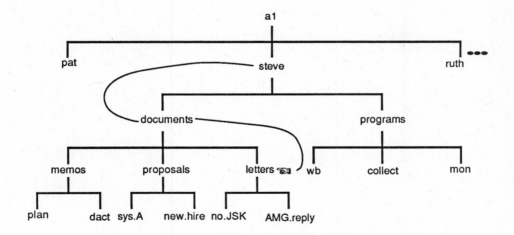

Fig. 4-7. cd documents/letters

You can get back up to the HOME directory with a single cd command as shown:

```
$ cd ../..
$ pwd
/a1/steve
$
```

Or you can get back to the HOME directory using a full path name instead of a relative one:

```
$ cd /a1/steve
$ pwd
/a1/steve
$
```

Finally, there is a third way to get back to the HOME directory that is also the easiest. Typing the command cd *without* an argument will *always* place you back into your HOME directory, no matter where you are in your directory path.

```
$ cd
$ pwd
/a1/steve
$
```

Now let's go back to the documents directory:

```
$ cd documents
$
```

What if you now wanted to change to the directory programs? You can go there directly by using a full path name:

```
$ cd /a1/steve/programs
$ pwd
/a1/steve/programs
$
```

or you can get there using a relative path name:

```
$ cd ../programs
$ pwd
/a1/steve/programs
$
```

Remember you always have a choice between a full and a relative path name. At first, choose the one that's easiest for you to understand; later—once you become more experienced using the UNIX system—you will naturally choose the one that's easiest to type.

More on the `ls` Command

By now you know that the `ls` command can be used to list your files. To be more specific, whenever you type the command `ls`, it is the files contained in the current working directory that are listed. But you can also use `ls` to obtain a list of files in other directories by supplying an argument to the command. First let's get back to your HOME directory:

```
$ cd
$ pwd
/a1/steve
$
```

Now let's take a look at the files in the current working directory:

```
$ ls
documents
programs
$
```

If you supply the name of one of these directories to the `ls` command, then you can get a list of the contents of that directory. So, you can find out what's contained in the `documents` directory simply by typing the command `ls documents`:

```
$ ls documents
letters
memos
proposals
$
```

Similarly, you can list the files contained in the `programs` directory as shown:

```
$ ls programs
collect
mon
wb
$
```

To take a look at the subdirectory memos, you follow a similar procedure:

```
$ ls documents/memos
dact
plan
$
```

If you specify a nondirectory file argument to the ls command, then you simply get that file name echoed back at the terminal:

```
$ ls documents/memos/plan
documents/memos/plan
$
```

There is an option to the ls command that enables you to determine whether a particular file is a directory, among other things. The -l option (the letter l) provides a more detailed description of the files in a directory. If you were currently in steve's HOME directory as indicated in Fig. 4-6, then the following would illustrate the effect of supplying the -l option to the ls command:

```
$ ls -l
total 2
drwxr-xr-x  5 steve  DP3725   80  Feb 25 13:27 documents
drwxr-xr-x  2 steve  DP3725   96  Feb 25 13:31 programs
$
```

The first line of the display is a count of the total number of *blocks* (1024 bytes) of storage that the listed files use. Each successive line displayed by the ls -l command contains detailed information about a file in the directory. The first character on each line tells whether the file is a directory. If the first character is d, then it is a directory; if it is − then it is an ordinary file; if it is anything else, it is a special file.

The next nine characters on the line tell how every user on the system can access the particular file. These *access modes* apply to the file's owner (the first three characters), other users in the same *group* as the file's owner (the next three characters), and finally to all other users on the system (the last three characters). They tell whether the user can read from the file, write to the file, or execute the contents of the file. Chapter 10 covers these modes in more detail.

The ls -l command tells who the owner of the file is (it is possible to have a file in your directory that you yourself do not own!), the name of the group owner of the file, how large the file is (i.e., how many characters are contained in it), and when the file was last modified. The information displayed last on the line is the file name itself.

```
$ ls -l programs
total 4
-rwxr--r--  1 steve  DP3725    358  Feb 25 13:31 collect
-rwxr--r--  1 steve  DP3725   1219  Feb 25 13:31 mon
-rwxr--r--  1 steve  DP3725     89  Feb 25 13:30 wb
$
```

The dash in the first column of each line indicates that the three files collect, mon, and wb are ordinary files and not directories.

Creating a Directory: the mkdir Command

In order to be able to create a directory, a special command called mkdir (make directory) must be used. The argument to this command is simply the name of the directory you want to make. As an example, assume that you are still working with the directory structure depicted in Fig. 4-7. Further suppose that you wish to create a new directory called misc *on the same level* as the directories documents and programs. Well, if you were currently in your HOME directory, then typing the command mkdir misc would achieve the desired effect:

```
$ mkdir misc
$
```

Now if you execute an ls command, you should get the new directory listed:

```
$ ls
documents
misc
programs
$
```

The directory structure will now appear as shown in Fig. 4-8. Since you haven't yet stored any files inside the misc directory, the following shows what will happen if you list the contents of the directory.

```
$ ls misc
$
```

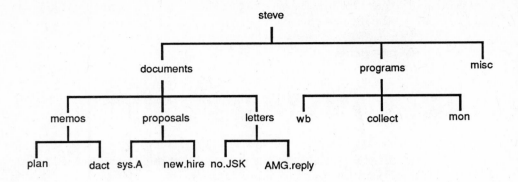

Fig. 4-8. Directory structure with newly created misc directory

Copying a File from One Directory to Another

You have seen how the cp command can be used to make a copy of a file. This command can also be used to make a copy of a file from one directory into another. For example, you can copy the file wb from the programs directory into a file called wbx in the misc directory as follows:

```
$ cp programs/wb misc/wbx
$
```

Since the two files are contained in different directories, it is not even necessary that they be given different names:

```
$ cp programs/wb misc/wb
$
```

When the destination file will have the same name as the source file (in a different directory, of course), then it is necessary to specify only the destination directory as the second argument:

```
$ cp programs/wb misc
$
```

When this command gets executed, the UNIX system recognizes that the second argument is the name of a directory and copies the source file into that directory. The new file is given the same name as the source file. You can copy more than one file into a directory using this technique. In such a case, the names of the files to be copied are listed before the name of the destination directory. The command:

```
$ cp wb collect mon ../misc
$
```

would copy the three files wb, collect, and mon into the misc directory, under the same names. If the last argument on the line is not a directory, then you will get the following:

```
$ cp wb collect mon
cp: Target must be directory
Usage: cp f1 f2
       cp f1 ... fn d1
$
```

To copy a file from another directory into your current one and give it the same name, use the fact that the current directory can always be referenced as '.':

```
$ pwd
/a1/steve/misc
$ cp ../programs/collect
$
```

The above command copies the file collect from the directory ../programs into the current directory (/a1/steve/misc).

Moving Files between Directories

You have learned that the mv command can be used to rename a file. However, when the two arguments to this command reference different directories, then the file is actually moved from the first directory into the second directory. For example, first change from the HOME directory to the documents directory:

```
$ cd documents
$
```

Suppose now you decide that the file plan contained in the memos directory is really a proposal and not a memo. So you would like to move it from the memos directory into the proposals directory. The following would do the trick:

```
$ mv memos/plan proposals/plan
$
```

The ls command can be used to verify that the file has indeed been moved:

```
$ ls memos
dact
$ ls proposals
new.hire
plan
sys.A
$
```

As with the cp command, if the destination file is to have the same name as the source file, then only the name of the destination directory need be supplied.

```
$ mv memos/plan proposals
$
```

Also like the cp command, a group of files can be simultaneously moved into a directory by simply listing all files to be moved before the name of the destination directory:

```
$ pwd
/a1/steve/programs
$ mv wb collect mon ../misc
$
```

This would move the three files wb, collect, and mon into the directory misc.

Remember the difference between the cp and mv commands: after the former command is executed, two copies of the file will exist; after the latter is executed, only a single copy of the file will exist (albeit perhaps under a new name).

Incidentally, you can also use the mv command to change the name of a directory. For example, the following will rename the directory programs to bin.

```
$ mv progams bin
$
```

Removing a Directory: the rmdir Command

Just as you can easily create a directory with the mkdir command, so can you easily remove one with the rmdir command. The only stipulation involved in removing a directory is that no files be contained in the directory. If there *are* files in the directory when rmdir is executed, then you will not be allowed to remove the directory. To remove the directory misc that you created earlier, the following could be used:

```
$ rmdir /a1/steve/misc
$
```

Once again, the above command will work only if no files are contained in the `misc` directory; otherwise, the following will happen:

```
$ rmdir /a1/steve/misc
rmdir: /a1/steve/misc non-empty
$
```

If this happened and you still wanted to remove the `misc` directory, then you would first have to remove all of the files contained in that directory before reissuing the `rmdir` command.

As an alternate method for removing a directory and the files contained in it, you can use the `-r` option to the `rm` command. The format is simple:

$$\text{rm } -r \; dir$$

where *dir* is the name of the directory that you want to remove. `rm` will remove the indicated directory and *all* files in it. Caution! You can easily remove all your files if you're not careful.

◆ An Introduction to the Editor ed[†] ◆

Up to now you've created files using the `cat` command, and you haven't had any way of altering them without retyping the entire file. The UNIX system provides you with a very helpful tool to change or *edit* your files. It is `ed`, the *text editor*.

`ed` is an environment all to itself. It has its own language to control operations on files, and once started is independent of the shell. To start it, you type in `ed` followed by the name of the file you want to edit:

```
$ ed names
27
```

`ed` prints out the number of characters contained in the file (27 in this case) and then waits for you to type in a command. Note that `ed` doesn't normally print any prompt to tell you that it's waiting for you to type something in. We can force `ed` to print a prompt by entering the `P` command.

---

† If you already know how to edit files with another UNIX editor (such as `vi`), then you may want to skip this section.

Entering ed Commands

The following examples that show how the editor works use the file names that we created earlier. First let's take another look at the file so you know what you're going to be working with:

```
$ cat names
Susan
Jeff
Henry
Allan
Ken
$
```

ed commands are single letters, optionally preceded by a line number or range of line numbers. (We'll discuss ranges later.) The ed command n prints out a line or group of lines:

```
$ ed names
27
P                                   Display prompt
*1n                                 Print line 1
1       Susan
*2n                                 Print line 2
2       Jeff
*4n                                 Print line 4
4       Allan
*1,3n                               Print lines 1 through 3
1       Susan
2       Jeff
3       Henry
*3,9n                               Print lines 3 through 9
?
```

The first ed command P asks ed to display a prompt whenever it's waiting for you to enter a command. ed uses an asterisk (*) as the prompt. The next ed command, 1n, asks the editor to display line 1 of the file. Notice that ed automatically precedes each line that is displayed by its number and some blank spaces. The command 1,3n asks for a *range* of lines to be displayed: from line 1 through line 3. The general format of a range specification is:

starting-line, ending-line

The 3,9n command produces a ? from ed. Since there is no line 9 in the file, ed just types back ?. This response is ed's way of saying "I'm sorry, but that doesn't make sense." From time to time, you'll get that response from ed. When you do don't worry about it; just look at what you typed for a possible mistake. Alternatively, type in the ''help'' command h to ask ed for an explanation:

```
*3,9n
?
*h                                Ask ed for an explanation
line out of range
```

There is also another help command in ed: H. This command causes ed to automatically print out explanations of error messages for the remainder of the editing session:

```
*H                                Automatically print explanations
*3,9n
?
line out of range
```

You may want to use the H command until you get comfortable with the syntax and use of ed commands. As soon as you start your editing session, type H to ''turn on'' this automatic help feature.

Returning to the n command, try using it on the file names. You can use the previous example as a starting point. When you're done, if you want to leave the editor and return to the shell, just type in a q. This is the quit command and it tells the editor that you are finished editing the file.

```
$ ed names
27
P
*1,5n
1       Susan
2       Jeff
3       Henry
4       Allan
5       Ken
*2n
2       Jeff
*q
$
```

When you get back your command prompt, $, you know that you are talking directly to the UNIX system again. Until that time, everything you type in is interpreted by ed.

Now that you've learned how to print the file you're editing, let's see how to make changes to the file. The ''delete'' command d is used to remove lines:

```
$ ed names
27
P
*1,5n
1       Susan
2       Jeff
3       Henry
4       Allan
5       Ken
*3,4d                              Delete lines 3 through 4
*1,3n
1       Susan
2       Jeff
3       Ken
```

As you can see, Henry and Allan (lines 3 and 4) were deleted. Also, you should note that Ken is now on line 3. As lines are deleted, the following ones move up to take their place.

```
*1,3n
1       Susan
2       Jeff
3       Ken
*1d
*1,2n
1       Jeff
2       Ken
```

Now there are two names left. So far, you have been making changes to the *editor's copy* of names; the file names has not been altered in any way. To make these changes permanent to names, you must "write" the editor's copy to the file. This is done with the w command:

```
*1,2n
1       Jeff
2       Ken
*w                                 Write the changes to the file
9
*q
$ cat names
Jeff
Ken
$
```

When the w command is typed, the number of characters written is displayed at the terminal. The original version of the file is then replaced by the edited copy.

Since you know how to delete lines, you should also know how to add them. The "append" command a allows you to add new lines at any point in a file:

```
$ ed names
9
P
*1,2n
1       Jeff
2       Ken
*1a                            Append after the first line
Nancy
George
Bill
.                              Leave append mode
*1,5n
1       Jeff
2       Nancy
3       George
4       Bill
5       Ken
```

Note that the command 1a adds the lines *after* line 1. All lines typed in after the a command are inserted in the file at that point. A single period tells the editor that you have finished your insertion. The period must be in the first column and alone on the line. Let's now write the changed file:

```
*w                             Write the changes to the file
27
*q                             and quit
$ cat names
Jeff
Nancy
George
Bill
Ken
$
```

Now let's look at a combination of delete and append:

```
$ ed names
27
P
*1,5n
1       Jeff
2       Nancy
3       George
4       Bill
5       Ken
*1,2d                                    Delete lines 1 and 2
*1,3n
1       George
2       Bill
3       Ken
*0a                                      Append before the first line
Steve
Jim
.                                        I'm done with my insertions
*1,$n                                    Display the entire file
1       Steve
2       Jim
3       George
4       Bill
5       Ken
*w                                       Write the file
26
*q                                       and quit
$
```

You should notice two odd things about the previous example. The first is that you are adding Steve and Jim after line *zero*. There is, of course, no line zero, but you are allowed to use this number to stick lines before the first line of a file. The second oddity is the $ in 1,$n. The $ in ed means the *last line* when used with the n, a, or d commands:

```
$ ed names
26
P
*1,$n
1       Steve
2       Jim
3       George
4       Bill
5       Ken
*3,$d                                    Delete lines 3 through the end
*1,$n                                    Display the file
```

```
1       Steve
2       Jim
*w
10
*q
$ cat names
Steve
Jim
$
```

ed can also be used to enter information into a new file. For example, assume you want to enter data into a new file called data_file:

```
$ ed data_file
?data_file                          This file doesn't exist
P
*a                                  Append a few lines
1.24
12
-117.677
199
.
*w
21
*q
$ cat data_file
1.24
12
-117.677
199
$
```

You'll remember that normally ed displays the number of characters in the file when it first starts. But since data_file didn't exist, ed displayed ?data_file instead.

There are a lot of other ed commands, but the ones shown here are all that are really necessary to create and modify files. The table that follows contains a summary of these commands. In the next chapter we'll cover more of the features in ed.

TABLE 4-2. Basic ed commands

Command	Function
n	Print line
a	Enter append text mode (use . as first and only character on the line to leave append mode)
d	Delete line
h	Explain last error
H	Automatically explain all errors
P	Display prompt (*) when waiting for commands
w	Save editing changes
q	Quit the editor

◆ Command Summary ◆

The following table summarizes all of the commands you have learned so far in this chapter. In this table, *file* refers to a file, *files* to one or more files, and *dir* to a directory.

TABLE 4-3. Command Summary

Command	Description
cat *file*	Display contents of *file*
cd *dir*	Change working directory to *dir*
cp *file$_1$ file$_2$*	Copy *file$_1$* to *file$_2$*
cp *files dir*	Copy *files* into *dir*
date	Display the date and time
echo *args*	Display *args*
ed *file*	Edit *file*
lp *file*	Print the contents of *file* on the line printer
ls *dir*	List files in *dir* or in current directory if *dir* is not specified
mkdir *dir*	Create directory *dir*
mv *file$_1$ file$_2$*	Move *file$_1$* to *file$_2$* (simply rename it if both reference the same directory)
mv *files dir*	Move *files* into directory *dir*
pg *file*	Display contents of *file* one screenful at a time
pwd	Display current working directory path
rm *files*	Remove *files*
rmdir *dir*	Remove empty directory *dir*
sort *file*	Alphabetize *file*
wc *file*	Count the number of lines, words and characters in *file*
who	Display who's logged in

Using the UNIX System

I n this chapter you will learn some more important concepts about the UNIX operating system. These include file name expansion, I/O redirection, and pipes. You will also learn more ed commands that will enable you to make changes to your files more efficiently.

♦　File Name Expansion　♦

The Asterisk

One very powerful feature of the UNIX system is *file name expansion*. It allows you to work with files collectively. For example, let's say your current directory has these files in it:

```
$ ls
chapt1
chapt2
chapt3
chapt4
$
```

Suppose you want to display their contents at the terminal. Well, you could execute four separate cat commands to get the required display:

```
$ cat chapt1
    .
    .
    .
$ cat chapt2
    .
    .
    .
$ cat chapt3
    .
    .
    .
$ cat chapt4
    .
    .
    .
```

Alternatively, you can take advantage of the fact that the cat command allows you to specify more than one file at a time. When this is done, the contents of the files are displayed at the terminal one after the other.

```
$ cat chapt1 chapt2 chapt3 chapt4
    .
    .
    .
$
```

But you can also type in:

```
$ cat *
    .
    .
    .
$
```

and get the same results. The UNIX system automatically *substitutes* the names of all of the files in the current directory for the *. The same expansion occurs if you use * with the echo command:

```
$ echo *
chapt1 chapt2 chapt3 chapt4
$
```

Here the * is again replaced with the names of all the files contained in the current directory, and the echo command simply displays them at the terminal. (As you can see, the command echo * provides a good way to obtain a *horizontal* list of your files.)

Any place that ＊ appears on the command line by itself, the UNIX system performs this expansion:

```
$ echo * : *
chapt1 chapt2 chapt3 chapt4 : chapt1 chapt2 chapt3 chapt4
```

The ＊ can also be used in combination with other characters to limit the file names that are substituted. For example, let's say that in your current directory you have not only chapt1 through chapt4 but also files a, b, and c:

```
$ ls
a
b
c
chapt1
chapt2
chapt3
chapt4
$
```

To display the contents of just the files beginning with chapt, you can type in:

```
$ cat chapt*
    .
    .
    .
$
```

The chapt＊ matches any file name that *begins* with chapt. All such matched file names are substituted on the command line by the UNIX system. Using ch＊ instead will match the same file names, since the only file names beginning with ch are chapt1 through chapt4:

```
$ echo ch*
chapt1 chapt2 chapt3 chapt4
$
```

The ＊ is not limited to the end of a file name; it can be used at the beginning or in the middle as well:

```
$ echo *t1                          File names ending in t1
chapt1
$ echo *t*                          File names containing a t
chapt1 chapt2 chapt3 chapt4
$ echo *x                           File names ending in x
*x
$
```

In the first echo the *t1 specifies all file names that end in the characters t1. In the second echo, the first * matches everything up to a t and the second everything after; thus, all file names containing a t are printed. Since there are no files ending with x, no expansion occurs in the last case. Therefore, the echo command simply displays *x.

Table 5-1 gives a few examples of how * can be used.

TABLE 5-1. File name expansion examples

Command	Description
echo a*	Display the *names* of the files beginning with a
cat *.c	Display the contents of all files ending in .c
rm *.*	Remove all files containing a period
ls −l x*	Give a long listing of all files beginning with x
rm *	Remove *all* files in the current directory (note: be careful when you use this)
echo a*b	Display the names of all files beginning with a and ending with b
cp ../programs/* .	Copy all the files from ../programs into the current directory

Matching Single Characters

The * matches *zero* or more characters, meaning that x* will match the file x as well as x1, x2, xabc, etc. This is usually fine, but sometimes you'll need to match a *single* character. The question mark (?) matches exactly one character. So cat ? will display the contents of all files with one-character names, just as cat x? will display the contents of all files with two-character names beginning with x.

```
$ ls
a
aa
aax
```

```
alice
b
bb
c
cc
report1
report2
report3
$ echo ?
a b c
$ echo a?
aa
$ echo ??
aa bb cc
$ echo ??*
aa aax alice bb cc report1 report2 report3
$
```

In the last example, the `??` matches two characters, and the `*` matches zero or more up to the end. The net effect is to match all file names of two or more characters.

Another way to match a single character is to give a list of the characters to use in the match inside square brackets `[]`. For example, `[abc]` matches *one* letter `a`, `b`, or `c`. It's similar to the `?`, but it allows you to choose the characters that will be matched.

```
$ echo *
a aa aax alice b bb c cc report1 report2 report3
$ echo [abcd]
a b c
$ echo report[13]
report1 report3
$ echo [ab]*
a aa aax alice b bb
$ echo *[0-9]
report1 report2 report3
$
```

The second `echo` matches any file whose name is `a`, `b`, `c` or `d`. In the next case, files whose name begin with `report` and end with either `1` or `3` are matched. The fourth case matches any file whose name begins with an `a` or `b`. The last case introduces a new twist. The specification `[0-9]` matches the characters 0 *through* 9. The only restriction in specifying a *range* of characters is that the first character must be alphabetically less than the last character, so that writing `[z-f]` is not a valid specification for the letters f through z.

By mixing and matching ranges and characters in the list, you can perform some very complicated expansions. For example, [a-np-z]* will match all files that start with the letters a through n *or* p through z (or more simply stated, any lowercase letter but o).

If you put an exclamation point (!) immediately after the left bracket, the sense of the match is *inverted*. For example, [!a-z]* will match all files that start with any character *except* a lowercase letter. The pattern *[!0-9] matches all files that end in any character other than a digit.

Here are some more examples of file name substitution:

```
$ ls
a
b
c
chapt1
chapt1.0
chapt1.1
chapt2.0
chapt3
chapt4
chapt4.1
chapt4.2
chapt5
chapt6
chapt7.1
x1
y1
z
$ echo [a-z]
a b c z
$ echo chapt1*
chapt1 chapt1.0 chapt1.1
$ echo chapt1.*
chapt1.0 chapt1.1
$ echo chapt[2-57]*
chapt2.0 chapt4 chapt4.1 chapt4.2 chapt5 chapt7.1
$ echo chapt?
chapt1 chapt3 chapt4 chapt5 chapt6
$ echo chapt*.*
chapt1.0 chapt1.1 chapt2.0 chapt4.1 chapt4.2 chapt7.1
$ echo [abx-z]*
a b x1 y1 z
$ echo [!c]*
a b x1 y1 z
$ echo *[!0-9]
a b c z
$ echo [d-f]*
[d-f]*
$
```

The **-i** Option to the **rm** Command

Table 5-1 notes that the command

```
rm *
```

will remove all the files in the current directory. If you want to remove all the files from your current directory that begin with the letters ch, you could type in

```
rm ch*
```

What do you suppose would happen if you typed in

```
rm ch *
```

by mistake; that is, if you accidentally typed a space between the ch and the *? The rm command would first try to remove a file called ch from your current directory (which may or may not exist), and then would proceed to remove all of the files from your current directory!

    The main point about the preceding example is that you must be very careful when using file name substitution with a destructive command like rm. The -i option to rm can help in such cases. With this interactive option, rm will present each file to you in turn and will ask for your approval before removing it. If you want to remove the file, you can type a y; if you don't want to remove it, you can type a n. Here's an example that shows how it works:

```
$ ls
bin
changes
chapt1
chapt2
checklist
docs
$ rm -i ch*            Remove all files that start with ch
changes: ? n          Don't remove
chapt1: ? y           Remove
chapt2: ? y           Remove
checklist: ? n        Don't remove
$ ls
bin
changes
checklist
docs
$
```

The grep Command

One command that is very useful when combined with file name substitution is the grep command. grep allows you to search one or more files for particular character patterns. The general format of this command is:

grep *pattern files*

Every line of each file that contains *pattern* is displayed at the terminal. If more than one file is specified to grep, then each line is also immediately preceded by the name of the file, thus enabling you to identify the particular file that the pattern was found in.

Let's start with an example of searching just a single file for a particular pattern. Let's say you have a directory filled with text files that make up a chapter of a book (this book, perhaps), and you want to find every occurrence of the word shell in the file ed.cmd:

```
$ grep shell ed.cmd
files, and is independent of the shell.
to the shell, just type in a q.
$
```

This output indicates that two lines in the file ed.cmd contain the word shell.

If the pattern does not exist in the specified file(s), then the grep command simply displays a new prompt:

```
$ grep cracker ed.cmd
$
```

Suppose you have a file called phone_book that you use to keep the phone numbers of people you frequently call:

```
$ cat phone_book
Farber, Ethan      445-4343
Iansito, Toby      937-1232
Levy, Steven       (907) 843-4432
Mead, John         864-5378
Sander, Rick       343-2109
Smith, George      723-2205
Snellen, Bart      331-9974
Weather info       976-1212
Wood, Pat          421-3193
Wood, Sam          778-3321
$
```

(We have shown a rather small phone directory here to conserve space.) When you need to look up a particular phone number, the grep command comes in handy:

```
$ grep Sander phone_book
Sander, Rick       343-2109
$
```

Look what happens when we look up `Wood`:

```
$ grep Wood phone_book
Wood, Pat       421-3193
Wood, Sam       778-3321
$
```

Two lines are printed, since there are more than two lines containing `Wood`. If you wanted, you could be more specific in the pattern to obtain only a single match from the directory:

```
$ grep 'Wood, Pat' phone_book
Wood, Pat       421-3193
$
```

In this case quote signs are *required* around the name because of the space that separates the two words `Wood,` and `Pat`. The quotes serve to join the two words together, so that the `grep` command sees them as a *single* pattern. See what happens if you omit the quotes:

```
$ grep Wood, Pat phone_book
grep can't open Pat
phone_book:Wood, Pat       385-3193
phone_book:Wood, Tom       778-3321
$
```

The `grep` command sees `Wood,` (and *just* `Wood,`) as the pattern and `Pat` and `phone_book` as the files to be searched. Since there is no file called `Pat`, `grep` displays the message `grep: can't open Pat`. `grep` then proceeds to search the file `phone_book` for the pattern `Wood,`. Since this pattern is in the file, the matching lines are displayed at the terminal.

The `grep` command is useful when you have a lot of files and you want to find out which ones contain certain words or phrases. The following example shows how the `grep` command can be used to search for the word `shell` in *all* files in the current directory:

```
$ grep shell *
cmdfiles:shell that enables sophisticated
ed.cmd:files, and is independent of the shell.
ed.cmd:to the shell, just type in a q.
grep.cmd:occurrence of the word shell:
grep.cmd:$ grep shell *
grep.cmd:every use of the word shell.
$
```

As mentioned previously, when more than one file is specified to grep, each output line is preceded by the name of the file containing that line.

The * can be replaced by any meaningful file list to determine which files will be searched:

```
$ grep shell *.cmd
ed.cmd:files, and is independent of the shell
ed.cmd:to the shell, just type in a q.
grep.cmd:occurrence of the word shell:
grep.cmd:$ grep shell *
grep.cmd:every use of the word shell.
$
```

If you want to be really clever, you can search for every occurrence of shell and Shell with grep:

```
$ grep [Ss]hell *
cmdfiles:shell that enables sophisticated
ed.cmd:files, and is independent of the shell
ed.cmd:to the shell, just type in a q.
grep.cmd:occurrence of the word shell:
grep.cmd:$ grep shell *
grep.cmd:every use of the word shell.
grep.cmd:occurrence of shell and Shell with grep:
grep.cmd:grep interprets [Ss]hell as Shell or
$
```

As you can see, grep uses the brackets for its pattern search in the same way the UNIX system uses them for file name matching;[†] grep interprets [Ss]hell as Shell *or* shell and goes its merry way through the files looking for the occurrence of either word.

Sifting through the output of grep can be a little tedious sometimes, particularly when there are a lot of occurrences of the pattern and you're interested only in the names of the files. Fortunately, grep has the -1 option to make it print just the names of the files containing the pattern:

[†] This is a simple example of writing a so-called *regular expression*. Regular expressions are recognized by several powerful UNIX commands, such as grep, ed, and sed. For a thorough discussion on this topic, consult *UNIX Shell Programming*.

```
$ grep -l [Ss]hell *
cmdfiles
ed.cmd
grep.cmd
$ grep -l [Ss]hell *.cmd
ed.cmd
grep.cmd
$
```

As you can see, the name of a file is printed only once if the pattern is found in it, no matter how many times it occurs.

One note of caution before we leave this discussion: it's generally a good idea to enclose your `grep` pattern inside a pair of *single* quotes to "protect" it from the UNIX system. For instance, if you want to find all the lines containing asterisks inside the file `stars`, then typing

```
grep * stars
```

will not work as expected because the UNIX system will see the asterisk and will automatically substitute the names of all the files in your current directory! Enclosing the asterisk in quotes, however, removes its special meaning from the system:

```
grep '*' stars
```

There are characters other than `*` that otherwise have a special meaning and must be quoted when used in a pattern. These include brackets (`[` and `]`), parentheses (`(` and `)`), semicolons (`;`), dollar signs ($), less-than and greater-than characters (< and >), and vertical bar characters (`|`). In the next chapter we'll go into more detail about these characters. For now, just remember to enclose them in quotes.

♦ The Editor ed Revisited ♦

In the last chapter, we went over the basic `ed` commands n (print text), a (append text), d (delete text), w (write text to file), and q (quit editing session). Now we'll look at some more `ed` commands that will help you make changes to files faster.

Searching for a String

One very helpful `ed` command is the *string search*. This is very much like searching with `grep`, except this command is built into `ed`. The way you search for a string in `ed` is to type in a slash (/), followed by the string to locate. So to search

for the string of characters `the`, you would simply type the `ed` command
`/the`:

```
$ ed names
10
P
*1,$n
1       Steve
2       Jim
*$a
Pat
George
Carol
Zebediah

.
*1,$n
1       Steve
2       Jim
3       Pat
4       George
5       Carol
6       Zebediah
*/Geo
George
*/ebed
Zebediah
*/Tony
?
```

Add some names at the end of the file

Find the line containing Geo

Find the line containing ebed

Find the line containing Tony

As you can see, `ed` prints out the line containing the string. If the string you
search for isn't in the file, `ed` prints out its usual I-don't-understand-you question mark.

The Current Line

After you have located a line using the string search command, you can delete it
by typing just a `d`.

```
*1,$n
1       Steve
2       Jim
3       Pat
4       George
5       Carol
6       Zebediah
*/Geo
```

Find the line containing Geo

```
George
*d                                          Delete it
*1,$n
1       Steve
2       Jim
3       Pat
4       Carol
5       Zebediah
```

Here the d was used without a preceding line number and the line containing George was deleted. This brings up the idea of a *current line*. Every ed command will work without a preceding line number by performing its action on the current line. When you search for a string, the current line is set to the line that contains the string. Typing d at that point will delete the line, typing n will print the line, and typing a will append new lines after the line.

```
*1,$n
1       Steve
2       Jim
3       Pat
4       Carol
5       Zebediah
*/Steve                                     Find the line containing Steve
Steve
*n
1       Steve
*/P                                         Find the line containing P
Pat
*a
Stan
Debbie
.
*n                                          Print the current line
5       Debbie
*1,$n
1       Steve
2       Jim
3       Pat
4       Stan
5       Debbie
6       Carol
7       Zebediah
```

As you can see, Stan and Debbie were appended after Pat, which was found in the previous string search. You should also note that the current line was changed to Debbie as indicated by the n command. Most ed commands make the *last line* accessed by the command the current line. For example, the a command makes the current line the last line entered; the n command makes it the last line printed out; and the d command makes it the line after the last one deleted.

The current line can be explicitly referenced with the period (.). Sometimes you may want to use the current line in a range. To do that, you use the period as if it were a line number. (Remember how the $ is used to represent the last line?)

```
*1,$n
1       Steve
2       Jim
3       Pat
4       Stan
5       Debbie
6       Carol
7       Zebediah
*/P                              Find the line containing P
Pat
*.,$n
3       Pat                      ⎫
4       Stan                     ⎪
5       Debbie                   ⎬  Print from the current line to the end
6       Carol                    ⎪
7       Zebediah                 ⎭
*/D                              Find the line containing D
Debbie
*.,$d                            Delete from the current line to the end
*n
4       Stan
*1,$n
1       Steve
2       Jim
3       Pat
4       Stan
```

Now you've deleted the lines from Debbie to the end. Right after the delete the current line is Stan, now the last line in the file.

When you perform a string search, the current line is set to the line that contains the string. We should also say that a string search starts on the line *after* the current line, so you can search through a file looking for all the lines containing a string:

```
*1n
1       Steve
*/t                              Find the next line containing t
```

```
Pat
*/t                                    Find the next line containing t
Stan
*/t                                    Find the next line containing t
Steve
*/t                                    Find the next line containing t
Pat
*/t                                    Find the next line containing t
Stan
```

As you can see, the string search goes from one line to the next that contains the string. Also, when it gets to the last line in the file, the search begins again on the first line. This is sometimes referred to as *wraparound*.

Substituting One String with Another

Another useful command in the editor is the substitute command s. It allows you to change parts of lines without deleting and retyping them:

```
*1,$n
1       Steve
2       Jim
3       Pat
4       Stan
*1n
1       Steve
*s/ve/phen/                            Change the ve to phen
*n
1       Stephen
*/Pat                                  Find the line containing Pat
Pat
*s/t/trick/                            Change the t to trick
*n
3       Patrick
```

Here the s command was used to change Steve to Stephen and Pat to Patrick. The s command is given two strings separated by slashes; ed scans the line for the first string and, if it finds it, replaces it with the second string:

$$s/string1/string2/$$

If it doesn't find *string1* in the line, ed prints out a ?.

Like other ed commands, the s command will perform its substitution on a range of lines:

```
*1,$n
1       Stephen
2       Jim
3       Patrick
4       Stan
*1,$s/t/xxx/                                    Change t to xxx on every line
*1,$n
1       Sxxxephen
2       Jim
3       Paxxxrick
4       Sxxxan
*1,$s/e/yyy/                                    Change e to yyy on every line
*1,$n
1       Sxxxyyyphen
2       Jim
3       Paxxxrick
4       Sxxxan
```

Note that when the s command was used to change all the e's to yyy that only
the first e on line 1 was changed. This is because the s command only changes
the *first* occurrence of the string that it finds on a line. To have it change *all*
occurrences of the string on the line you have to add the letter g (for global) at
the end of the s command. So

```
s/,/;/g
```

would change all commas to semicolons in the current line, and

```
1,$s/,/;/g
```

would do it for the entire file.

If you decide that you don't want your editing changes permanently
recorded, you can leave ed without writing the file:

```
*q
?
*q
$
```

The first time you type in q, ed prints out a ?. Once changes have been made
to a file, ed considers quitting before writing the changes to be an error. (And
you know what ed types back when it sees an error!). The second time, however, ed assumes you know what you're doing and returns to the shell.

The Backslash (\)

Sometimes you'll want to put some special characters in a file. For example, you might want to have a list of items and prices:

```
hamburger @ $2.89/lb
eggs @ .99/doz
milk @ .59/qt
```

The only problem is getting the @ into the file, since normally it's the line kill character. If you try to type in the @ while in the append mode in ed, all you'll do is wipe out the line you typed in. Of course since there are plenty of @'s sprinkled throughout this text, there must be a way of putting them in files. This is done with the help of the *backslash* (\). The backslash has a very different meaning to the UNIX system than the regular slash (/), which is used to separate directories in a path name. As you can see, the regular slash leans to the right (/) and the backslash leans to the left (\).

The purpose of the backslash is to remove the special meaning that the UNIX system gives to certain characters. This is done by *preceding* the special character with a backslash:

```
$ ed groceries
?groceries
P
*a                              Add some lines with special characters
hamburger \@ $2.89/lb
eggs \@.99/doz
milk \@ .59/qt
groceries -- check \# 4437       # is erase character

.
*1,$n
1   hamburger @ $2.89/lb
2   egg @ .99/doz
3   milk @ .59/qt
4   groceries -- check # 4437
```

As you can see, the backslash removed the special meaning of the @ and # so they could become part of the file like any other character. Also note that the backslash disappeared. In the process of removing the special meaning of a character, the backslash goes away. To get a backslash in your file, simply type two in a row. (The first backslash removes the special meaning of the second.)

Writing to a New File

After making some changes to a file, you may decide that you don't want to overwrite the contents of the original file. The w command can also be used to write a *new* file. This is done by simply specifying a file name argument to the w command. As an example, suppose after editing names you wanted to write to a new file names1 and leave names intact:

```
$ ed names
10
P
*1,$n
1   Steve
2   Jim
*a
Sam
Bill
.
*w names1                          Write to new file names1
19
*q
$ cat names1
Steve
Jim
$ cat names1
Steve
Jim
Sam
Bill
$
```

This way you can keep both the old and new versions of a file.

Table 5-2 summarizes the ed commands you have learned.

TABLE 5-2. Summary of basic ed commands

Command	Function
a	Enter append text mode (to leave append mode, use . as first and only character on the line)
d	Delete line
h	Explain last error
H	Automatically explain all errors
n	Print line
P	Display prompt (*) when waiting for next command
q	Quit the editor
/string/	Search for *string* starting from the current line
s/string1/string2/	Change *string1* to *string2*
w *file*	Save editing changes in *file*

♦ Displaying the End of a File: `tail` ♦

The `tail` command is an interesting one—its purpose is to display the end of a file. For example, you can use it to display the last ten lines of a file. It seems to be a curiosity, a command that has little use. In time you will see that it is indispensable.

For now, let's see how it works. First, let's make a "big" file for it to work on:

```
$ ed tailfile
?tailfile
P
*$a
now we will
begin to
add a few
lines to
the file
tailfile.
Perhaps five
or
six more
lines will
do the
trick.
.
```

```
*w tailfile
100
*q
$
```

Now let's try `tail`:

```
$ tail tailfile
add a few
lines to
the file
tailfile.
Perhaps five
or
six more
lines will
do the
trick.
$
```

As you can see, `tail` displayed the last 10 lines of `tailfile`. You can have it display fewer or more than 10 lines with the *–number* option. For example, to have `tail` display the last five lines of `tailfile`, you can type:

```
$ tail -5 tailfile
or
six more
lines will
do the
trick.
$
```

And to have it display just the last line of `tailfile`, you can type:

```
$ tail -1 tailfile
trick.
$
```

◆ Comparing Two Files: `sdiff` ◆

The `sdiff` command allows you to perform a side by side comparison of two files. Let's use `ed` to create a few files that will be used to illustrate the `sdiff` command:

```
$ ed names
10
P
*1,$d                                    Delete all lines
*a
Pat
Tony
Ruth                                     Put new names in names
Bill
.
*w
19
*$a
Tom
John
.
*w names1
28
*4d                                      Delete Bill
*1,$n
1  Pat
2  Tony
3  Ruth
4  Tom
5  John
*w names2
23
*q
$
```

Now let's look at the files that were created:

```
$ cat names
Pat
Tony
Ruth
Bill
$ cat names1
Pat
Tony
Ruth
Bill
Tom
John
```

```
$ cat names2
Pat
Tony
Ruth
Tom
John
$
```

So now you have some files that have some lines in common and some that are unique. This is a good time to introduce the sdiff command. sdiff prints two files side by side marking the differences:

```
$ sdiff names names1
Pat          Pat
Tony         Tony
Ruth         Ruth
Bill         Bill
        >    Tom
        >    John
$
```

The > marks a line that appears only in the second file. Similarly, a < marks a line that appears only in the first file, and a | marks lines that are in both files but are different.

```
$ sdiff names1 names2
Pat          Pat
Tony         Tony
Ruth         Ruth
Bill    <
Tom          Tom
John         John
$ sdiff names names2
Pat          Pat
Tony         Tony
Ruth         Ruth
Bill    |    Tom
        >    John
$
```

When comparing large files, you can use the -s option with sdiff; it suppresses the printing of identical lines, considerably reducing the amount of output.

```
$ sdiff -s names names2
4c4,5
Bill        |   Tom
            >   John
$
```

The rather cryptic first line is actually an edit-style command that describes the difference between the two files. Don't worry about it.

```
$ sdiff -s names1 names2
4d3
Bill        <
$
```

Here you see that the only difference between names1 and names2 is that Bill appears in the former file and not in the latter.

In case you're interested, there's another command similar to sdiff that's called diff. Unlike sdiff, diff does not generate a side-by-side comparison of the two files.

◆ Standard Input, Standard Output, and I/O ◆

Standard Input and Standard Output

Most commands in the UNIX system take input from your terminal and send the resulting output back to your terminal. A command normally reads its input from a place called *standard input*, which happens to be your terminal by default. Similarly, a command normally writes its output to *standard output*, which is also your terminal by default. This concept is depicted in Fig 5-1.

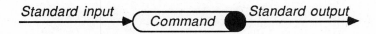

Fig. 5-1. Typical UNIX command

Let's take an example of an actual command. You will recall that executing the who command results in the display of the currently logged-in users. More formally, the who command writes a list of the logged-in users to standard input. This is depicted in Fig. 5-2.

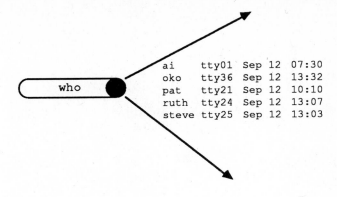

Fig. 5-2. who command

If a sort command is executed *without* a file name argument, then the command will take its input from standard input. As with standard output, this is your terminal by default.

When entering data to a command from the terminal, the CTRL and D keys (denoted *CTRL-d* in this text) must be simultaneously pressed after the last data item has been entered. This tells the command that you have finished entering data. As an example, let's use the sort command to sort the following four names: Tony, Barbara, Harry, Dick. Instead of first entering the names into a file as you did before, this time we will enter them directly from the terminal:

```
$ sort
Tony
Barbara
Harry
Dick
CTRL-d
Barbara
Dick
Harry
Tony
$
```

Since no file name was specified to the sort command, the input was taken from standard input, the terminal. After the fourth name was typed in, the CTRL and D keys were pressed to signal the end of the data. At that point, the sort command sorted the four names and displayed the results on the standard output device, which is also the terminal. This is depicted in Fig. 5-3.

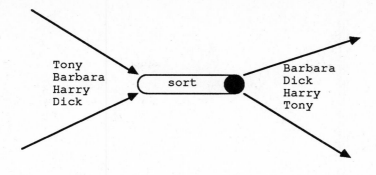

Fig. 5-3. `sort` command

Output Redirection

Under the UNIX system, the output from a command normally intended for standard output can be easily "diverted" to a file instead. This capability is known as *output redirection*.

Suppose you wanted to store the names of the logged-in users inside a file.

If the notation > *filename* is appended to *any* command that normally writes its output to standard output, then the output of that command will be written into the specified file instead of to your terminal:

```
$ who > users
$
```

This command line causes the who command to be executed and its output to be written into the file users. You will notice that no output appears at the terminal. This is because the output has been *redirected* from the default standard output device (the terminal) into the specified file. You can now examine the contents of the users file with the cat command to see if the redirection did in fact work:

```
$ cat users
oko        tty01 Sep 12 07:30
ai         tty15 Sep 12 13:32
ruth       tty21 Sep 12 10:10
pat        tty24 Sep 12 13:07
steve      tty25 Sep 12 13:03
$
```

As another example of output redirection, you can store the current date and time inside a file called now as follows:

```
$ date > now
$ cat now
Tue Sep 12 14:20:26 EDT 1988
$
```

The echo command also writes to standard output, which means that it can be redirected:

```
$ echo line 1 > x
$ cat x
line 1
$
```

Consider the following example:

```
$ echo line 1 > x
$ cat x
line 1
$ echo line 2 > x
$ cat x
line 2
$
```

If a command has its output redirected to a file and the file already contains some data, then that data will be lost. Therefore, the contents of x (the line line 1) were lost when the second echo command was executed. Now consider this example:

```
$ echo line 1 > x
$ cat x
line 1
$ echo line 2 >> x
$ cat x
line 1
line 2
$
```

The second echo command uses a different type of output redirection indicated by the characters >>. This character pair causes the standard output from the command to be *appended* to the specified file. Therefore the previous contents of the file are not lost and the new output simply gets added onto the end.

More on the cat Command

You will recall that the first file in the last chapter was created using the command `cat > names`. Now you can understand precisely how that command worked. Like most other commands, the `cat` command takes its input from standard input and writes its output to standard output by default. This means that if no file name is supplied to the `cat` command then this command will expect its input to come from the terminal. The following example illustrates this idea:

```
$ cat
line one
line one
line two
line two
etc.
etc.
CTRL-d
$
```

Since no file name argument was specified, `cat` read its input from the terminal. As each line was read, it was written to standard output. The net effect was to simply `echo` each line typed in. The *CTRL-d* signaled the end of the input to `cat`. Redirection of the output with a command such as

```
cat > junk
```

would have caused the three lines that were typed to be redirected to the file `junk`. So you can see how the use of output redirection on the `cat` command enables you to have text typed in from the terminal stored in a file.

By using the redirection append characters `>>`, you can use `cat` to append the contents of one file onto the end of another:

```
$ cat file1
This is in file1.
$ cat file2
This is in file2.
$ cat file1 >> file2          Append file1 to file2
$ cat file2
This is in file2.
This is in file1.
$
```

Recall that specifying more than one file name to `cat` results in the display of the first file followed immediately by the second file, and so on:

```
$ cat file1
This is in file1.
$ cat file2
This is in file2.
$ cat file1 file2
This is in file1.
This is in file2.
$ cat file 1 file2 > file3        Redirect it instead
$ cat file3
This is in file1.
This is in file2.
$
```

Now you can see where the cat command gets its name: when used with more than one file its effect is to *concatenate* the files together.

One thing you should note: a command such as

```
cat file2 file1 > file1
```

will *not* work correctly, and you'll lose the original contents of file1. If you want to do this sort of thing, use a temporary file for the output and then mv the file where you want it. For example, to concatenate file1 to the end of file2 and have the result go to file1 use the following sequence:

```
$ cat file2 file1 > temp
$ mv temp file1
$
```

You can see how output redirection enables the cat command to be used for purposes other than displaying files. Table 5-3 summarizes these uses. Study each command in the table until you feel comfortable with how it works.

TABLE 5-3. Output Redirection with the cat command

Command	Description
cat f_1	Display f_1
cat $f_1 f_2 > f_3$	Concatenate f_1 and f_2, placing result into f_3
cat $> f_1$	Enter data typed in from terminal (up to *Ctrl-d*) into f_1
cat $f_1 > f_2$	Copy f_1 to f_2 (like the cp command)
cat $f_1 >> f_2$	Copy f_1 to the end of file f_2

Input Redirection

Just as the output of a command can be redirected to a file, so can the input of a command be redirected from a file. And as the greater-than character > is used for output redirection, the less-than < character is used to redirect the input of a command. Of course, only commands that normally take their input from standard input can have their input redirected from a file in this manner.

In order to redirect the input of a command, you type the < character followed by the name of the file that the input is to be read from. So, for example, to count the number of lines in the file `users`, you know that you can execute the command `wc -l users`:

```
$ wc -l users
   5 users
$
```

Or, you can count the number of lines in the file by redirecting the input of the wc command from the terminal to the file `users`:

```
$ wc -l < users
   5
$
```

You will note that there is a difference in the output produced by the two forms of the wc command. In the first case, the name of the file `users` is listed with the line count; in the second case, it is not. This points out the subtle distinction between the execution of the two commands. In the first case wc knows it is reading its input from the file `users`. In the second case, it knows only that it is reading its input from standard input. The shell redirects the input from the terminal to the file `users`. As far as wc is concerned, it doesn't know whether its input is coming from the terminal or from a file!

Input and Output Redirection

As you might expect, you can simultaneously redirect the input and the output of a command—provided of course the command reads its input from standard input *and* writes its output to standard output.

```
$ cat users
oko        tty01 Sep   12   07:30
ai         tty15 Sep   12   13:32
ruth       tty21 Sep   12   10:10
pat        tty24 Sep   12   13:07
steve      tty25 Sep   12   13:03
```

```
$ sort < users > sorted_users
$ cat sorted_users
ai          tty15 Sep  12  13:32
oko         tty01 Sep  12  07:30
pat         tty24 Sep  12  13:07
ruth        tty21 Sep  12  10:10
steve       tty25 Sep  12  13:03
$
```

In this example, the `sort` command's input was redirected from the file `users` and its output was redirected to the file `sorted_users`.

◆ Pipes ◆

As you will recall, the file `users` that was created previously contains a list of all the users currently logged onto the system. Since you know that there will be one line in the file for each user logged onto the system, you can easily determine the *number* of users logged in by simply counting the number of lines in the `users` file:

```
$ who > users
$ wc -l < users
    5
$
```

This output would indicate that there were currently five users logged in. Now you have a command sequence you can use whenever you want to know how many users are logged in.

There is another approach to determine the number of logged-in users that bypasses the use of a file. The UNIX system allows you to effectively "connect" two commands together. This connection is known as a *pipe,* and it enables you to take the output from one command and feed it directly into the input of another command. A pipe is effected by the character |, which is placed between the two commands. So to make a pipe between the `who` and `wc -l` commands, you simply type `who | wc -l`:

```
$ who | wc -l
    5
$
```

The pipe that is effected between these two commands is depicted in Fig. 5-4.

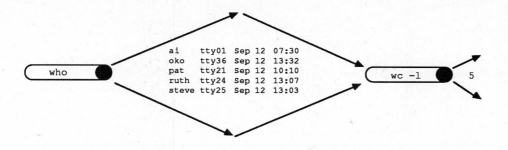

Fig. 5-4. Pipeline process: who | wc −l

When a pipe is set up between two commands, the standard output from the first command is connected directly to the standard input of the second command. You know that the who command writes its list of logged-in users to standard output. Furthermore, you know that if no file name argument is specified to the wc command then it takes its input from standard input. Therefore, the list of logged-in users that is output from the who command automatically becomes the input to the wc command. Note that you never see the output of the who command at the terminal, since it is *piped* directly into the wc command. This is depicted in Fig. 5-5.

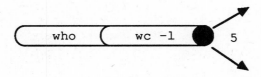

Fig. 5-5. Pipeline process

A pipe can be made between *any* two programs under the UNIX system, provided the first program writes its output to standard output, and the second program reads its input from standard input.

As another example of a pipe, suppose you wanted to count the number of files contained in your directory. Knowledge of the fact that the ls command displays one line of output per file enables you to use the same type of approach as before:

```
$ ls | wc -l
    10
$
```

The output indicates that the current directory contains 10 files.

The following counts the number of files that end with the characters .c:

```
$ ls *.c | wc -l
    3
$
```

Given the fact that sort takes its input from standard input by default, you can use the following pipeline to get a sorted list of the logged-in users:

```
$ who | sort
adn             tty27 Feb 22 08:56
ai              tty05 Feb 22 09:43
clf             tty11 Feb 22 08:59
console         tty04 Feb 22 09:00
dianne          tty14 Feb 22 08:45
dji             tty20 Feb 22 09:44
fes             tty22 Feb 22 09:31
jcm             tty06 Feb 22 08:19
rcc             tty37 Feb 22 08:27
ruth            tty17 Feb 22 09:44
steve           tty15 Feb 22 08:45
ws              tty13 Feb 22 08:25
$
```

And to save the sorted list of users in a file called users you can use output redirection on the sort command:

```
$ who | sort > users
$ cat users
adn        tty27 Feb 22 08:56
ai         tty05 Feb 22 09:43
clf        tty11 Feb 22 08:59
    .
    .
    .
$
```

Suppose you were interested in finding the *number* of files in your current directory that contained the word shell. The first part of the sentence implies that the wc command should probably be used, while the latter part indicates that the grep command should be used. A command sequence such as:

```
$ grep shell * | wc -l
    6
$
```

is close to what you want, but when you think about it for a while, what this sequence is doing is counting the total number of lines (and not files) that contain the word `shell`—not quite what you want. What you really need is one line of output from `grep` for each file containing `shell`. Recalling the `-l` option to `grep`, this is precisely what you get:

```
$ grep -l shell * | wc -l
    3
$
```

So the output of this pipeline sequence indicates that precisely three files in your current directory contain the word `shell`.

You can use `grep` on the other side of the pipe to quickly scan through the output of a command for something. For example, suppose you want to find out if the user `jim` is logged in. You can type in `who` and scan the output for his id; however, if there are a lot of users logged in or if you're using a slow terminal, you won't want to look at all that output. You do have a faster way to look for him by using `grep`:

```
$ who | grep jim
jim    tty16 Feb 20 10:25
$
```

Note that by not specifying a file to search, `grep` automatically scans its standard input. Naturally, if the user `jim` were not logged in, then you would simply get back a new prompt, because `grep` would not find `jim` in `who`'s output:

```
$ who | grep jim
$
```

It is also possible to form a pipeline consisting of several programs, with the output of one program feeding into the input of the next. Let's take a look at a double pipeline. Suppose every user working on a project called *amps* has a user id in the format

$$amps abc$$

where *abc* represents the initials of the particular user. Executing a `who` command might give the following results:

```
$ who
frj          tty04 Feb 27 13:45
kjc123       tty06 Feb 27 13:08
s5841lm      tty07 Feb 27 14:10
ampsphw      tty08 Feb 27 09:03
aps          tty10 Feb 27 13:19
ampsoko      tty11 Feb 27 14:39
mack         tty12 Feb 27 14:26
arrizzo      tty14 Feb 27 14:32
ampssgk      tty15 Feb 27 08:40
jam402       tty16 Feb 27 14:20
ampsclf      tty18 Feb 27 10:26
monitor      tty19 Feb 27 14:45
g311bij      tty20 Feb 27 14:24
ruth         tty17 Feb 27 09:14
wl           tty23 Feb 27 14:27
k43htb3      tty29 Feb 27 10:03
s700fwm      tty41 Feb 27 07:29
$
```

So at the time this command was executed there were four users in the *amps* project logged in, with users id's `ampsphw,` `ampsoko,` `ampssgk,` and `ampsclf.`

By using a pipeline, you can more readily find the *amps* users:

```
$ who | grep amps
ampsphw   tty08 Feb 27 09:03
ampsoko   tty11 Feb 27 14:39
ampssgk   tty15 Feb 27 08:40
ampsclf   tty18 Feb 27 10:26
$
```

To obtain a sorted list of the users in the *amps* project, the following double pipeline could be used:

```
$ who | grep amps | sort
ampsclf   tty18 Feb 27 10:26
ampsoko   tty11 Feb 27 14:39
ampsphw   tty08 Feb 27 09:03
ampssgk   tty15 Feb 27 08:40
$
```

The output of `who` is fed into the input of `grep`, which *filters* out only those id's containing the pattern `amps`. These lines are then fed into `sort`, where they are alphabetized and the results displayed at the terminal. This pipeline process is depicted in Fig. 5-6.

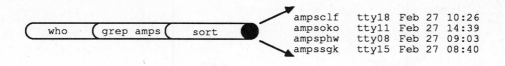

```
                                       ampsclf   tty18  Feb 27  10:26
                                       ampsoko   tty11  Feb 27  14:39
 who      grep amps      sort          ampsphw   tty08  Feb 27  09:03
                                       ampssgk   tty15  Feb 27  08:40
```

Fig. 5-6. Pipeline `who | grep amps | sort`

(Why can you interchange the `grep` and `sort` commands in this pipeline and still get the same output?)

The term *filter* is often used in UNIX terminology to refer to any program that can take input from standard input, perform some operation on that input, and write the results to standard output. More succinctly, a filter is any program that can be used between two other programs in a pipeline. So in the above pipeline, `grep` and `sort` are both considered filters. `who` is not, since it does not read its input from standard input. As other examples `cat` and `wc` are filters, while `ls`, `date`, `cd`, `pwd`, `echo`, `rm`, `mv`, and `cp` are not.

As a slight variation on the previous pipeline, consider the task of finding the *number* of logged-in *amps* users:

```
$ who | grep amps | wc -l
    4
$
```

The flow of data through this pipeline is depicted in Fig. 5-7.

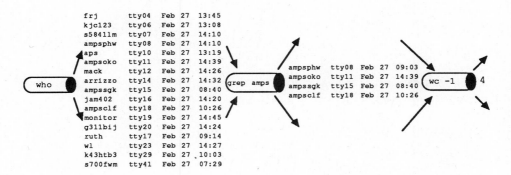

Fig. 5-7. Data flow through pipeline `who | grep amps | wc -l`

Capturing the Output in a Pipe: tee

We have stressed the fact that any output from a command that gets piped into another command is not seen at the terminal. Sometimes, you may wish to save the output that is produced in the middle of a pipe. For example, suppose you wanted to save the names of the logged-in *amps* users in a file, as well as count them. The tee command enables you to do this easily. The format of this command is simple enough:

tee file

The tee command simply copies the data coming in on standard input to standard output, in the meantime saving a copy in the specified *file*. Figure 5-8 will give you a better understanding of how this command works and where it gets its name.

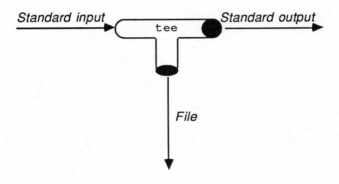

Fig. 5-8. The tee command

So you can insert the tee command right after the grep in the previous pipeline to save the user names in a file:

```
$ who | grep amps | tee ampsusers | wc -l
     4
$
```

This pipeline works the same way as the previous one, except in this case the tee command saves the output of the grep command in the file ampsusers:

```
$ cat ampsusers
ampsphw   tty08 Feb 27 09:03
ampsoko   tty11 Feb 27 14:39
ampssgk   tty15 Feb 27 08:40
ampsclf   tty18 Feb 27 10:26
$
```

Operation of this particular process is depicted in Fig. 5-9.

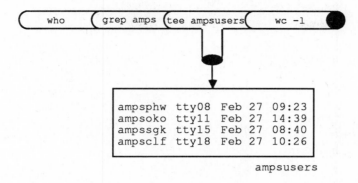

Fig. 5-9. Pipeline process containing **tee**

You can also insert a `tee` at the *end* of a pipeline to see the results of an operation while saving them in a file at the same time:

```
$ who | grep amps | sort | tee ampsusers
ampsclf   tty18 Feb 27 10:26
ampsoko   tty11 Feb 27 14:39
ampsphw   tty08 Feb 27 09:03
ampssgk   tty15 Feb 27 08:40
$
```

Here the output from `sort` is piped into `tee`, which simultaneously copies its input to the terminal (standard output) and to the file `ampsusers`.

♦ Selecting Fields from a Line: cut ♦

Suppose in the previous examples that you were interested only in the names of the logged-in *amps* users, and couldn't care less about their `tty` numbers or about the date and time they logged in. So instead of the output that you got, you would really prefer to see the following:

```
ampsclf
ampsoko
ampsphw
ampssgk
```

There is an easy way to just "cut out" the user names from the output of the `who` command, and this is done with an appropriately named UNIX command called `cut`.

The basic format of the `cut` command is:

cut −c*list files*

The `−c` option to `cut` specifies that you want to cut out specific character positions from *each* line of the specified *files*. *list* tells which character positions to cut. For example, the command

cut -c1 names

would cut out the first character of each line from the file `names`:

```
$ cat names
Pat
Tony
Ruth
Bill
$ cut -c1 names
P
T
R
B
$
```

And in the following example, the second character is cut from each line of the same file:

```
$ cut -c2 names
a
o
u
i
$
```

Naturally, you can cut more than one character from each line. To do this, you simply list the character positions to be cut, separated by commas:

```
$ cut -c1,2 names
Pa
To
Ru
Bi
$
```

A range of consecutive character positions can also be specified by using the notation:

start-end

The following example cuts the first through third character from each line:

```
$ cut -c1-3 names
Pat
Ton
Rut
Bil
$
```

To specify that a cut is to be made from a specified character position to the end of the line, leave out the ending number:

```
$ cut -c2- names
at
ony
uth
ill
$
```

In this example cut is used to cut characters two through the end of the line—in other words, all but the first character.

Of course, the character positions that are cut do not *have* to be consecutive:

```
$ cut -c1,3 names
Pt
Tn
Rt
Bl
$
```

As you might expect, cut takes its input from *standard input* and writes its output to *standard output* by default. This means, of course, that it can be used in a pipeline:

```
$ who | cut -c1-8
frj
kjc123
s58411m
ampsphw
aps
```

```
ampsoko
mack
arrizzo
ampssgk
jam402
ampsclf
monitor
g311bij
ruth
wl
k43htb3
s700fwm
$
```

Here you can see cut used to extract just the first eight characters from each line of the who command's output. So this pipeline displays just the user ids of the logged-in users. Recalling the problem that was introduced at the start of this section, now you know how to get a list of just the names of the logged-in *amps* people:

```
$ who | cut -c1-8 | grep amps
ampsphw
ampsoko
ampssgk
ampsclf
$
```

Of course, you can also tack a sort onto the end to get a sorted list:

```
$ who | cut -c1-8 | grep amps | sort
ampsclf
ampsoko
ampsphw
ampssgk
$
```

There is a sister command to cut called paste. This command is used to merge characters into single lines. See your *UNIX User's Manual* for details.

Now that you are familiar with pipes you may realize why the UNIX system is typically so terse: so that the output of a program can be easily used as the input to another program. Just think about how much more difficult it would be to do this if the output from commands included "extraneous" information such as headings, for instance. (Think about counting the number of logged-in users if who printed headings; or counting the number of files in your current directory if ls printed headings.) Indeed, most UNIX commands were designed with the realization that the output from the command may very well be the input to another command in a pipe.

♦ Standard Error ♦

In addition to standard input and standard output there is another place known as *standard error*. This is where most UNIX commands write their error messages. And as with the other two "standard" places, standard error is associated with your terminal by default. In most cases, you never know the difference between standard output and standard error:

```
$ ls n*                         list all files beginning with n
n* not found
$
```

Here the "not found" message is actually being written to standard error and not standard output by the ls command. You can verify that this message is not being written to standard output by redirecting the ls command's output:

```
$ ls n* > foo
n* not found
$
```

So you see you still get the message printed out at the terminal, even though you redirected standard output to the file foo.

The above example shows the raison d'etre for standard error: so that error messages will still get displayed at the terminal even if *standard output* is redirected to a file or piped to another command.

Although it won't be described here, you should note that you can also redirect standard error to a file if you like. Consult *UNIX Shell Programming* for more details.

♦ More on Commands ♦

In this section you'll learn some more about the format of the commands you type in.

Typing More Than One Command on a Line

You can type more then one command on a line provided you separate each command with a semicolon. For example, you can find out the current time and also your current working directory by typing in the date and pwd commands on the same line:

```
$ date; pwd
Wed Apr 25 20:14:32 EST 1988
/a1/pat/progs
$
```

You can string out as many commands as you like on the line, as long as each command is delimited by a semicolon.

Continuing a Command on the Next Line

Sometimes you may have a command that is too long to fit on a line. Well, you can insert a backslash character at the end of the line and continue the command on the next line. The backslash at the end of the line (and it must be the *last* character that you type on the line before the RETURN) tells the UNIX system that you want to continue this command on the next line. The following shows a highly manufactured example.

```
$ echo one\
> two\
> three
one two three
$
```

You'll note that the prompt character changed from $ to > on the two continuation lines of the echo command. This is the UNIX system's way of telling you that it's waiting for you to finish typing the command. As soon as you end a line without a backslash, the UNIX system takes this as the end of the command and executes it.

Sending a Command to the Background

Normally, you type in a command and then wait for the results of the command to be displayed at the terminal. For all the examples you have seen thus far, this waiting time is typically quite short—maybe a second or two. However, you may have to run commands that require many seconds or even minutes to execute. In those cases, you'll have to wait for the command to finish executing before you can proceed further *unless you execute the command in the background*.

If you type in a command followed by the ampersand character &, then that command will no longer tie up your terminal and you can then proceed with other work. The standard output from the command will still be directed to your terminal; however in most cases the standard input will be dissociated from your terminal. If the command does try to read any input from standard input, it will be as if *CTRL-d* were typed.

```
$ sort data > out &                    Send the sort to the background
1258                                    Process id
$ date                                  Your terminal is immediately available
Thu Apr 26 17:45:09 EST 1988
$
```

When a command is sent to the background, the UNIX system automatically displays a number, called the *process id* for that command. In the above example, 1258 was the process id assigned by the system. This number uniquely identifies the command that you sent to the background, and can be used to obtain status information about the command. This is done with the ps command, described in detail in Chapter 12. You are also referred to that chapter for more information about the process id.

As noted, sending a command to the background for execution is most often used for commands that require a significant amount of time to execute as it frees up your terminal for other work. However, you shouldn't abuse this feature if you have more than one user logged in to your system. In such a case, having many commands executing in the background is discourteous to other users since you will be using a disproportionate amount of the computer's resources.

◆ Changing Your Erase Character ◆

As promised in Chapter 4, now you'll see how to change your erase character from # to something else. To do this, you must use the stty command in the following format:

```
stty echoe erase char
```

where *char* is the character you want as your character erase. Most often, you'll want this to be the BACKSPACE. In fact, if your erase character is not #, then it has probably been changed to BACKSPACE for you. Here's how simple it is to change your erase character:

```
$ stty echoe erase CTRL-h
$
```

The BACKSPACE key has been shown as *CTRL-h* since that's what the system actually "sees" when this key is pressed. Your cursor will probably move back one character when you press this BACKSPACE; don't be concerned about this, the stty command will interpret things properly. After the above stty command has been executed, you can use the BACKSPACE key to erase characters. The # key will no longer erase characters—it's special meaning to the system has been removed.

Your newly defined erase character will remain effective as long as you're logged in. However, next time you log in, it'll be # again. In the next chapter you'll see how you can have your erase character changed automatically whenever you log in.

♦ Command Files ♦

One of the most powerful features of the UNIX system is a capability that effectively enables you to define your own commands. For example, you have seen how you can easily determine the number of users currently logged into the system by simply piping the output of the who command into the input of the wc command:

```
$ who | wc -l
    14
$
```

This output indicates that 14 users are currently logged in. It is quite conceivable that you might want to execute this command several times throughout the day. In order to avoid some extra typing, you can first type the above command sequence into a file called perhaps nu (for number of users):

```
$ cat > nu
who | wc -l
CTRL-d
$
```

Now that you have stored this command sequence in the file nu you can simply type in nu at the terminal whenever you want to know the number of logged-in users:

```
$ nu
nu: cannot execute
$
```

Oops! We forgot to mention one thing. Before you can execute the commands contained in the nu file, you must first tell the UNIX system that this file contains commands that can be executed. This is done with the chmod (*change mode*) command. This command is described in more detail in Chapter 10. For now, simply remember its syntax and the fact that it must be used to tell the UNIX system that you have just created a file that contains commands you want to execute.

```
$ chmod +x nu
$
```

The option +x says "make the file executable." This enables you to subsequently execute the commands contained in that file by simply typing the name of the file:

```
$ nu
    14
$
```

That's better! Your newly defined "command" behaves like any other UNIX command. For example, you can redirect its output in the normal fashion:

```
$ nu > out
$ cat out
    14
$
```

The following shows a slight enhancement to the nu command:

```
$ ed nu
12
P
*1,$n
1   who | wc -l
*0a
echo Number of users logged in:
.
*1,$n
1   echo Number of users logged in:
2   who | wc -l
*w
44
*q
$ nu
Number of users logged in:
    14
$
```

Edit the command file

Execute it

When nu is typed at the terminal, the commands inside that file are executed in turn. So the echo command is executed first, which displays the phrase Number of users logged in: at the terminal. Then the pipeline who | wc -l is executed, which displays a count of the number of logged-in users.

You can put any commands at all inside a file, change the mode of the file to make it executable, and then use it like any other command. And as you will see in the next chapter, there even exists a special language in the UNIX system that enables you to create more sophisticated command files.

The Old Shell Game

Those chapter delves into more details about the operation of the shell. It also introduces the unique shell programming language. A more complete treatment of the shell is offered in *UNIX Shell Programming*.

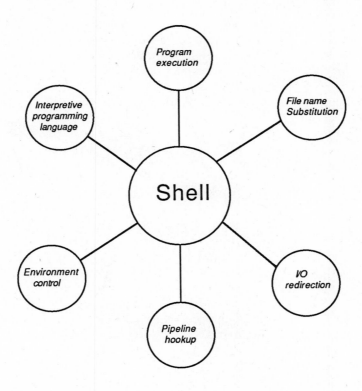

Fig. 6-1. Functions of the shell

In Chapter 2 you learned that the shell is the UNIX system's command inter-preter. But the shell actually does a lot more than just interpret commands. The functions served by the shell are depicted in Fig. 6-1.

Program execution
Just about everything you type in at the terminal is interpreted by the shell. Whenever the shell is waiting for you to type in a command, it displays your command prompt $. After you type in your command and press RETURN, the shell then proceeds to analyze the line you typed in. This line is commonly called the *command line*.

Every command that is executed under the UNIX system has the same general format, as far as the shell is concerned:

command   arguments

The shell treats the first characters on the line up to the first blank (or to the end of the line if there are none) as the name of the command to be executed. Any characters appearing after the command name are interpreted as the commands arguments (except for I/O redirection specifications—see below). Arguments are delimited by blanks. So for example, in the command

```
grep Wood phone_book
```

grep is the command and Wood and phone_book the arguments. As you saw in Chapter 5, quotes can be used to group blank-separated characters together:

```
grep "Wood, Pat" phone_book
```

Here grep also has two arguments: Wood, Pat and phone_book.

The shell is responsible for ensuring that the arguments you type in get properly "handed over" to the program being executed. It then starts execution of the program. After the program has completed execution, control goes back to the shell. At that point, your com-mand prompt is displayed as the shell's way of telling you it is await-ing your next command.

File name substitution
If file name substitution is specified on the command line with the characters *, ?, or [...], then the shell performs the substitu-tion. This happens *before* the program gets executed; the program itself never has to worry about it.

I/O redirection

If input and/or output redirection is specified on the command line, then this too is handled by the shell. On input redirection, the shell opens the file for reading and "connects" it to the standard input of the program. Once again, this happens before execution of the program begins, so the program doesn't even know (or care) that its input has been redirected. All it needs to do is read its input from standard input; the shell has taken care of the rest.

If output redirection is specified, then the shell creates the file if necessary and "connects" it to the program's standard output. If the file already exists, then the previous contents of the file are lost, unless the append characters >> are used for the redirection. Just like input redirection, the program itself never has to worry about output redirection; it just writes its output to standard output in the normal fashion.

Pipeline hookup

If the command line contains two programs connected by a pipe as in:

```
who | wc -1
```

then the shell takes responsibility for connecting the standard output of the first program to the standard input of the second. It then starts execution of both programs. As with I/O redirection, the fact that these two programs have been connected by a pipe is unbeknownst to either—the first program simply writes its output to standard output and the second program reads its input from standard input.

Environment control

The shell gives you some flexibility in customizing your "environment" to suit your needs. This environment includes the path name of your HOME directory, the directories that will be searched by the shell whenever you type the name of a program to be executed, and even the particular character that is used by the shell as your command prompt.

Interpretive programming language

The shell provides a powerful programming language. Statements in this language can be typed in directly at the terminal for execution, or they can first be entered into a file. You saw how the latter function was performed at the end of the last chapter when the concept of command files was introduced.

One of the greatest testaments to the power and flexibility of the UNIX system is the fact that the operating system is not tied to a particular command interpreter. Actually, since the shell is a program, several different "flavors" of the shell have evolved. Each differs slightly in the features that it provides and in the syntax of the command language. There are currently three popular shells:

- the "Bourne shell" sh
- the "C shell" csh
- the "Korn shell" ksh

The first and third shells get their names from their inventors, Stephen Bourne and David Korn, respectively. The second shell was developed at the University of California at Berkeley and gets its name from its programming language, which resembles the C programming language in syntax.

The Bourne shell is the shell that is currently distributed with standard UNIX systems. In later releases of the UNIX system, the Korn shell will most likely become the "standard shell". The Korn shell is compatible with the Bourne shell; the C shell is not. (A good indication that you're running under the C shell is given by your command prompt. If it's a percent sign (%), then you're probably using the C shell.)

The remainder of this chapter introduces you to the command language provided in the the standard Bourne Shell sh. Since the Korn shell is compatible with the Bourne shell, everything you learn here will work with that shell as well. If you have access to the Korn shell, at the end of the chapter we'll show you how to exploit two of the nicest features of this shell: command-line editing and the history mechanism. If you're using the C shell, you may want to check with your system administrator to see if the standard shell sh is available. If it is, you should use that shell while reading through this chapter. Then, after you've learned how to program in the standard shell, you can easily apply what you've learned to the C shell.

◆ Shell Variables ◆

Variable Names

As with other programming languages, the shell provides the user with the ability to define *variables* and to assign values to them. A shell variable name begins with a letter (upper or lowercase) or underscore character and optionally is followed by a sequence of letters, underscore characters or numeric characters.

```
i5
length
Input_file
HOMEDIR
_cflag
```

are examples of valid shell variable names, whereas the names:

`5i`	*Cannot begin with a numeric character*
`.length`	*'.' is not a valid character*
`file name`	*Embedded spaces are not permitted*

are not for the reasons stated.

Assigning Values to Variables

Values can be assigned to shell variables by writing the variable name followed immediately by the assignment operator = followed by the value to be assigned to the variable:

```
length=80
```

This statement assigns 80 to the shell variable `length`. Note that embedded spaces are *not* allowed either before or after the equals sign. The shell command

```
file_name=ai.memo
```

assigns `ai.memo` to the shell variable `file_name`. When assigning a string of characters to a shell variable, it's generally a good idea to enclose the string within a pair of *double* quotes. In fact, if the string of characters contains embedded spaces, then the quotes are *mandatory*:

```
message="The system will be shut down at 18:00 for PM"
```

Later in this chapter you'll learn more about the different types of quoting mechanisms that are built into the shell.

You should note that unlike other programming languages, there is no "type" associated with a shell variable. Every value that you assign to a variable is simply treated as a string of characters by the shell.

Displaying the Value of a Shell Variable

Now that you know how to assign values to shell variables, let's see how you can use these variables. The first thing you will want to learn is how to access the value that is stored in a shell variable. The shell is unlike most other programming languages in this respect. To access the value stored inside a shell variable, you must immediately precede the name of the variable by a dollar sign, as in $length or $file_name.

To display the value that has been assigned to a shell variable at the terminal, use the echo command. So to assign 80 to the shell variable length and then display its value using the echo command, the following sequence could be used:

```
$ length=80
$ echo $length
80
$
```

The first command assigns the value 80 to the shell variable length. In the next line, the echo command displays the value of this variable. This same technique is used in the next example.

```
$ message="System shutdown in 5 minutes."
$ echo $message
System shutdown in 5 minutes.
$
```

Whenever the shell encounters a dollar sign followed by a variable name, the value of that variable gets substituted at that precise point by the shell. This explains the output from the follwing sequence of commands.

```
$ length=80
$ echo The length is $length
The length is 80
$
```

Let's see what happens if you try to display a shell variable that was never assigned a value:

```
$ echo $noval

$ echo :$noval:
::
$
```

The last echo demonstrates that an unassigned variable has *no* value. In shell programming terminology, this is known as the *null* value.

Using Shell Variables

Shell variables are frequently used as command arguments:

```
$ file="ai.memo"
$ wc -l $file
    115 ai.memo
$
```

First the string `ai.memo` is assigned to the shell variable `file`. Then the `wc` command is executed. The file name argument to the command is given by the *value* of the shell variable `file`. Since you assigned the string `ai.memo` to this variable, the number of lines contained in the file `ai.memo` is counted and displayed at the terminal, exactly as if the command:

```
wc -l ai.memo
```

had been typed in instead. The following provides a further extension to the previous example.

```
$ option="-l"
$ file="ai.memo"
$ wc $option $file
    115 ai.memo
$
```

As a final example along the same lines, consider the following:

```
$ command="wc"
$ option="-l"
$ file="ai.memo"
$ $command $option $file
    115 ai.memo
$
```

The value of a shell variable can be assigned to another shell variable in the expected fashion:

```
$ file="ai.memo"          Assign ai.memo to file
$ save_file=$file         Assign value of file to save_file
$ echo $save_file         Display the value of save_file
ai.memo
$
```

A shell variable should almost always be preceded by a dollar sign, except if it appears on the left side of an equals sign.

```
$ file="ai.memo"
$ option="-l"
$ command="wc $option $file"
$ echo $command                    Display the contents of command
wc -l ai.memo
$ $command                         Execute the contents of command
    115 ai.memo
$
```

Another common use for shell variables is for assigning symbolic names to directory paths. For example, recall the directory structure from previous chapters:

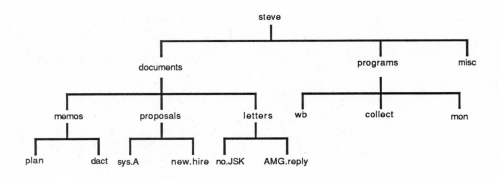

Fig. 6-2. Directory structure

Suppose you had to do a lot of work between two directories, such as between the `misc` directory and the `proposals` directory. Your command sequence might include the following types of commands:

```
$ cd /a1/steve/documents/proposals
$ cp sys.A /a1/steve/misc/sys.A_save
$ ls /a1/steve/misc
    .
    .
    .
$ cd /a1/steve/misc
    .
    .
    .
```

Even using relative path names, the typing can get a little tedious when performing operations between directories, such as moving or copying files or simply switching between them.

You can assign path names to shell variables and then use them in subsequent commands to help reduce typing. For example, in

```
$ p=/a1/steve/documents/proposals
$ m=/a1/steve/misc
$
```

the path name /a1/steve/documents/proposals is assigned to the shell variable p and the path name /a1/steve/misc to the shell variable m. Now you can avoid some typing in future commands:

```
$ ls $p
new.hire
sys.A
$ cd $m
$ pwd
/a1/steve/misc
$
```

The next example shows how easily you can move or copy a file between the two directories:

```
$ cp $p/sys.A $m
$ ls $m
sys.A
$
```

It's generally a good idea to use more meaningful variable names than those shown. This is particularly important when writing command files. Meaningful variable names will help make your shell programs more understandable—to both you and others.

♦ The for Statement ♦

All programming languages provide mechanisms that enable you to execute repeatedly a group of statements. The shell is no exception, as it provides three such language statements: the for, the while, and the until.

The general format of the for statement in the shell is:

```
for variable in list
do
    command
    command
    command
    ...
done
```

variable is any shell variable that you choose. It is listed *without* a leading dollar sign. The number of items specified in *list* determines the number of times the *commands* enclosed between the do and done will be executed. Each time the loop is executed, the next value in *list* is assigned to *variable*.

As an example of the for, consider the following:

```
for index in 1 2 3 4 5
do
    echo $index
done
```

In this example, *list* consists of the five values 1, 2, 3, 4, and 5. Therefore, the loop will be executed a total of five times. Each time through the loop, the next value in *list* will be assigned to the shell variable index. The "body" of the loop consists of the single command echo $index, which has been indented to visually identify it as belonging to the loop.

Let's see what happens if you type this for loop in at the terminal:

```
$ for index in 1 2 3 4 5
> do
>     echo $index
> done
1
2
3
4
5
$
```

You probably noticed that the prompt changed from $ to > after the first line of the for was typed. This is the shell's way of telling you that it is expecting more input. The > continues to be displayed by the shell until you type done, thus closing the for statement. At that point, the shell proceeds to execute the loop.

Execution of the for begins with index getting assigned the first value in the list: 1. The body of the loop—the echo command—is then executed. This results in the display of the value of index—1—at the terminal.

After the `echo` command has been executed, the next value in the list, 2, gets assigned to `index`. The `echo` command is once again executed to display the value of `index` at the terminal, and execution of the loop then continues. The last time through the loop, the value 5 gets assigned to `index`, the `echo` command displays its value at the terminal, and then the loop terminates. At this point the normal `$` command prompt is displayed by the shell.

One of the real uses of the `for` is to apply a command or series of commands to a group of files. Let's assume you have files `names`, `names1`, and `names2` in your current directory and that their contents are as illustrated on pages 77-78.

```
$ ls name*
names
names1
names2
$
```

The following example shows that any value at all can form the *list* in a `for`:

```
$ for file in names names1 names2
> do
>    echo $file
> done
names
names1
names2
$
```

The next example shows how file name substitution can be used in the list specification:

```
$ for file in name*
> do
>    echo $file
> done
names
names1
names2
$
```

Even though there appears to be only one item in the list, the shell sees the `*` in `name*` and expands it into `names`, `names1`, and `names2`. This is verified by the output of the `echo` commands.

In the following example, the contents of the files `names`, `names1` and `names2`, are separately sorted:

```
$ for file in name*
> do
>    sort $file
> done
Bill
Pat
Ruth
Tony
Bill
John
Pat
Ruth
Tom
Tony
John
Pat
Ruth
Tom
Tony
$
```

Well, you got the results you wanted, but it's not very readable! The following is certainly an improvement:

```
$ for file in name*
> do
>   echo "======================================="
>   echo "          Sorted contents of $file"
>   echo "======================================="
>   sort $file
>   echo
> done
=======================================
          Sorted contents of names
=======================================
Bill
Pat
Ruth
Tony


=======================================
          Sorted contents of names1
=======================================
```

```
Bill
John
Pat
Ruth
Tom
Tony


===========================================
        Sorted contents of names2
===========================================
John
Pat
Ruth
Tom
Tony

$
```

That's more like it. The purpose of the `echo` that was typed after the `sort` is simply to insert a blank line in the display. As you will recall, this is the effect of executing an `echo` with no arguments.

♦ All about Quotes ♦

The shell is a unique programming language with respect to the way quote signs work. The shell interprets four different characters on your keyboard as "quote characters":

- the double quote mark "
- the single quote mark '
- the backslash character mark \
- the single *back* quote mark `

Each of these quote marks has a special and *different* meaning to the shell. Understanding the distinctions between them is important.

The Double Quote Mark

Suppose your current directory contained the following files:

```
$ ls
documents
misc
programs
$
```

Now consider the output from the following two echo commands:

```
$ echo *
documents misc programs
$ echo "*"
*
$
```

In the first case, the shell substituted * with the names of all the files in the directory. In the second case, no substitution occurred. Obviously, the double quotes had something to do with this. The fact of the matter is that if the shell sees a pair of double quote marks, then *no file name substitution will occur between the pair of double quotes.*

The following example implies that an even greater generalization can be made:

```
$ echo >
syntax error: 'newline or ;' unexpected
$ echo ">"
>
$
```

In the first echo, the shell thought you were redirecting the output from the echo and looked for a file name to follow. Since none was specified, the (rather cryptic) error message was generated. In the second case, the double quote marks surrounding the > had the effect of *removing the special meaning of the character to the shell.*

This is the key behind the double quotes: any character that is otherwise special to the shell (such as *, ?, >, <, >>, and |) loses its special meaning when it appears between a pair of quote marks. The *exceptions* to this rule are the dollar sign $, the back quote `, and the *backslash* \ (but only if the backslash precedes a $, ", `, newline, or another \; otherwise it *does* lose its special meaning to the shell).

Double quotes also preserve *white-space* characters by removing their special meaning to the shell. These characters are blank spaces, tab characters, and newline characters. You saw double quotes used for this purpose in Chapter 5 when the grep command was taught:

```
$ grep "Wood, Pat" phone_book
```

Without the quotes around `"Wood, Pat,"` the shell thinks that `Wood,` is the first argument to `grep`, `Pat` is the second argument, and `phone_book` is the third argument. With the quotes, `grep` sees `"Wood, Pat"` as the first argument because the special meaning of the space (that is, as argument separator) is removed from the shell.

The Single Quote Mark

Study the output of the following:

```
$ message="hello there"
$ echo $message
hello there
$ echo "$message"
hello there
$
```

In both cases, the value of the shell variable `message`—hello there —was echoed at the terminal. This is because the shell does substitute the value of shell variables *inside* double quotes. Now look at the following:

```
$ echo '$message'
$message
$
```

As you can see, when a shell variable is enclosed within *single* quote marks, its value is not substituted by the shell. Furthermore, the following example shows that special shell characters enclosed within single quotes also get ignored:

```
$ echo '< > * ? >> |'
< > * ? >> |
$
```

The shell does not process any characters enclosed within single quotes; that is, they are guaranteed to remain unchanged. Study the following output very carefully to see the subtle differences between no quotes, double quotes, and single quotes.

```
$ echo *
names names1 names2
$ echo * "*" '*'
names names1 names2 * *
$ var=hello
$ echo $var "$var" '$var'
hello hello $var
$
```

The Backslash Character

In Chapter 5 you learned that to enter a special character such as # into a text file using ed it is necessary to precede the character by a backslash \. Preceding any character by a backslash removes the special meaning of that character to the shell. In other words, \ followed by any character *c* is similar to writing '*c*'. Here are some examples:

```
$ echo \$foo                          Don't treat the $ specially
$foo
$ echo \< \> \" \' \` \$ \| \* \?
< > " ' ` $ | * ?
$ echo \\
\
$
```

The last example shows that even a backslash can be preceded by a backslash to remove its special meaning.

The Back Quote Mark

One of the most unusual features of the shell is the way it handles back quote marks. Enclosing a command inside a pair of back quotes causes the command to be executed and its output to be inserted at that precise point on the command line. For example, consider the following:

```
$ echo The date is `date`
The date is Sun Mar 19 13:27:33 EST 1989
$
```

When the shell processes the command line, it notices the back quote marks. The shell then proceeds to execute whatever is enclosed between these quotes: the date command. The output from date, Sun Mar 19 13:27:33 EST 1989, is then substituted by the shell at that point on the command line and the echo command is then executed. echo isn't even aware that any of this is happening. In fact, echo sees as its arguments the following characters: The date is Sun Mar 19 13:27:33 EST 1989.

Let's take a look at another example:

```
$ echo Your current working directory is `pwd`
Your current working directory is /a1/steve/programs
$
```

In this case, the pwd command was executed and its output inserted in the command line. To be more precise, it was the standard output of pwd that was inserted by the shell.

You can even have a pipeline executed in this fashion. The entire pipeline must be enclosed inside the back quotes. The following shows a one-line version of the `nu` program:

```
$ echo There are `who | wc -l` users logged in.
There are 5 users logged in.
$
```

One very powerful feature of the back quote mechanism is the ability to assign the output from a command to a shell variable:

```
$ now=`date`
$ echo $now
Sun Mar 19 13:34:20 EST 1989
$
```

In the first line, the `date` command is executed and its output assigned to the shell variable `now`. In the next line, the value of `now` is displayed. Look at another example:

```
$ users=`who | wc -l`
$ echo There are $users users logged in.
There are 5 users logged in.
$
```

The result of the pipeline `who | wc -l` is assigned to the variable `users` in the first line, and the value of `users` is subsequently displayed with an `echo` command.

Can you explain the output from the following?

```
$ cat names
Pat
Tony
Ruth
Bill
$ list=`cat names`
$ echo $list
Pat Tony Ruth Bill
$
```

The output from the `echo` appears on one line because the shell "got to" the newline characters in `list` before `echo` had a chance to see them. Recall that the shell "gobbles" up multiple spaces, newlines and tabs. In order to preserve the newline characters inside `list`, you must enclose `list` inside double quotes (why not single quotes?) so that `echo` can see them:

```
$ echo "$list"
Pat
Tony
Ruth
Bill
$
```

Back-quoted commands can be inserted just about anywhere. For example, here one is used to form the list in a shell `for` statement:

```
$ for name in `cat names`
> do
>   echo Hello, $name
> done
Hello, Pat
Hello, Tony
Hello, Ruth
Hello, Bill
$
```

The following table summarizes the different quoting mechanisms in the shell.

TABLE 6-1. Quote characters

Character	Meaning
"	Removes special meaning of `'`, `<`, `>`, `#`, `*`, `?`, `&`, `|`, `;`, `(`, `)`, `[`, `]`, `^`, blank spaces, newlines, and tabs; `$`, `` ` ``, and `\` are interpreted (*see* `\` *below*)
'	Same as " except also removes special meaning of `$`, `` ` ``, `"`, and `\`
\	Removes special meaning of character that follows; inside double quotes, removes special meaning of `$`, `"`, `` ` ``, and `\` (but is otherwise not interpreted)
`	Causes enclosed command to be executed and its standard output to be inserted at that point

Don't worry if this discussion of quotes seems a bit complicated, because it is! Even experienced UNIX users still have difficulty getting their quotes straight at times. It's only to be expected that you'll experience the same difficulties.

◆ More on echo ◆

The echo command gives special meaning to certain characters that are preceded by a backslash \. These characters give you more flexibility and control in your output displays and therefore are quite useful. A complete list of these characters is provided in Section 1 of your *UNIX User's Manual*. Here, three of the most often used characters are discussed.

Moving to the Next Line: \n

If the echo command sees a backslash character followed immediately by the letter n, then at that point a new line will be displayed; that is, the cursor will go to the beginning of the next line. The following examples will help make this point clear. One word of caution before you proceed: in order to remove the special meaning to the shell of the backslash character, any of these special echo characters *must* be quoted (either single or double quotes will do).

```
$ echo "one\ntwo\nthree"
one
two
three
$ echo this is what happens\nif you forget the quotes
this is what happensnif you forget the quotes
$ echo 'skip a\n\nline'
skip a

line
$
```

In the last example, the first \n causes the cursor to move to the beginning of the next line, and the second one causes it to go down another line. The net effect is to insert a blank line between skip a and line.

Staying on the Same Line: \c

Normally, after echo displays its last argument it goes to the beginning of the next line. This is usually what you want. However, suppose you wanted to display one part of a message and then later in the program display another part of the message *on the same line*. Or, as you'll see later, suppose you wanted to display a message and then have the user enter some data right after that message on the same line.

If you tack the characters \c to the end of an echo command, then echo will *not* automatically go to the beginning of the next line; instead, it will stay right where it is. Once again, some examples will help you understand:

```
$ echo "stay on this line\c"
stay on this line$
```

The \c causes the echo command to suppress the newline. Therefore, the shell's prompt was printed right after the last character displayed by echo.

Type the following commands into a file called testx:

```
echo "one\c"
echo "two\c"
echo "three"
```

Now change the mode on the file so that it can be executed and then run it.

```
$ chmod +x testx
$ testx
onetwothree
$
```

As a final example, type the lines:

```
for i in 0 1 2 3 4 5 6 7 8 9
do
    echo "$i\c"
done

echo
```

into a file called test2 and then execute it:

```
$ chmod +x test2
$ test2
0123456789
$
```

The string $i\c was enclosed in double quotes rather than single quotes so that the value of the shell variable i would be substituted by the shell. (Of course, $i"\c" or $i'\c' could have been used instead.)

The purpose of the last echo is simply to go to the next line. If it hadn't been included, then the shell's prompt, $, would have appeared right after the 9.

Moving to the Next Tab Stop: \t

Try pressing the key labeled TAB at your terminal and see what happens. (If your terminal doesn't have this key, simultaneously type CTRL and I instead.) If your terminal is like most others, then each time you press this key, the cursor will move across the screen. On most terminals, the cursor moves over eight character positions each time the TAB key is pressed. The "first" tab position is column 1, the second column 9, the third column 17 and so on. Tabs are useful for aligning data in columnar format. You can move to the *next* tab position on the line in an echo command by using the characters \t:

```
$ echo "1\t2\t3\t4\t5"
1       2       3       4       5
$
```

As mentioned, tabs are very useful for aligning data. Type the following lines into the file inventory:

```
echo
echo "Item\tNumber"
echo "----\t-----"
echo "Widgets\t1,020"
echo "Pipes\t5,730"
echo "Filters\t3,097
echo "Tees\t2,912"
echo
```

and then execute it:

```
$ chmod +x inventory
$ inventory

Item    Number
----    ------
Widgets 1,020
Pipes   5,730
Filters 3,097
Tees    2,912

$
```

I think you get the idea of how the tab character works. The phone book shown on page 64 was created with tab characters so that the phone numbers all lined up. Each name and number is separated by two tab characters.

◆ Passing Arguments to Shell Programs ◆

Arguments greatly increase the flexibility and usefulness of any program. You can have your shell programs take arguments the same way other UNIX commands take them. When the program is executed, you simply list the arguments on the command line in the normal fashion:

```
add Pennino 985-0987
```

This indicates to the shell that the program add is to be executed and that it has two arguments: Pennino and 985-0987. To reference arguments from inside a shell program, the notation:

$$\$i$$

is used, where *i* is an integer from 1 through 9 that identifies the first through ninth arguments, respectively. So typing the line:

```
add Pennino 985-0987
```

would cause the add program to be executed with the arguments Peninno and 985-0987 assigned to $1 and $2 respectively. The add program would treat these arguments like any other shell variables. For instance, to display the value of the second argument (985-0987) the following line might appear inside add:

```
echo $2
```

To search the file phone_book for the occurrence of the first argument (Pennino), this line might appear inside add:

```
grep $1 phone_book
```

Suppose you type the following shell program into a file called arg1:

```
# shell command file to display argument 1
```

```
echo "Argument one is :$1:"
```

The first line is known as a *comment* and its sole purpose is to document the purpose of this shell program. Whenever the shell encounters a # character, it simply ignores the remainder of the line; therefore, you can type whatever you please. (Recall that to enter the # character into a file using ed you must first enter a \ so that the # is not interpreted as a character erase.)

```
$ ed arg1
?arg1
P
*a
\# shell command file to display argument 1

echo "Argument one is :$1:"
```

```
*w
73
*q
$
```

Remember what has to be done before you can execute the commands contained in `arg1`?

```
$ chmod +x arg1
$
```

That's right! You have to explicitly tell the UNIX system that this file contains commands to be executed. Now let's experiment with this file to see exactly what the shell considers to be the first argument.

```
$ arg1 abc
Argument one is :abc:
$
```

The colons were placed around the display of `$1` in `arg1` to see precisely what characters are included. For example:

```
$ arg1
Argument one is ::
$
```

If no argument is supplied, then the value of `$1` is null.

```
$ arg1 one two three
Argument one is :one:
$
```

The shell always delimits arguments by blank spaces. Therefore, only one is assigned to `$1`. As is the case with standard UNIX commands, if you want to include blanks in an argument, then it must be surrounded by a pair of quotes (either single or double):

```
$ arg1 "one two three"
Argument one is :one two three:
$
```

You can even assign just blanks to an argument, as long as they are quoted:

```
$ arg1 "  "
Argument one is :  :
$
```

Again, as with standard UNIX commands, file name substitution can be used:

```
$ ls
arg1
collect
mon
nu
wb
$ arg1 c*
Argument one is :collect:
$ arg1 ??
Argument one is :nu:
$
```

In the last example, ?? gets expanded to the names of all files that are exactly two characters long: nu and wb. Since the shell separates these by a blank and alphabetizes the result, only the first name in the list, nu, gets assigned to $1.

Now let's see a practical use of a shell program that takes an argument. Recall the phone directory file called phone_book:

```
$ cat phone_book
Farber, Ethan      445-4343
Iansito, Toby      937-1232
Levy, Steven       (907) 843-4432
Mead, John         864-5378
Sander, Rick       343-2109
Smith, George      723-2205
Snellen, Bart      331-9974
Weather info       976-1212
Wood, Pat          421-3193
Wood, Sam          778-3321
$
```

You saw how the grep command could be used to look up an entry in this file:

```
$ grep "Iansito, Toby" phone_book
Iansito, Toby  937-1232
$
```

Here's a simple shell program that takes a name as its argument and does a lookup of the name inside the phone_book:

```
# lookup a person's phone number

grep "$1" phone_book
```

The quotes around $1 are needed so that grep sees a name with embedded blanks as a single argument.

If you type these lines into a file called lu (for lookup) and change the mode on the file to make it executable, then the following would depict typical operation of the program:

```
$ lu "Iansito, Toby"
Iansito, Toby  937-1232
$ lu "Master, Rich"
$
```

The last example shows what happens when a name isn't found in the phone book: you just get back your command prompt.

Now that you have a shell program to look up someone's number, it might be nice also to have a program to add a new entry to the phone book, as well as to remove an entry from the phone book. Call the former program add and the latter rem. The add program will be developed in the text; it's left as an exercise for you to write the rem program (hint: read the description of sed at the end of this chapter).

Before proceeding, it might be a good idea to make a separate directory for the phone book file and its associated programs. Call the directory phone and create it at the same level as the documents, programs, and misc directories (refer to Fig. 6-2):

```
$ cd                                    Return to HOME directory
$ mkdir phone                           Make the new directory
$ mv misc/phone_book misc/lu phone      Move the two files in
$ cd phone                              Change to the new directory
$ ls                                    and take a look
lu
phone_book
$
```

After executing this sequence of commands, the directory structure will appear as shown in Fig. 6-3:

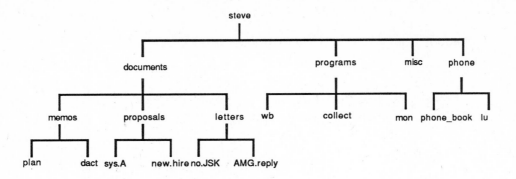

Fig. 6-3. Directory structure with the new phone directory

Now that your files are better organized, let's develop the add program. The program should be straightforward enough. You can have it take two arguments: the name and the number to be added. These two arguments can then simply be appended to the end of the phone_book file:

```
#
# add a name and number to the phone book
#

echo "$1\t\t$2" >> phone_book
echo "$1 has been added to the phone book."
```

Type the above shell program into the file add, change its mode, and execute it:

```
$ add "Gualtieri, Dave" 867-5394
Gualtieri, Dave has been added to the phone book.
$ lu Gualtieri
Gualtieri, Dave        867-5394
$
```

It seems to be working just fine. Let's take a closer look at the new phone_book file:

```
$ cat phone_book
Farber, Ethan          445-4343
Iansito, Toby          937-1232
Levy, Steven           (907) 843-4432
Mead, John             864-5378
Sander, Rick           343-2109
Smith, George          723-2205
Snellen, Bart          331-9974
```

```
Weather info          976-1212
Wood, Pat             421-3193
Wood, Sam             778-3321
Gualtieri, Dave       867-5394
$
```

Gualtieri was added to the end of the file, as we intended. However, you'll notice that the file is no longer in alphabetical order. This isn't necessarily a problem, but you could modify your add program to sort the phone book after adding a new entry. This change is shown next:

```
#
# add a name and number to the phone book
#

echo "$1\t\t$2" >> phone_book    # add name and number
sort phone_book -o phone_book    # sort the phone book
echo "$1 has been added to the phone book."
```

You can't have the output of the sort go directly to phone_book using a statement such as:

```
sort phone_book > phone_book
```

because of the way output redirection works. If the designated file already exists, then any previous contents get destroyed. So the shell would first "zero out" the phone_book file and then execute the sort. sort would then try to sort phone_book, which would not contain any information. The net result of the entire operation would be a phone_book file that did not contain any data. This explains why we used the -o option to sort, which is followed by the name of the output file. When using this option, it is valid to specify the same name for the output file as the file being sorted. This enables the sort command to sort the phone_book file without losing its contents.

Let's see what happens when you add another entry to the phone book:

```
$ add "Barker, Barry" 439-7776
Barker, Barry has been added to the phone book.
$ cat phone_book
Barker, Barry     439-7776
Farber, Ethan     445-4343
Gualtieri, Dave   867-5394
Iansito, Toby     937-1232
Levy, Steven      (907) 843-4432
Mead, John        864-5378
Sander, Rick      343-2109
```

```
Smith, George      723-2205
Snellen, Bart      331-9974
Weather info       976-1212
Wood, Pat          421-3193
Wood, Sam          778-3321
$
```

$# and $*

The shell has two "variables" that are automatically set whenever you execute a shell program. The first one is $# and it is set to the *number* of arguments that were passed to the program. The second one is $* and it is set to *all* of the arguments that were passed.

To see how $# gets set, type the following into a file called num and make it executable:

```
echo Number of arguments is $#.
```

Now let's experiment:

```
$ num one
Number of arguments is 1.
$ num one two three
Number of arguments is 3.
$ num "one two three"
Number of arguments is 1.
$ num
Number of arguments is 0.
$
```

So that you see that $# tells you the number of arguments that were passed to the program. This information is useful when you write a shell program that expects a precise number of arguments. You'll see shortly how you can test the value of this variable to see if the correct number were supplied to the program.

Now it's time to turn your attention to $*. As you'll recall, this variable contains the *entire* list of arguments passed to a program.

Edit the num program and add the following line at the end:

```
echo They are :$*:
```

So the file num should now look like this:

```
echo Number of arguments is $#.
echo They are :$*:
```

Let's try it out:

```
$ num one
Number of arguments is 1.
They are :one:
$ num one two three
Number of arguments is 3.
They are :one two three:
$ num "one two three"
Number of arguments is 1.
They are :one two three:
$ num
Number of arguments is 0.
They are ::
$ num *
Number of arguments is 5.
They are :arg1 collect mon nu wb:
$ num ??
Number of arguments is 2.
They are :nu wb:
$
```

$* is useful in shell programs that take a variable number of arguments. In such programs it's not unusual to see $* used as the list specification in a `for` statement, for instance, to sequence through each of the arguments. As an example, the following shell program takes a variable number of file arguments. Each argument is the name of a file that is to be sorted, preceded by an appropriate heading:

```
#
# shell program to sort files
#

for file in $*
do
    echo "========================================="
    echo "        Sorted contents of $file"
    echo "========================================="
    sort $file
    echo
done
```

If you type this program into a file called `sortf`, then the following shows the results you might get from executing the program:

```
$ sortf names
===========================================
         Sorted contents of names
===========================================
Bill
Pat
Ruth
Tony

$ sortf name*
===========================================
         Sorted contents of names
===========================================
Bill
Pat
Ruth
Tony


===========================================
         Sorted contents of names1
===========================================
Bill
John
Pat
Ruth
Tom
Tony


===========================================
         Sorted contents of names2
===========================================
John
Pat
Ruth
Tom
Tony

$ sortf
$
```

The last example shows what happens when no arguments are supplied. In that case, the value of $* is *null*, so the `for` statement inside `sortf` has an "empty" list. The shell simply ignores the entire `for` statement if the list is empty, thus explaining the output.

◆ The if Statement ◆

Every programming language provides at least one statement that lets you conditionally perform some actions based on the results of a question. In the shell, the if statement performs this function. The general format of the if statement is:

```
if condition
then
    command
    command
    . . .
fi
```

If the value of *condition* is valid or *TRUE*, then the commands enclosed between the then and the fi will be executed; otherwise they will be skipped. *condition* might be a test to determine if a shell variable has a particular value or if a certain file exists, for example. Such tests are enclosed inside a pair of brackets. So the general format is:

[*test-expression*]

As an example, the following sequence will display the message Hello, steve if the value of the variable user is equal to steve (assume here that it *is*):

```
$ if [ $user = steve ]
> then
>   echo Hello, steve
> fi
Hello, steve
$
```

The *condition*, [$user = steve], (and note that the blanks after the [, around the =, and before the] are all required) tests if the shell variable user is equal to the character string steve. If it is, then the echo command is executed; otherwise, it is ignored.

There are other *relational operators* that you can use besides the equality operator =. The more commonly used operators are summarized in Table 6-2.

TABLE 6-2. Summary of relational operators

Operator	Used to test if	Example
=	two strings are equal	"$user" = steve
!=	two strings are not equal	"$group" != GP
−n	a string has nonzero length	−n "$file"
−z	a string has zero length	−z "$name"
−ne	two integers are not equal	"$line" −ne 0
−lt	one integer is less than another	"$i" −lt 100
−le	one integer is less than or equal to another	"$i1" −le "$i2"
−gt	one integer is greater than another	"$count" −gt 0
−ge	one integer is greater than or equal to another	"$a" −ge "$b"
−f	a file is an ordinary file	−f data_file
−d	a file is a directory	−d "$DATADIR"
−s	a file has nonzero length	−s grepout

In addition, an expression can be joined with either the *and* operator −a or the *or* operator −o. So the expression

```
[ $i -gt 5 -a $i -le 100 ]
```

will be *TRUE* only if the value of the shell variable i is greater than 5 and less than or equal to 100. The expression

```
[ $env = UNIX -o $group = GP ]
```

will be *TRUE* if the shell variable env equals UNIX *or* the variable group equals GP.

(There are also other operators that have not been described here. For more information, look under the program test in Section 1 of your *UNIX User's Manual*, or consult *UNIX Shell Programming*.)

In general, you should enclose shell variables used on either side of a relational operator within a pair of double quotes. Otherwise, in most cases the shell will issue an error message if the variable is null or contains blanks:

```
$ user=""                          Intentionally set user null
$ if [ $user != steve ]
> then
>   echo I was expecting steve
> fi
test: argument expected
$
```

Executing an `if` statement directly from the terminal is usually quite useless. However, this statement is very useful inside command files.

The else Clause

The shell provides an `else` clause to the `if` that can be used to cause execution of statements to occur if the specified test proves *FALSE*. The general format of the `if-else` is:

```
if condition
then
    command
    command
    ...
else
    command
    command
    ...
fi
```

If the result of *condition* is *TRUE*, then the commands enclosed between the `then` and `else` get executed; otherwise, the statements between the `else` and `fi` get executed. In either case, only one set of commands gets executed, never both.

As an example of the use of the `else` and also of the `$#` variable, let's modify the lookup program `lu` to include a test to ensure that exactly one argument is supplied on the command line:

```
# lookup a person's phone number in the phone book

if [ $# -ne 1 ]
then
    echo "\nUsage: lu name\n"
else
    grep "$1" phone_book
fi
```

If the number of arguments does not equal 1, then the `echo` command displays the proper command usage to the user; otherwise the `grep` gets executed to search `phone_book` for the specified name.

```
$ lu

Usage: lu name

$ lu Iansito, Toby

Usage: lu name
```

```
$ lu "Iansito, Toby"
Iansito, Toby  937-1232
$ lu "Master"
$
```

The last example reminds you that the program doesn't display anything if a name is not found in the phone book. It might be nice to change the program to display a message if it couldn't find someone's name.

You know that `grep` simply produces no output when it doesn't find any lines that match the given pattern. Using this fact and the back quoting mechanism, you can assign the output of the `grep` to a shell variable and then test the variable to see if it is null (i.e., has zero length) or not. If it is null, then you know that `grep` couldn't find the name in the file. In that case, you can display a message to this effect at the terminal. If it isn't null, then the variable will contain the result of the `grep`; so you can simply display its value at the terminal.

Here's the (once again) modified `lu` program:

```
# lookup a person's phone number in the phone book

if [ $# -ne 1 ]
then
    echo "\nUsage: lu name\n"
else
    output=`grep "$1" phone_book`

    if [ -z "$output" ]
    then
        echo "I couldn't find $1 in the phone book"
    else
        echo "$output"
    fi
fi
```

It's perfectly valid to include `if`s inside other `if`s. In fact, the nesting can go as deep as you like. Just remember that for each `if` you must include a corresponding `fi`.

```
$ lu Sander
Sander, Rick   343-2109
$ lu Archer
I couldn't find Archer in the phone book
$ lu Wood
Wood, Pat      421-3193
Wood, Sam      778-3321
$
```

The output from the last example explains why you had to include $out-put inside double quotes in the echo command of the program. Had you not done so, then the shell would have removed the newline characters from out-put before being passed as an argument to echo, thus resulting in the display of the two Wood entries on the same line.

The elif Construct

Suppose you wanted to create a shell program that displayed the salutation "Good morning." if it's anytime after midnight but before noon; the phrase "Good afternoon." if it's from noon to 6 P.M.; and the phrase "Good evening." if it's anytime from 6 P.M. to midnight.

If you think about writing a shell program to perform this task, you will realize that its structure should look something like this:

```
if  it's after midnight and before noon
then
     display Good morning.
else
    if  it's after noon and before 6 PM
    then
        display Good afternoon.
    else
        display Good evening.
    fi
fi
```

You can directly translate the above into a shell program. First you have to fig-ure out how to make the tests on the time of day. Well, you know that the date command gives you the time (plus some other information);

```
$ date
Sun Mar 19 13:43:00 EST 1989
$
```

For this program, all you really need to know is the hour of the day. You can use the cut command to get the hour of the day out of date given the fact that the hour always appears in columns 12-13 of date's output:

```
$ date | cut -c12-13
13
$
```

Now that you have this technique, you can write the program. Before proceed-ing, however, let's introduce the elif construct. As the name implies, this con-struct is actually a marriage of the else and if. Its general format is:

```
if condition
then
    command
    command
    ...
elif   condition
then
    command
    command
    ...
fi
```

You can include as many `elif`s as you need. At the end of it all you can place an `else` so that a set of commands can be executed if none of the preceding test expressions is *TRUE*. Now here is a shell program to print the salutation. Call the program `salute`:

```
#
# shell program to execute date and then display
# Good morning, Good afternoon, or Good evening, as
# appropriate
#

hour=`date | cut -c12-13`

if [ $hour -ge 0 -a $hour -lt 12 ]
then
    echo "Good morning."
elif [ $hour -ge 12 -a $hour -lt 18 ]
then
    echo "Good afternoon."
else
    echo "Good evening."
fi
```

Let's see if it works for the present time:

```
$ date
Sun Mar 18 13:59:11 EST 1984        We know it's afternoon
$ salute
Good afternoon.                     Seems okay
$
```

◆ Arithmetic Operations with Shell Variables ◆

The standard shell does not provide any built-in mechanisms to enable you to perform arithmetic operations on shell variables. You may think this quite unusual for a programming language. It is unusual; but then, no one ever claimed that the shell was your usual programming language!

Suppose you had a shell variable called count and you set it equal to 0 with the statement:

```
count=0
```

If you attempted to add 1 to count, this is what you'd get:

```
$ count=$count+1
$ echo $count
0+1
$
```

Once again, the shell doesn't know how to add 1 to a variable in the manner akin to most programming languages. All is not lost, however, as there is a command called expr that is used by shell programmers to evaluate expressions in shell programs. Let's experiment with this command:

```
$ expr 1 + 2
3
$ expr 5 "*" 10
50
$ expr 1+2
1+2
$ count=100
$ expr $count + 1
101
$
```

The expr command evaluates the expression given by its arguments and writes the result to standard output. In the first case, expr is given three arguments, 1, +, and 2. The result of the addition, 3, is then displayed.

In the second example the * operator—used to multiply two integers —*must* be quoted to prevent the shell from substituting the names of all of the files in the current directory on the command line. You could not place quotes around the entire expression, as in

```
expr "5 * 10"
```

since this would only be seen by expr as *one* argument and not three. (Try it and see what happens.)

The third example shows that `expr` does not interpret

```
1+2
```

as you might expect. This has to do with the same point made in the previous sentence: `expr` expects to see each term and operator as separate arguments.

The fact that `expr` writes its result to standard output is the key to performing arithmetic operations in the shell. By using the backquote mechanism, you can assign `expr`'s result to a shell variable:

```
$ result=`expr 1 + 2`
$ echo $result
3
$
```

And the following shows how you can use `expr` to add 1 to a shell variable:

```
$ count=100
$count=`expr $count + 1`          Add 1 to count
$ echo $count
101
$
```

You should note that the Korn shell `ksh` *does* provide built-in integer arithmetic operations, and also allows you to work with integers expressed in different bases.

♦ The `while` Statement ♦

The `while` is another looping statement provided by the shell. It enables you to repeatedly execute a set of commands `while` a specified condition is *TRUE*. The format of the `while` is:

```
while condition
do
    command
    command
    ...
done
```

The `condition` part is the same as it is for the `if` statement. It is tested first when the `while` loop starts. If it is `true`, then the commands enclosed between the `do` and `done` are executed. Each time after the commands are executed, condition is again tested. The commands enclosed between the do and done will continue to be executed until *condition* proves *FALSE*. At that time, the while loop will be terminated.

The following illustrates use of the while loop and also the method that was outlined for performing arithmetic with shell variables.

```
$ count=1
$ while [ "$count" -le 10 ]
> do
>   echo $count
>   count=`expr $count + 1`
> done
1
2
3
4
5
6
7
8
9
10
$
```

Before leaving this brief discussion of the while statement, you should note that the shell also provides a statement called until that is very similar in operation to the while. Consult *UNIX Shell Programming* for more details.

◆ Reading Data from the Terminal ◆

When writing shell programs you may come across the need to have the user enter some data from the terminal. The shell statement read exists for this purpose. Its general format is simple enough:

read *variable-list*

Execution of this statement causes the shell to read in a line from the terminal and assign the values read to the shell variables specified in *variable-list*. If only one variable is listed, then the entire line is assigned to that variable. Values typed in are delimited by blanks or tabs. Let's experiment with read at the terminal:

```
$ read a b c
one     two     three
$ echo ":$a:$b:$c:"
:one:two:three:                        Blanks got removed
$read line                             Only one variable
this is a line of text     !!!
$ echo "$line"
this is a line of text     !!!         Entire line was assigned
$ read a b
first and then the rest
$ echo ":$a:$b:"
:first:and then the rest               Extra data gets stored in last variable
$
```

Now let's put the read statement to work in an actual program. The purpose of this program is to show how you can develop your own commands that prompt the user for information. You'll create a program called copy to copy files. The program will not take any arguments but instead will prompt the user for the names of the source and destination files. After this information has been entered, the copy program will simply call the cp command to perform the copy.

```
#
# Program to copy files
#

echo "Source file: \c"
read source

echo "Destination file: \c"
read destination

cp $source $destination
```

The \c characters were placed in the two echos so that the user can enter the data on the same line as the prompt message.
    Now to test it:

```
$ ls                                   Let's see what's around
names
names1
names2
$ copy
Source file: names
Destination file: test
$ ls
```

```
names
names1
names2
test                              The new file is there
$ sdiff -s names test            and it's identical to the original
$
```

A subtle point worth noting about the `copy` program: since you were careful *not* to enclose the shell variables `destination` and `source` inside quotes in the `cp` command, the shell will perform file name substitution on these arguments if specified:

```
$ ls *2
names2
$ copy
Source file: *2
Destination file: test2
$ sdiff -s names2 test2
$
```

Some interesting modifications can be made to the `copy` program to make it more useful. One might be to allow the user to enter the arguments on the command line if desired. The program could then test for this condition and directly call the `cp` command with the arguments typed on the line (remember `$*` ?).

Another worthwhile change might test to see if the destination file already existed. If it did, then the user could be asked if he or she wanted to proceed with the copy. If the user decided not to proceed, the program could simply ignore the copy request. This would be helpful for novice UNIX users, as it could help keep them from accidentally overwriting their files. (You can even make your own version of the `mv` command to do the same type of check.)

The main point to be remembered from all of this is that the UNIX system provides you with the power and flexibility to effectively customize UNIX commands. The fact that `cp` is a built-in UNIX command while `copy` is a custom-written command can remain unknown to other users.

◆ The case Statement ◆

The shell `case` statement is useful when you want to compare a value against a whole series of values. You know that this can be done with an `if-elif` statement chain, but the `case` statement is more concise and also easier to write and read. The general format of this statement is:

```
case value
in
    pattern₁ )    command
                  command
                  ...
                  command;;
    pattern₂ )    command
                  command
                  ...
                  command;;
                  ...
    pattern n )   command
                  command
                  ...
                  command;;
esac
```

Operation of the `case` proceeds as follows: *value* is successively compared against $pattern_1$, $pattern_2$, ..., $pattern_n$. As soon as a match is found, the commands listed after the matching patterns are executed, until a double semicolon (; ;) is reached. At that point, the `case` statement is terminated. If *value* does not match any of the specified patterns, then no action is taken, and the entire `case` is effectively "skipped." If the special pattern ✶ is included as the *last* pattern in the `case`, then the commands that follow will be executed whenever none of the preceding patterns match.

As a simple example of the use of the `case`, the following program displays the English equivalent of a number from 0 through 9. This number is given as an argument to the command. If a value other than 0 through 9 is specified, then the program displays the message `Invalid argument`.

```
#
# Display the English equivalent of a digit
#

case "$1"
in
    0 )    echo zero;;
    1 )    echo one;;
    2 )    echo two;;
    3 )    echo three;;
    4 )    echo four;;
    5 )    echo five;;
    6 )    echo six;;
    7 )    echo seven;;
    8 )    echo eight;;
    9 )    echo nine;;
    * )    echo Invalid argument;;
esac
```

If you call this program digit, then the following represents some sample uses:

```
$ digit 5
five
$ digit x
Invalid argument
$ digit 8
eight
$
```

The case statement is frequently used by shell programmers in writing programs that take options. For example, the following shell statements might appear in a program that took options -l, -c, and -w, plus a list of file name arguments. The for that surrounds the case enables you to supply a variable number of options and arguments, in any order.

```
loption=""
coption=""
woption=""
filelist=""

for arg in $*
do
    case $arg
    in
        -l)    loption=1;;
        -w)    woption=1;;
        -c)    coption=1;;
         *)    filelist="$filelist $arg";;
    esac
done
```

This code sequence assumes that any file argument typed on the command line that's not -l, -w, or -c is a file name. At the end of execution of these statements, the shell variable loption will be set to 1 if -l were typed on the command line, the variable woption to 1 if -w were typed, and the variable coption to 1 if -c were typed. The shell variable filelist will contain a list of files typed on the command line.

If this sequence of statements occurred in a program called coop, for instance, then the following shows sample command lines that would get properly interpreted:

```
coop -w -c file1
coop -w f* -c -l
coop -l
coop file1 file2 name*
```

The patterns that are specified inside a `case` statement are matched by the shell the same way file names are. This means, for example that the pattern

    na*

would match any value that begins with `na`; the pattern

    ?x

would match any two-character value that ends in `x`; and the pattern

    [a-z]

would match any lower-case letter.

An *Or*ing of patterns is effected by separating patterns with a vertical bar `|`. So, for example, the following pattern will match the value `hp` *or* `hp-2621` *or* `2621`:

    hp | hp-2621 | 2621

And as a final example, the following pattern matches any values that begin with the characters `fig` *or* `tbl`:

    fig* | tbl*

◆ Your Environment ◆

Whenever you log onto the system, you are given your own copy of the shell program. You are also set up in your own little world known as your *environment*. Included in this environment are special shell variables that are specific to you. For example, there is a shell variable `HOME` that contains the path to your `HOME` directory; another variable called `PATH` describes to the UNIX system the directories that are to be searched whenever a command is executed; two shell variables called `PS1` and `PS2` describe your first and second "level" command prompts.

There's No Place Like HOME

The shell variable `HOME` is automatically set to your home directory path as soon as you log into the system. Try printing out the value of this variable at your terminal and see what happens:

```
$ echo $HOME
/a1/steve
$
```

The HOME variable is used by several UNIX commands to locate your HOME directory. For example, you will recall that typing just the command cd with no argument places you in your HOME directory. The cd command determines where this directory is by examining your HOME variable. Study the following example:

```
$ pwd
/a1/steve/documents
$ cd                          Change to HOME directory
$ pwd
/a1/steve
$ HOME=/a1/steve/misc         Change the value of HOME
$ cd                          Now see what happens
$ pwd
/a1/steve/misc
$
```

As you can see, changing the value of the shell variable HOME has an effect on the execution of the cd command. Be careful—operation of other commands may be effected as well.

PS1 and PS2

By now you're used to getting a dollar sign prompt printed whenever the shell is waiting for you to type a command. But what if you don't want your prompt to be a dollar sign? Well, you can easily change your prompt character at any time simply by changing the value of the shell variable PS1. First, let's see what value this variable currently has:

```
$ echo prompt is $PS1
prompt is $
$
```

Now let's see what happens when you change it:

```
$ PS1=">"
>date
Mon Mar 20 16:16:05 EST 1989
>
```

(You will recall from the discussion on quotes that you must include > in quotes when assigning it to PS1; otherwise, the shell thinks you're trying to redirect output.) As you can see, as soon as you change the value of PS1, the value it is changed to becomes your new prompt character for *all* subsequent commands. You can change the command prompt to any characters at all, as the next few examples illustrate:

```
>PS1="> "      Add an extra blank space to the end
> date
Mon Mar 20 16:19:55 EST 1989
> PS1="=> "
=> PS1="Enter your command: "
Enter your command: date
Mon Mar 20 16:20:25 EST 1989
Enter your command:
```

The last prompt, Enter your command:, may seem a little extreme, but it does illustrate the point.

As you probably guessed, the prompt that is printed whenever the shell is expecting more input (normally >) can also be changed. This prompt character is stored in the variable PS2:

```
Enter your command: echo $PS2
>
Enter your command:PS1="$ "      Change this back
$
```

Now that you've changed your PS1 prompt to something more reasonable, change the value of PS2:

```
$ PS2="====> "
$ for n in 1 2 3
====> do
====> echo $n
====> done
1
2
3
$
```

Any value that is assigned to either PS1 or PS2 remains in effect throughout your login session. Next time you log in, the default values of $ and > will be used. You'll see shortly how you can keep these changes across login sessions.

Your PATH

Probably the most important shell variable is the one called PATH. This variable tells the shell exactly *where* to find *any* command that you execute. Whenever you log in, your PATH variable is set to some default value. See what it is set to now:

```
$ echo $PATH
/bin:/usr/bin:
$
```

The PATH variable contains a list of *all* directories that will be searched whenever you type in the name of a program to be executed. It also specifies the order in which the search will be performed. The directories listed in the PATH variable will be searched by the shell from left to right. A colon (:) separates one path from the next in the list. A colon at the end of the list means that the current directory is to be searched last.

The value of the PATH variable shown indicates that three directories are to be searched whenever you type in the name of a program to be executed. First the directory /bin is searched, then the directory /usr/bin, and finally the current directory. As soon as the shell finds the program in one of these directories, it executes it. However, if it doesn't find it in any of these directories, then it prints the message *command*: not found.

The nice thing about the PATH variable is that you can change its value to control the order of the search, or to add new directories to be searched. For example, the directory structure depicted in Fig. 6-3 contains a directory called programs that you can assume contains programs that can be executed. So you probably would place your nu (to count the number of users) and Salute (to print "Good morning," "Good afternoon," or "Good evening,") programs inside this directory (see Fig. 6-4).

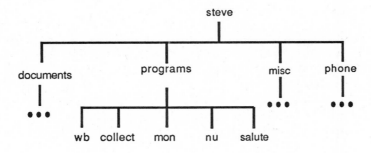

Fig. 6-4. Local program directory programs

Without using the PATH mechanism, you have to explicitly tell the shell where it can find the nu program whenever you want to find out how many users are logged in.

```
$ pwd
/a1/steve/documents/memos
$ nu                                    Execute the program nu
nu: not found                           The shell couldn't find it
$ /a1/steve/programs/nu
There are 9 users logged in.
$
```

The first time you tried to execute nu, the shell used the PATH variable to deter-mine where to search for the program. So first it looked inside the current direc-tory /a1/steve/documents/memos for nu. Since no executable file of that name was to be found in that directory, it continued its search with the directory /bin and then with the directory /usr/bin. Since nu couldn't be found in these two directories either, the shell printed its not found message at the ter-minal.

The next time, a full path to the nu program was specified (a relative path could have been used as well). So the shell went directly to the directory /a1/steve/programs to find nu, since specifying a path to a program always overrides the PATH variable.

Instead of having to explicitly tell the shell where to find nu each time you want to use it, you can add the programs directory to your PATH so that the shell will automatically search this directory. To do this, you can explicitly assign the new search path to PATH:

```
PATH=/bin:/usr/bin::/a1/steve/programs
```

(note the two adjacent colons in the PATH to specify the current directory) or you can equivalently "tack" your new directory onto the end of the existing PATH:

```
PATH=$PATH:/a1/steve/programs
```

This last method saves some typing. Now you can execute a program contained in your programs directory from *anywhere*:

```
$ pwd
/a1/steve/documents/memos
$ PATH=$PATH:/a1/steve/programs     Add programs to the PATH
$ echo $PATH
/bin:/usr/bin::/a1/steve/programs
$ nu
There are 9 users logged in.        This time the shell found it
$ salute
Good morning.
$
```

Recall the programs lu, add, and rem to look up, add, and remove
entries, respectively, from the phone book. We stored these programs, together
with the phone_book file in a directory that we called phone. It would be nice
if you could execute the lu, add, and rem programs from anywhere in your
directory path. So let's add /a1/steve/phone to your PATH:

```
$ PATH=$PATH:/a1/steve/phone
$ echo $PATH
/bin:/usr/bin::/a1/steve/programs:/a1/steve/phone
$
```

Now let's go back to the HOME directory /a1/steve and try to look someone
up in the phone book:

```
$ cd
$ lu Gualtieri
grep: couldn't open phone_book
I couldn't find Gualtieri in the phone book
$
```

What happened? The output says that grep couldn't open the file
phone_book. This happened because the grep inside the lu program looked
for the phone_book file only in the *current working directory* /a1/steve and
couldn't find it there. Remember, PATH only specifies directories to be searched
for programs, and not for other files. And unless a relative or full path name is
specified for a file, only the current working directory will be searched for that
file.

As you might expect, add and rem probably have the same problem as
the lu program. These programs will work only if executed from inside the
phone directory, since that is where the phone_book file resides.

There are several ways to solve this problem. One way is to edit each program to specify a full path to the phone_book file wherever it is used. So, for
example, the lu program would now appear as shown:

```
# lookup a person's phone number in the phone book

if [ $# -ne 1 ]
then
    echo "Usage: lu name"
else
    output=`grep "$1" /a1/steve/phone/phone_book`

    if [ -z "$output" ]
    then
        echo "I couldn't find $1 in the phone book"
    else
        echo "$output"
    fi
fi
```

Now this program will work from anywhere:

```
$ pwd                           See where we are
/a1/steve
$ lu Gualtieri
Gualtieri, Dave    867-5394
$
```

Another solution is to have each program change its working directory to the phone directory as soon as it begins execution. In this way, the `phone_book` file *will* be found in the current directory:

```
# lookup a person's phone number in the phone book

if [ $# -ne 1 ]
then
    echo "Usage: lu name"
else
    cd /a1/steve/phone

    output=`grep "$1" phone_book`

    if [ -z "$output" ]
    then
        echo "I couldn't find $1 in the phone book"
    else
        echo "$output"
    fi
fi
```

It is interesting to note that executing a `cd` from inside a shell program only changes the working directory for that program. It has no effect on *your* current working directory. The following verifies this fact:

```
$ pwd
/a1/steve
$ lu Barker
Barker, Barry   338-7776
$ pwd
/a1/steve                       It didn't change
$
```

The second technique for solving our problem—namely `cd`'ing to the phone directory is very useful when dealing with shell programs that need to reference many files in a particular directory. By changing to that directory, you are saved from the "bother" of having to fully qualify all of these files in the program.

Before leaving this discussion, you should note that the shell uses the `PATH` variable to find standard UNIX commands as well. These are stored in the directories `/bin` and `/usr/bin`. If you did something naughty such as assigned the null string to `PATH`, then the system would not be able to find *any* command:

```
$ PATH=""                          ⎫  Wipe out the PATH
$ date                             ⎪
date: not found                    ⎬  The shell can't find anything now
$ who                              ⎪
who: not found                     ⎭
$ PATH=/bin:/usr/bin:
$ date
Tue Mar 21 09:41:23 EST 1989         That's better!
$
```

As with the `PS1`, `PS2`, and `HOME` shell variables, any changes made to `PATH` will not be there next time you log in.

Exported Variables

Whenever you execute a shell program, the shell creates an entirely separate environment for that program to run in. This means that the program gets its own distinct set of variables. Any variables that you assigned values to before executing the program cannot be accessed or changed by the program. And when the program finishes execution, its environment goes away with it. So any variables set by that program do not exist after that program has completed execution. The following illustrates an example:

```
$ cat > foo                        ⎫
echo :$x:                          ⎬  Create a program to display the value of x
CTRL-d                             ⎪
$ chmod +x foo                     ⎭
$ x=100
$ echo $x
100
$ foo
::
$
```

The `foo` program couldn't access the value of `x`. Furthermore, if `foo` had assigned a value to a variable called `x`, then that would have had no effect on the variable `x` that was assigned the value 100 before `foo` was executed—its value would still be 100 after execution of `foo` was completed.

There *is* a way to access the value of a shell variable from another program. A shell statement called `export` must be used; its format is:

export *variable-list*

where *variable-list* is a blank separated list of variables (*not* preceded by dollar signs). Any program that subsequently gets executed can access the value of the exported variables—but it still cannot permanently change them.

Let's go back to the foo program:

```
$ echo $x
100                                      It's still there
$ export x
$ foo
:100:                                    This time foo knows about x
$
```

Now add a line to the beginning of foo so that it looks like this:

```
x=50
echo :$x:
```

Here's what happens when you execute foo:

```
$ echo $x
100
$ foo
:50:
$ echo $x
100
$
```

So you see that foo could not permanently change the value of x; it merely changed its own copy of x that existed in its environment.

Your .profile

Suppose you've made several changes to your environment and you would like to have them saved; that is, you want these changes to still be there the next time you log in. In order to be able to do this, the shell has adopted the following convention: Every time you log in, the shell automatically looks in your HOME directory for a file called .profile. If the file is there, then the shell automatically executes it. And since this file gets executed in a different way from other shell programs, any variables that get set or exported inside the .profile remain in effect even after execution of the .profile has completed.

You probably have a .profile right now without even being aware of it! First, go to your HOME directory:

```
$ cd
$ pwd
/a1/steve
$
```

Now see if there's a `.profile` there:

```
$ ls .profile
.profile
$
```

Apparently, `steve` does have one. But look what happens if he does an `ls` to list all the files in his directory:

```
$ ls
documents
misc
phone
programs
$
```

The `.profile` file is *not* listed when the `ls` command is executed. This is because the `ls` command does not normally list file names that begin with a period. You can explicitly list such "hidden" files with a command such as `ls .profile`, or you can use the `-a` option to the `ls` command:

```
$ ls -a
.
..
.profile
documents
misc
phone
programs
$
```

You see that the directory file `..` as well as the current directory file `.` are both listed when the `-a` option is used.

Getting back to the `.profile` file, let's assume that you don't have one. Let's set one up to include the `programs` and `phone` directories in your `PATH`, change `PS1` to `"=>"`, change your erase character from `#` to BACKSPACE (*CTRL-h*), print a salutation, and then tell us how many users are logged in:

```
# Add "programs" and "phone" to the search path and
# export it so other programs know about it

PATH=$PATH:/a1/steve/programs:/a1/steve/phone
export PATH

# Now change PS1

PS1="=> "
```

```
# Set erase character to Backspace

stty echoe erase CTRL-h

# Print salutation

echo
salute

# Tell how many people are logged in

nu
```

The shell will be able to find the `salute` and `nu` programs since your PATH will be changed by the time you execute these programs.

If you typed the above lines into a `.profile` file in your HOME directory, the following shows what would happen *whenever* you subsequently logged in.

```
login: steve
Password: iop098

Good morning.
There are 5 users logged in.
=>
```

◆ Using the Korn Shell ◆

As noted earlier in this chapter, the Korn shell is a relatively new shell developed by David Korn. He designed this shell to be "upwards compatible" with the System V shell, so that programs written for the Bourne shell also run under the Korn shell. Except for a few minor differences, the Korn shell provides you with all of the Bourne shell's features, as well as many new ones.

The main added features in the Korn shell are:

1. The ability to edit your command line using `vi` or `emacs` commands.

2. The ability to easily recall previously entered commands, make changes to them, and re-execute them.

3. Built-in integer arithmetic and string manipulation capabilities.

4. The ability to assign alternate names to commands and command sequences.

5.   Arrays.

6.   The ability to automatically monitor and control programs executing in the background.

In this chapter we'll tell you how to get started using the Korn shell and exploit the first capability listed above.

Running the Korn Shell

Normally, when you log in, you will be running the Bourne shell. Since the Korn shell isn't yet a standard feature of the UNIX system, not all systems have it, and those that do may not keep it in a standard directory.

    You can check to see if you're already running the Korn shell by typing in the following command:

```
$ echo $RANDOM $RANDOM
```

If you're not running the Korn shell, you will get a blank line displayed as the output from the above command.

```
$ echo $RANDOM $RANDOM

$
```

If two different numbers are displayed, you're already running the Korn shell:

```
$ echo $RANDOM $RANDOM
10113 17515
$
```

If you're not running the Korn shell, it's usually called ksh, so you can try to run it by typing in:

```
$ ksh
```

If you get the message ksh: not found, you may have to go hunting for it. Likely hiding places are in /usr/lbin, /usr/local, /usr/add-on, and the like. If you search for it for a while and can't find it, you may want to ask your system administrator where the Korn shell is on your system.

    Once you've found it, you can either add the directory it's in to your PATH, or you can invoke it by typing its full path name, e.g.,

```
$ /usr/lbin/ksh
```

If you don't have the Korn shell on your system, you can obtain a copy and have it installed (or install it yourself). Once you've been using the Korn shell for a while, you may want to make it your *default* login shell. Talk to your system administrator about how this can be done.

When you start up the Korn shell, it looks for an exported variable called ENV. If it is set, the file specified by ENV will be executed, much like the .pro-file is executed when logging in. The ENV file usually contains commands to set up the Korn shell's environment. One thing you should start with is to have it set the SHELL variable to the Korn shell. This way, as long as you're in the Korn shell, new shells that get started will be the Korn shell and not the Bourne shell:

```
$ cat $ENV
SHELL=/usr/lbin/ksh
export SHELL
$
```

The vi Line Edit Mode

With the Korn shell, you can edit your command line if you spot a mistake before you hit the RETURN key. The Korn shell supports two different types of editing commands: vi and emacs. Here we'll just talk about vi edit mode.

In order to be able to use the Korn shell's built-in editing capabilities, you first have to select an edit mode. The set command with the −o *mode* option may be used to turn on one of the line edit modes.

```
$ set -o vi                          Turn on vi mode
```

Note that you can put this line into in your ENV file to automatically start up the Korn shell with vi edit mode turned on. After turning on the vi line editor, you will be placed in *input* mode. You probably won't even notice anything different about input mode, as you can type in and execute commands the same as before you started the vi line editor:

```
$ set -o vi
$ echo hello
hello
$ pwd
/usr/steve
$
```

To make use of the line editing capabilities, you must enter *command* mode, by pressing the ESC key, usually in the upper left-hand corner of the keyboard. When you enter command mode, the cursor will move to the left one space, to the last character typed in (just as it does when you are using vi). The *current character* is whatever character the cursor is on. Once in command mode, you can enter `vi` commands. *Note that* `vi` *commands are not followed by a* RETURN.

One of the problems often encountered when typing in long commands is that you may notice an error in a command line after you finish typing it in. Invariably, the error is at the beginning of the line. In command mode, you can move the cursor around *without disturbing the command line.* Once you've moved the cursor to the place where the typo is, you can change the letter or letters to whatever you want.

In the examples that follow, the underline (_) represents the cursor. A command line will be shown, followed by one or more keystrokes, followed by what the line looks like after applying the keystrokes:

before   keystrokes   after

First, let's look at moving the cursor around. The `h` key will move the cursor to the left and the `l` key will move it to the right. You should try this out by entering command mode and pressing the `h` and `l` keys a few times. The cursor should move around on the line. If you try to move the cursor past the left or right side of the line, the Korn shell will "beep" at you.

```
$ mary had a little larb_      ESC      $ mary had a little larb
$ mary had a little larb       h        $ mary had a little larb
$ mary had a little larb       h        $ mary had a little larb
$ mary had a little larb       l        $ mary had a little larb
```

Once the cursor is on the character you want to change, you can use the `x` command to delete the current character ("X" it out).

```
$ mary had a little larb       x        $ mary had a little lab
```

Note that the `b` moved to the left when the `r` was deleted and is now the current character.

To add characters to the command line, you can use the `i` and `a` commands. The `i` command adds characters *before* the current character, and the `a` command adds characters *after* the current character. Both of these commands put you back into input mode; you must press ESC again to go back to command mode.

```
$ mary had a little lab        im       $ mary had a little lamb
$ mary had a little lamb       m        $ mary had a little lammb
$ mary had a little lammb      ESC      $ mary had a little lammb
$ mary had a little lammb      x        $ mary had a little lamb
$ mary had a little lamb       a        $ mary had a little lamb_
$ mary had a little lamb_      da       $ mary had a little lambda_
```

If you think that moving the cursor around by repeatedly hitting h and l is slow, you're right. The h and l commands may be preceded by a number that specifies the number of spaces to move the cursor.

```
$ mary had a little lambda_    ESC     mary had a little lambda
$ mary had a little lambda     10h     $ mary had a little lambda
$ mary had a little lambda     13h     $ mary had a little lambda
$ mary had a little lambda     5x      $ had a little lambda
```

As you see, the x command can also be preceded by a number to tell it how many characters to delete.

You can easily move to the end of the line by typing the $ command:

```
$ had a little lambda          $       $ had a little lambda
```

To move to the beginning of the line, you use the 0 (that's a zero) command:

```
$ had a little lambda          0       $ had a little lambda
```

Two other commands useful in moving the cursor are the w and b commands. The w command moves the cursor forward to the beginning of the next word, where a word is a string of letters, numbers, and underscores delimited by blanks or punctuation. The b command moves the cursor backward to the beginning of the previous word. These commands may also be preceded by a number to specify the number of words to move forward or backward.

```
$ had a little lambda          w       $ had a little lambda
$ had a little lambda          2w      $ had a little lambda
$ had a little lambda          3b      $ had a little lambda
```

At any time you can enter RETURN and the current line will be executed as a command.

```
$ had a little lambda                  Hit RETURN
ksh: had:  not found
$ _
```

After a command is executed, you are placed back in input mode.

So far, you've learned how to edit the current line. As we said before, the Korn shell keeps a history of recently entered commands. To access these commands, you can use the vi commands k and j. The k command replaces the current line on your terminal with the previously entered command, putting the cursor at the beginning of the line. Let's assume that these commands have just been entered:

```
$ pwd
/usr/pat
$ cd /tmp
$ echo this is a test
this is a test
$ _
```

Now go into command mode and use k to access them:

```
$ _                        ESC k        $ echo this is a test
```

Every time k is used, the current line is replaced by the previous line from the command history.

```
$ echo this is a test       k          $ cd /tmp
$ cd /tmp                    k          $ pwd
```

To execute the command being displayed, just press the RETURN key.

```
$ pwd        Hit RETURN
/tmp
$ _
```

The j command is the reverse of the k command and is used to display the next command in the history.

The / command is used to search through the command history for a command containing a string. If the / is entered, followed by a string, then the Korn shell will search backward through its history to find the most recently executed command that contains that string anywhere on the command line. The command will then be displayed. If there is no line in the history containing the string, the Korn shell will "beep" the terminal. When the / is entered, the current line is replaced by a /.

```
/tmp
$ _                        ESC /test     /test_
```

The search is begun when the RETURN key is pressed.

```
/test_                     RETURN       $ echo this is a test
```

To execute the command that results from the search, RETURN must be pressed again.

```
$ echo this is a test     Hit RETURN again
this is a test
$ _
```

If the command that's displayed isn't the one you're interested in, then you can continue the search through the command history by simply typing in / and pressing RETURN. The shell will use the string that you entered the last time you executed the search command.

When you've found the command in the history (either by k, j, or /), you can edit the command using the other vi commands we've already discussed. Note that you don't actually change the command in the history; that command cannot be changed once it is entered. Instead, you are editing a copy of the command in the history, which will itself be entered in the history when you hit RETURN.

Table 6-3 summarizes the basic vi line edit commands.

TABLE 6-3. Basic vi line edit commands

Command	Meaning
h	Move left one character
l	Move right one character
b	Move left one word
w	Move right one word
0	Move to start of line
$	Move to end of line
x	Delete character at cursor
a	Enter input mode and enter text after the current character
i	Enter input mode and insert text before the current character
k	Get previous command from history
j	Get next command from history
/*string*	Search history for the most recent command containing *string*; if *string* is omitted the previous string will be used

The r Command

There is a simple Korn shell command that allows you to re-execute previous commands using even a fewer number of keystrokes than described. If you simply type in the r command, the Korn shell will re-execute your last command:

```
$ date
Tue Jan 10 21:56:47 EDT 1989
$ r                                    Re-execute previous command
date
Tue Jan 10 21:57:13 EDT 1989
$
```

When you type in the `r` command, the Korn shell redisplays the previous command and then immediately executes it.

If you give the `r` command the name of a command as an argument, the Korn shell will re-execute the most recent command line from your history that *begins* with the specified argument:

```
$ cat docs/planA
  . . .
$ pwd
/usr/steve
$ r cat                              Rerun last cat command
cat docs/planA
  . . .
$
```

Once again, the Korn shell redisplays the command line from its history before automatically re-executing it.

The final form of the `r` command allows you to substitute the first occurrence of one string with the next. To re-execute the last `cat` command on the file `planB` instead of `planA` you could type:

```
$ r cat planA=planB
cat docs/planB
  . . .
$
```

or even more simply, you could have typed:

```
$ r cat A=B
cat docs/planB
  . . .
$
```

As noted, there are many other features of the Korn shell that are not described here. For more information, check Appendix B.

◆ The Stream Editor sed ◆

It's worthwhile taking a slight diversion at this point to describe a program that's commonly used when writing shell programs. The `sed` program allows you to perform a one-pass edit on a file. The general format of `sed` is:

sed *ed-command file*

where *ed-command* is an `ed`-style command that is to be applied to the contents of *file*. Unless explicit line numbers are referenced by this command, the command will be sequentially applied to every line of *file*. The output of `sed` goes to standard output, which as you know may be redirected if desired.

As an example, consider the following file called `test`.

```
$ cat test
The Unix operating system was
pioneered in the late 1960's.
Today Unix runs on a variety of systems.
$
```

The following shows how `sed` can be used to change all occurrences of the string `Unix` to the string `UNIX` in the file `test`:

```
$ sed s/Unix/UNIX/g test
The UNIX operating system was
pioneered in the late 1960's.
Today UNIX runs on a variety of systems.
$
```

The `g` was placed at the end of the substitute command just in case the string `Unix` occurred more than once on any line. (Remember from the discussions of `ed` that the `s` command will only change the first occurrence of a string on a line unless the "global" option `g` is used.)

You don't have to specify a line range to the `s` command (as in `1,$s/Unix/UNIX/g`) since `sed` automatically applies the editor command to every line of the file by default.

If you wanted to *permanently* change all occurrences of `Unix` to `UNIX` in the file `test`, then you would have to redirect `sed`'s output to a file and then `mv` the file back:

```
$ sed s/Unix/UNIX/g test > foo        Make the edit changes
$ mv foo test                         Replace the old file with the new one
$ cat test                            Verify that it worked
The UNIX operating system was
pioneered in the late 1960's.
Today UNIX runs on a variety of systems.
$
```

Redirecting the output of `sed` directly to `test` would have messed things up royally. This two step process must be used.

The following example shows how line 3 from the file `test` can be deleted:

```
$ sed 3d test
The UNIX operating system was
pioneered in the late 1960's.
$
```

Remember that in order to get this change reflected back in the file `test` you have to go through the redirection and moving scheme outlined above.

To delete all lines from `test` that contain the string `UNIX`, you can use the following `sed` command:

```
$ sed /UNIX/d test
Today UNIX runs on a variety of systems.
$
```

`sed` is often used to "edit" the value stored in a shell variable. For example, the following takes the value of the shell variable `VAL` and changes all minus signs to plus signs:

```
$ echo $VAL
a--b--c
$ echo $VAL | sed s/-/+/g
a++b++c
$
```

The `echo` is used to write the value of the shell variable `VAL` to standard output so that it can be piped into the `sed` command, which takes its input from standard input if no file name is supplied.

You can assign the output of the above command sequence back to `VAL` by using the shell's back-quoting mechanism:

```
$ echo $VAL
a--b--c
$ VAL=`echo $VAL | sed s/-/+/g`
$ echo $VAL
a++b++c
$
```

This works as before, except the result of the `sed` is stored back in the shell variable `VAL`.

The `cut` command is also commonly used to "edit" shell variables. In the following example, the first character contained in the shell variable `filename` is extracted and assigned to the variable `ch1`:

```
$ echo $filename
s.main.c
$ ch1=`echo $filename | cut -c1`
$ echo $ch1
s
$
```

As previously mentioned, this chapter has not attempted to cover all of the features provided by the shell. Rather, it has attempted to introduce you to its wonderfully rich and powerful programming language. A thorough treatment is given in *UNIX Shell Programming*. Among the features not covered here are sub-shells, functions, more advanced types of parameter substitutions, and the special shell commands ., break, continue, eval, exec, exit, set, shift, trap, and wait.

C H A P T E R
7

Screen Editing with `vi`

E diting is one of the most frequently used functions of a general purpose computer. No matter what you're planning to do, basic editing is sure to be the first step. Currently, the UNIX system supports a line editor, `ed`, which was discussed in Chapters 4 and 5. Many prefer to use a *screen editor* to create or modify their files. The only restriction of a screen editor is that the user must have a video (screen) terminal.

A screen editor allows you to see portions of your file on the terminal's screen and to modify characters and lines by simply typing at the current *cursor* position. The cursor is the little blinking line or box that shows where the next character will be printed, either by you or the system. In a screen editor, you move the cursor around your file until you find the part you want to modify, then you add or change the text to your liking.

The screen editor supplied with the UNIX System V Release 3 is called `vi`. `vi` was developed by the University of California at Berkeley and is also supplied with the Berkeley distribution of the UNIX system and with Xenix.

This chapter is divided into three parts. The first is an introduction to `vi`. It is meant to get you started using `vi` and to familiarize you with cursor motions and simple editing. The second section is more advanced and is meant to teach many of the more useful `vi` commands that can make you more effective at using `vi`. There are fewer examples and more "meat" in the second section. The third section is devoted to advanced and miscellaneous `vi` commands that can greatly improve your editing speed. It covers the commands quickly, and it should be read after you've spent a few hours using the commands in the first two sections. We have also put a `vi` command summary at the end of this chapter.

◆ Introduction to `vi` ◆

Before you can use `vi`, you must let it know what type of terminal you are using. The way you let `vi` know about your terminal is with the shell variable `TERM`. By setting `TERM` to your terminal type, `vi` will know what features, capabilities, and quirks your terminal has:

```
$ echo $TERM                          Is it already set?
                                      I guess not

$ TERM=hp2621                         A popular terminal made by Hewlett-Packard
$ export TERM                         Make the variable TERM available to vi
$
```

For `vi`, just remember that you *must* set `TERM` to the terminal type you're using, and you *must* export it as well. If you want, you can put the `TERM=` and export in your `.profile` as well. You will find a discussion of shell variables, the `export` command, and the `.profile` in Chapter 6.

There is a table at the end of this chapter of the more popular terminals that `vi` can be used with. This list is hardly complete, as some UNIX administrators will add terminals at the request of users. If you don't recognize your terminal in the list, ask your system administrator whether your terminal is supported.

Entering `vi`

Now you can run `vi` just like any other UNIX command. When you start `vi`, it will print out the file name, number of lines, and number of characters at the bottom of the screen:

```
$ date
Sat Mar 10 14:46:38 EST 1984
$ cat names
John
Jim
Pat
Steve
$ vi names




















"names" 4 lines, 19 characters☐
```

Then it will clear your screen and fill it with the file you're editing:

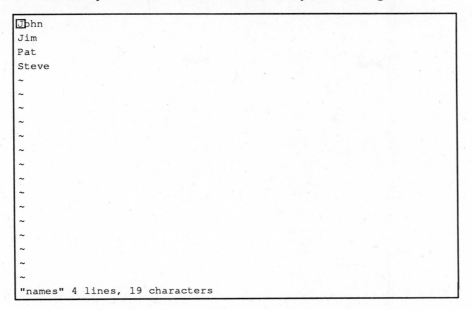

```
John
Jim
Pat
Steve
~
~
~
~
~
~
~
~
~
~
~
~
~
~
"names" 4 lines, 19 characters
```

The four lines from the file names and a message line at the bottom are listed. A ~ in the first column means that the file doesn't have enough lines to fill up the screen. The cursor is depicted by a box (□) and is placed in the upper left corner when vi starts. The bottom line is the *message line*. It will sometimes print things, but this depends on the command. There will be more about the message line as the chapter progresses.

Conventions Used in this Chapter

The screens shown previously are only 20 lines long and about 60 characters wide. Most video terminals are at least 24 lines by 80 characters, but in the interest of saving space and giving clearer examples, our windows will be 8 lines by about 26 characters.

The way we'll show vi commands and responses is as follows. Two screens will be shown side by side. The first shows the screen before the vi command is entered; listed between the screens is the vi command that is entered; and the second shows the screen after the command:

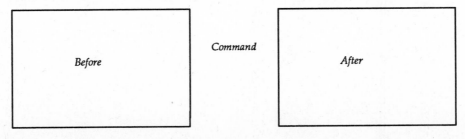

Before   *Command*   *After*

When running vi, the RETURN key is seldom used except when entering text. For all of the following vi screens, the RETURN key is not entered at the end of a command or line unless it is explicitly shown with CR (see Table 7-1). vi uses control characters extensively (remember the *CTRL-d*?), so the shorthand ^LETTER will be used in place of *CTRL-LETTER*.

TABLE 7-1. Special characters for vi

Character	vi *representation*
cursor	□
RETURN	CR
ESCAPE	ESC
CTRL-d	^D
CTRL-b	^B
CTRL-f	^F
CTRL-l	^L

Moving Around

The first thing you need to learn about using vi is how to move the cursor around on the screen. Once you know how to do that, you can position it wherever you want to make additions or changes.

Let's start by running vi on the file names:

```
$ vi namesCR




"names" 4 lines, 19 charac
```

So you will have a screen that looks like this:

```
□ohn
Jim
Pat
Steve
~
~
~
"names" 4 lines, 19 charac
```

The basic screen motion commands are h, j, k, and l. You might notice they are situated next to each other on the right side of the keyboard. The motions for h, j, k, and l are left, down, up, and right, respectively (see Fig. 7-1).

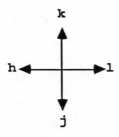

Fig. 7-1. Basic Cursor Motions

Here are a few examples; note that the commands are not echoed on the screen — the only thing vi shows on the screen (except for the message line) is *the contents of the file.*

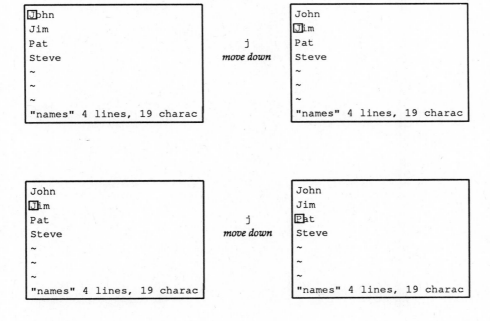

```
John
Jim
Pat
Steve
~
~
~
"names" 4 lines, 19 charac
```

l
move right

```
John
Jim
Pat
Steve
~
~
~
"names" 4 lines, 19 charac
```

```
John
Jim
Pat
Steve
~
~
~
"names" 4 lines, 19 charac
```

k
move up

```
John
Jim
Pat
Steve
~
~
~
"names" 4 lines, 19 charac
```

```
John
Jim
Pat
Steve
~
~
~
"names" 4 lines, 19 charac
```

l
move right

```
John
Jim
Pat
Steve
~
~
~
"names" 4 lines, 19 charac
```

```
John
Jim
Pat
Steve
~
~
~
"names" 4 lines, 19 charac
```

k
move up

```
John
Jim
Pat
Steve
~
~
~
"names" 4 lines, 19 charac
```

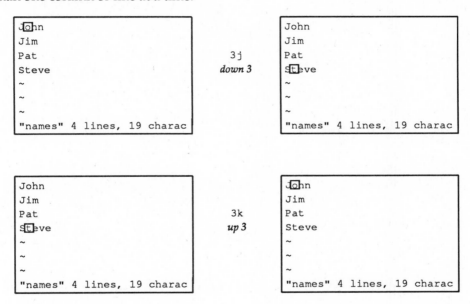

You can precede these keys with numbers, which allows you to move more than one column or line at a time:

If you try to move past the beginning or end of the file, vi will "beep" at you. In general, when vi doesn't like one of your commands, it will beep. In the previous example, if you try to move up with another k, vi will cause your terminal to beep and leave the cursor where it is.

Some people prefer to use the SPACE bar instead of the l key to move right. The SPACE bar has *exactly* the same effect on the cursor as the l key. To avoid confusion, however, this chapter uses the l key exclusively.

Some versions of vi will let you use the arrow keys, if your terminal has them. You can try them out, and if they work, you can use them. Don't get too attached to them, as older versions of vi may not understand the arrow keys and may actually think they're trying to do something else. Also, you probably won't be able to use the arrow keys in input mode (see the next section).

Adding Text

Once you've become comfortable with moving the cursor with the h, j, k, and
l keys, you can try adding some text. The way you add text is to position the
cursor over a character and type an a. This puts you in a special mode of operation called *insert mode*. (Remember how the a command put you in a special
mode in ed?) Now everything you type in is *appended* to the text *after* the character the cursor was positioned over.

```
John                               Joxxyyzzhn
Jim                                Jim
Pat            axxyyzz             Pat
Steve          add xxyyzz          Steve
~                                  ~
~                                  ~
~                                  ~
"names" 4 lines, 19 charac         "names" 4 lines, 19 charac
```

When you're done adding text, you press the ESC key.

```
Joxxyyzzhn                         Joxxyyzzhn
Jim                                Jim
Pat              ESC               Pat
Steve                              Steve
~                                  ~
~                                  ~
~                                  ~
"names" 4 lines, 19 charac         "names" 4 lines, 19 charac
```

When you press the ESC key, the cursor moves back to the last character you
entered. This way, you know that you are no longer in insert mode.

   You can even put RETURNs in the added text, and new lines appear, almost
magically:

```
Joxxyyzzhn                         Joxxyyzzone
Jim                                twohn
Pat            aoneCR              Jim
Steve          twoESC             Pat
~              embedded CR         Steve
~                                  ~
~                                  ~
"names" 4 lines, 19 charac         "names" 4 lines, 19 charac
```

The appending started between the z and hn of the first line, causing the hn to
be carried to the next line when the CR was pressed.

There's another way of adding text. It's with the i command. i works like the a command, but it *inserts* instead of appending, meaning the characters you type in are placed *before* the current character position. (You might have noticed that it's impossible to add text at the *beginning* of a line with the a command.) i also puts you in insert mode, requiring an ESC to finish inserting.

```
Joxxyyzzone
twohn
Jim
Pat
Steve
~
~
"names" 4 lines, 19 charac
```

3j
down 3

```
Joxxyyzzone
twohn
Jim
Pat
Steve
~
~
"names" 4 lines, 19 charac
```

```
Joxxyyzzone
twohn
Jim
Pat
Steve
~
~
"names" 4 lines, 19 charac
```

iabc**ESC**
insert abc

```
Joxxyyzzone
twohn
Jim
Pat
Stabceve
~
~
"names" 4 lines, 19 charac
```

After the ESC is pressed, the cursor moves back to the last character inserted, just as with the a command.

Deleting Text

Now that you can add text to a file, the next thing to learn is how to delete text. Basically, there are two commands that delete text in vi: x and d.

To delete one character, you use the x command. x deletes the character at the current cursor position, moving the rest of the line left into the void created by the deleted character:

```
Joxxyyzzone
twohn
Jim
Pat
Stabceve
~
~
"names" 4 lines, 19 charac
```

x
delete "c"

```
Joxxyyzzone
twohn
Jim
Pat
Stabeve
~
~
"names" 4 lines, 19 charac
```

```
Joxxyyzzone                              Joxxyyzzone
twohn                                    twohn
Jim                          x           Jim
Pat                      delete "e"      Pat
Stabeve                                  Stabve
~                                        ~
~                                        ~
"names" 4 lines, 19 charac               "names" 4 lines, 19 charac
```

```
Joxxyyzzone                              Joxxyyzzone
twohn                                    twohn
Jim                         2x           Jim
Pat                     delete "ve"      Pat
Stabve                                   Stab
~                                        ~
~                                        ~
"names" 4 lines, 19 charac               "names" 4 lines, 19 charac
```

As you can see, the x command can be preceded by a number to indicate how many characters you want to delete. If you get rid of all the characters on a line and keep hitting x, you will get beeps because you are trying to delete non-existent characters:

```
Joxxyyzzone                              Joxxyyzzone
twohn                                    twohn
Jim                        xxxx          Jim
Pat                    delete "Stab"     Pat
Stab                                     □
~                                        ~
~                                        ~
"names" 4 lines, 19 charac               "names" 4 lines, 19 charac
```

```
Joxxyyzzone                              Joxxyyzzone
twohn                                    twohn
Jim                         2x           Jim
Pat                       "beep"         Pat
□                                        □
~                                        ~
~                                        ~
"names" 4 lines, 19 charac               "names" 4 lines, 19 charac
```

Note that each x of the xxxx is done at the end of the line. When x is used at the end of a line, it deletes the character at the current cursor position and then moves the cursor *left* to what is now the new end of the line.

Deleting characters is all well and good, but sometimes you want to delete an entire line. The x command will get rid of all the characters on a line, but it won't get rid of the line itself. To delete a line, you use the dd command. (That's two d's in a row.) The dd command is just a special case of a more general delete that is discussed in the second half of this chapter. It can be preceded by a number to indicate the number of lines to delete.

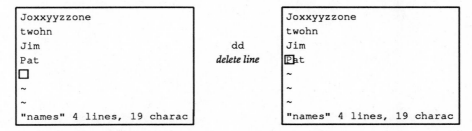

Here the last line was deleted and replaced on the screen with a ~ (meaning nothing's there).

Now move up to the top of the screen and delete a few lines. Notice how the lines following those deleted move up:

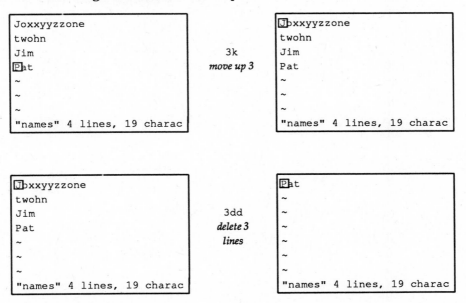

OOPS!! We really didn't want to delete all those lines! We need to *undo* that delete command:

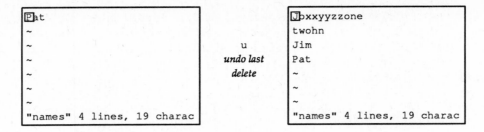

That's better. As you can see, if you make a mistake with vi, you can just type a u and undo the change. The u will undo the last x or dd command. It also works with other commands that change the file.

Saving the file

Like ed, vi also changes a copy of the file (sometimes referred to as a *buffer*) that must be written before the original file is actually changed. There are several ways to write files in vi, but the easiest is with the zz command. When you type in two capital z's, vi will automatically write the file *and* quit, putting you back in the shell. (Notice how the top line scrolls off the top of the screen when the $ is printed.)

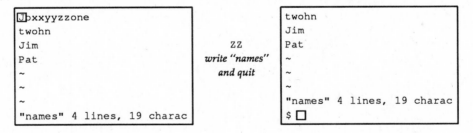

Once you're back in the shell, all the special screen editing features go away.

TABLE 7-2. Summary of basic **vi** commands

Command	Operation
h	← Move cursor left
j	↓ Move cursor down
k	↑ Move cursor up
l	→ Move cursor right
a	Append after cursor (end with ESC)
i	Insert before cursor (end with ESC)
x	Delete character at current cursor position
dd	Delete current line
zz	Write file and quit

◆ Using **vi** ◆

This part of the chapter covers some of the more advanced features of **vi**. The next section covers some advanced **vi** commands that aren't as widely used but are very useful to users who have gained some proficiency with **vi**.

Scrolling

The term *scrolling* refers to the property of video terminals that makes the top line leave the screen as each new line is displayed at the bottom. If you are listing a file at the terminal, the top of it will disappear from the screen as more of the file is displayed. Screen editors use scrolling to edit large files. Only the first 23 lines are displayed by **vi** when you start it on a large file. As you work with the file and move about in it, the top lines will sometimes scroll up off the screen as more lines are displayed at the bottom; sometimes the lines at the bottom will scroll down off the screen as more lines are listed at the top.

The following example illustrates how simple scrolling works in **vi**:

```
$ cat jokes
A few years ago,
Quasimodo (the
hunchback of Notre
Dame) was looking
for a replacement.
He put an ad in the
paper, and this guy
showed up to apply
for the job.
The only problem was
this guy had no arms
so Quasi asked him
how he was going to
ring the bells.
The guy said "I run
up and hit the bells
with my head," and
ran right into a
bell with his fore-
head.  Then he took
a step back and went
for the BIIIIG bell;
tripping, he fell
headlong to the
pavement.  A crowd
gathered in front of
the church, as a
```

```
police inspector
came by and asked
Quasi "who is this
guy?"
Quasi replied, "I
don't know, but his
face rings a bell."
$
```

```
police inspector
came by and asked
Quasi "who is this
guy?"
Quasi replied, "I
don't know, but his
face rings a bell."
$ vi jokesCR
```
start vi
```
A few years ago,
Quasimodo (the
hunchback of Notre
Dame) was looking
for a replacement.
He put an ad in the
paper, and this guy
"jokes" 34 lines, 625 char
```

```
A few years ago,
Quasimodo (the
hunchback of Notre
Dame) was looking
for a replacement.
He put an ad in the
paper, and this guy
"jokes" 34 lines, 625 char
```
6j
down 6 lines
```
A few years ago,
Quasimodo (the
hunchback of Notre
Dame) was looking
for a replacement.
He put an ad in the
paper, and this guy
"jokes" 34 lines, 625 char
```

```
A few years ago,
Quasimodo (the
hunchback of Notre
Dame) was looking
for a replacement.
He put an ad in the
paper, and this guy
"jokes" 34 lines, 625 char
```
j
down 1 line
```
Quasimodo (the
hunchback of Notre
Dame) was looking
for a replacement.
He put an ad in the
paper, and this guy
showed up to apply
```

```
Quasimodo (the
hunchback of Notre
Dame) was looking
for a replacement.
He put an ad in the
paper, and this guy
showed up to apply
```
j
down 1 line
```
hunchback of Notre
Dame) was looking
for a replacement.
He put an ad in the
paper, and this guy
showed up to apply
for the job.
```

As you can see, when you try to move past the bottom of the screen, vi scrolls the screen up a line. After a scroll, the text on the mesage line usually gets clobbered. As you might expect, you can precede the command with a number to scroll the screen several lines:

```
hunchback of Notre
Dame) was looking
for a replacement.
He put an ad in the
paper, and this guy
showed up to apply
for the job.
```
4j
down 4 lines
```
paper, and this guy
showed up to apply
for the job.
The only problem was
this guy had no arms
so Quasi asked him
how he was going to
```

Similarly, you can scroll up the screen with the k command.

vi also supplies you with commands for scrolling several lines at a time. The ^D and ^U scroll half a screen down or up if there are enough lines in the file to do so:

```
paper, and this guy
showed up to apply
for the job.
The only problem was
this guy had no arms
so Quasi asked him
how he was going to
```
^D
*down ½
screen*
```
this guy had no arms
so Quasi asked him
how he was going to
ring the bells.
The guy said "I run
up and hit the bells
with my head," and
```

```
this guy had no arms
so Quasi asked him
how he was going to
ring the bells.
The guy said "I run
up and hit the bells
with my head," and
```
^D
*down ½
screen*
```
The guy said "I run
up and hit the bells
with my head," and
ran right into a
bell with his fore-
head.  Then he took
a step back and went
```

```
The guy said "I run
up and hit the bells
with my head," and
ran right into a
bell with his fore-
head.  Then he took
a step back and went
```
^U
up ½ screen
```
this guy had no arms
so Quasi asked him
how he was going to
ring the bells.
The guy said "I run
up and hit the bells
with my head," and
```

You also have the commands ^F and ^B that scroll forward and back one full screen, respectively.

String Searching

vi can search for strings just like ed does. You type in a / followed by the string you want to search for followed by a CR. vi then scans for the next occurrence of the string:

```
this guy had no arms
so Quasi asked him
how he was going to
ring the bells.
The guy said "I run
up and hit the bells
[w]ith my head," and
```

/QuasiCR
search for
"Quasi"

```
police inspector
came by and asked
[Q]uasi "who is this
guy?"
Quasi replied, "I
don't know, but his
face rings a bell."
```

```
police inspector
came by and asked
[Q]uasi "who is this
guy?"
Quasi replied, "I
don't know, but his
face rings a bell."
```

/QuasiCR
search for
"Quasi"

```
police inspector
came by and asked
Quasi "who is this
guy?"
[Q]uasi replied, "I
don't know, but his
face rings a bell."
/Quasi
```

When you type in a /, vi puts a / on the message line at the bottom of the screen. As you type in the characters you want to search for, vi puts these characters on the message line, so you can see the string you're searching for. As you can see, the second search didn't scroll the screen because the next "Quasi" was already on the screen. vi simply moved the cursor down two lines. Since the screen wasn't scrolled, the message line remained intact with /Quasi.

The / command searches *forward* or down through a file, finding the next occurrence of a string. If you want to find the *previous* occurrence of a string, you can use the ? command. It works the same as /, but it searches up through the file for the string:

```
police inspector
came by and asked
Quasi "who is this
guy?"
[Q]uasi replied, "I
don't know, but his
face rings a bell."
/Quasi
```

?QuasiCR
search for
previous "Quasi"

```
police inspector
came by and asked
[Q]uasi "who is this
guy?"
Quasi replied, "I
don't know, but his
face rings a bell."
?Quasi
```

To facilitate searching through a file more than once for a particular string, vi provides you with the n command. After you search for a string with the / command, you can use the n command to look for the next occurrence of that string without typing in the string again. This allows you to search down through a file quickly. If you used the ? instead of the /, then n would search up for the previous string. You might say that n repeats the most recent / or ?.

Words

vi knows about objects called *words* that are simply letters and numbers separated by blanks, tabs, or punctuation marks. vi allows you to move from word to word, delete them, and change them with simple commands. The w command moves the cursor to the next word, the b command moves the cursor backward a word, and the e command moves the cursor to the end of a word:

```
police inspector
came by and asked
Quasi "who is this
guy?"
Quasi replied, "I
don't know, but his
face rings a bell."
?Quasi
```
w
go to
next word
```
police inspector
came by and asked
Quasi "who is this
guy?"
Quasi replied, "I
don't know, but his
face rings a bell."
?Quasi
```

```
police inspector
came by and asked
Quasi "who is this
guy?"
Quasi replied, "I
don't know, but his
face rings a bell."
?Quasi
```
e
go to
end of word
```
police inspector
came by and asked
Quasi "who is this
guy?"
Quasi replied, "I
don't know, but his
face rings a bell."
?Quasi
```

```
police inspector
came by and asked
Quasi "who is this
guy?"
Quasi replied, "I
don't know, but his
face rings a bell."
?Quasi
```
e
go to
end of word
```
police inspector
came by and asked
Quasi "who is this
guy?"
Quasi replied, "I
don't know, but his
face rings a bell."
?Quasi
```

```
police inspector
came by and asked
Quasi "who i[s] this
guy?"
Quasi replied, "I
don't know, but his
face rings a bell."
?Quasi
```

w
go to
next word

```
police inspector
came by and asked
Quasi "who is [t]his
guy?"
Quasi replied, "I
don't know, but his
face rings a bell."
?Quasi
```

```
police inspector
came by and asked
Quasi "who is [t]his
guy?"
Quasi replied, "I
don't know, but his
face rings a bell."
?Quasi
```

b
go back to
previous word

```
police inspector
came by and asked
Quasi "who [i]s this
guy?"
Quasi replied, "I
don't know, but his
face rings a bell."
?Quasi
```

(You might notice that since none of the previous commands scrolled the screen, the ?Quasi remains on the message line.) The w command goes to the next line when you move past the end of a line and the b command goes to the previous line when you move past the beginning of a line:

```
police inspector
came by and asked
Quasi "who [i]s this
guy?"
Quasi replied, "I
don't know, but his
face rings a bell."
?Quasi
```

2w
go forward
two words

```
police inspector
came by and asked
Quasi "who is this
[g]uy?"
Quasi replied, "I
don't know, but his
face rings a bell."
?Quasi
```

Deleting and Changing Text

vi provides you with several ways to delete and change text. One method of deleting text is with the d command. The d command is *always* followed by another character that specifies what will be deleted. If it is followed by a w, for example, a word will be deleted. If it is followed by an l (letter l), the current character is deleted. if it is followed by a $, the current position to the end of the line is deleted, because $ moves the cursor to the end of the line. In general, the d is followed by a cursor motion, and whatever lies in that motion is deleted:

```
police inspector                           police inspector
came by and asked                          came by and asked
Quasi "who is this          dw             Quasi "who is this
⬚uy?"                    delete            ▢'
Quasi replied, "I         one word         Quasi replied, "I
don't know, but his                        don't know, but his
face rings a bell."                        face rings a bell."
?Quasi                                     ?Quasi
```

```
police inspector                           police inspector
came by and asked                          came by and asked
Quasi "who is this          d$             Quasi "who is this
▢'                      delete to          ▢
Quasi replied, "I        end of line       Quasi replied, "I
don't know, but his                        don't know, but his
face rings a bell."                        face rings a bell."
?Quasi                                     ?Quasi
```

The dd is a special case of the d command that deletes the current line. Other commands that use cursor motions to determine what is to be affected often use two command letters in a row to "do it to the current line." One of these commands is the c command.

The c command *changes* whatever lies in the specified motion. It puts you in input mode so you can type in your changes. Of course, you must hit the ESC key to get back into command mode. As you might guess, cc changes the entire line. Here is an example of the c command:

```
police inspector                           police inspector
came by and asked                          came by and asked
Quasi "who is ⬚his          cw             Quasi "who is ⬚hi$
                          change
Quasi replied, "I         a word           Quasi replied, "I
don't know, but his                        don't know, but his
face rings a bell."                        face rings a bell."
?Quasi                                     ?Quasi
```

Note that a $ is displayed at the last character affected by the change.

```
police inspector                           police inspector
came by and asked                          came by and asked
Quasi "who is ⬚hi$       a test**ESC**     Quasi "who is a tes⬚
                        enter change
Quasi replied, "I                          Quasi replied, "I
don't know, but his                        don't know, but his
face rings a bell."                        face rings a bell."
?Quasi                                     ?Quasi
```

Control Commands

There are certain commands in vi that are preceded by a colon (:). These are control commands that have to do with external file manipulation (reading and writing files) and some special functions of vi.

The file manipulation commands include :q, which quits vi; :w, which writes the file without quitting vi (unlike ZZ); and :q!, which quits vi without writing, discarding all changes (:q won't quit if changes have been made to the file).

The control commands that perform special functions include :*number*, which moves the cursor to the specified line number, scrolling if necessary (for example, :1 moves the cursor to the beginning of the file) and :*ed-command*, which causes the ed command *ed-command* to be executed. Here are a few examples of these special control commands:

```
police inspector
came by and asked
Quasi "who is a test

Quasi replied, "I
don't know, but his
face rings a bell."
```

:1**CR**
go to
line 1

```
A few years ago,
Quasimodo (the
hunchback of Notre
Dame) was looking
for a replacement.
He put an ad in the
paper, and this guy
```

```
A few years ago,
Quasimodo (the
hunchback of Notre
Dame) was looking
for a replacement.
He put an ad in the
paper, and this guy
```

:5**CR**
go to
line 5

```
A few years ago,
Quasimodo (the
hunchback of Notre
Dame) was looking
for a replacement.
He put an ad in the
paper, and this guy
```

```
A few years ago,
Quasimodo (the
hunchback of Notre
Dame) was looking
for a replacement.
He put an ad in the
paper, and this guy
```

:s/a/is/**CR**
change "a"
to "is"

```
A few years ago,
Quasimodo (the
hunchback of Notre
Dame) was looking
for is replacement.
He put an ad in the
paper, and this guy
```

```
┌─────────────────────────┐                    ┌─────────────────────────┐
│ A few years ago,        │                    │ A few years ago,        │
│ Quasimodo (the          │         u          │ Quasimodo (the          │
│ hunchback of Notre      │                    │ hunchback of Notre      │
│ Dame) was looking       │    undo change     │ Dame) was looking       │
│ ▣or is replacement.     │                    │ ▣or a replacement.      │
│ He put an ad in the     │                    │ He put an ad in the     │
│ paper, and this guy     │                    │ paper, and this guy     │
└─────────────────────────┘                    └─────────────────────────┘


┌─────────────────────────┐                    ┌─────────────────────────┐
│ A few years ago,        │                    │ police inspector        │
│ Quasimodo (the          │      :$CR          │ came by and asked       │
│ hunchback of Notre      │     go to          │ Quasi "who is a test    │
│ Dame) was looking       │    last line       │                         │
│ ▣or a replacement.      │                    │ Quasi replied, "I       │
│ He put an ad in the     │                    │ don't know, but his     │
│ paper, and this guy     │                    │ ▣ace rings a bell."     │
└─────────────────────────┘                    └─────────────────────────┘


┌─────────────────────────┐                    ┌─────────────────────────┐
│ police inspector        │                    │ police inspector        │
│ came by and asked       │      :wCR          │ came by and asked       │
│ Quasi "who is a test    │    write file      │ Quasi "who is a test    │
│                         │                    │                         │
│ Quasi replied, "I       │                    │ Quasi replied, "I       │
│ don't know, but his     │                    │ don't know, but his     │
│ ▣ace rings a bell."     │                    │ ▣ace rings a bell."     │
└─────────────────────────┘                    │ "jokes" 34 lines, 618 char
                                               └─────────────────────────┘
```

The :set command allows you to turn certain features of vi on and off. For example, :set number makes vi precede each line on the display with the line number:

```
┌─────────────────────────┐                    ┌─────────────────────────┐
│ police inspector        │                    │ 28  police inspector    │
│ came by and asked       │  :set numberCR     │ 29  came by and asked   │
│ Quasi "who is a test    │    turn on         │ 30  Quasi "who is a test│
│                         │  line numbering    │ 31                      │
│ Quasi replied, "I       │                    │ 32  Quasi replied, "I   │
│ don't know, but his     │                    │ 33  don't know, but his │
│ ▣ace rings a bell."     │                    │ 34  ▣ace rings a bell." │
│ "jokes" 34 lines, 618 char                   │ :set number             │
└─────────────────────────┘                    └─────────────────────────┘
```

Note that these numbers aren't added to the file, they are there for information purposes only. Line number mode can be turned off by using :set nonumber. In fact, the other vi modes that you can toggle are all turned off by preceeding the mode with no.

The `showmode` mode causes `vi` to tell you when you're in an input mode (any mode that requires an ESC to exit):

```
28   police inspector            28   police inspector
29   came by and asked           29   came by and asked
30   Quasi "who is a test        30   Quasi "who is a test
31                               31
32   Quasi replied, "I           32   Quasi replied, "I
33   don't know, but his         33   don't know, but his
34   face rings a bell."         34   face rings a bell."
:set number                      :set showmode
```

:set showmodeCR
turn on
"show" mode

```
28   police inspector            28   police inspector
29   came by and asked           29   came by and asked
30   Quasi "who is a test        30   Quasi "who is a test
31                               31
32   Quasi replied, "I           32   Quasi replied, "I
33   don't know, but his         33   don't know, but his
34   face rings a bell."         34   face rings a bell."
:set showmode                    :set showmode   APPEND MODE
```

a
enter append
mode

```
28   police inspector            28   police inspector
29   came by and asked           29   came by and asked
30   Quasi "who is a test        30   Quasi "who is a test
31                               31
32   Quasi replied, "I           32   Quasi replied, "I
33   don't know, but his         33   don't know, but his
34   face rings a bell."         34   face rings a bell."
:set showmode   APPEND MODE      :set showmode
```

ESC
leave append
mode

To turn off `showmode`, simply use `:set noshowmode`.

♦   **Odds and Ends**   ♦

`vi` provides many commands that are not really necessary. You can use other commands or combinations of other commands to perform the same functions. (Actually, almost all of the commands are unecessary except for `x`, `dd`, `i`, `a` and `ZZ`.) For example, you have the `o` and `O` commands. `o` creates a new line after the current one, places the cursor at the beginning of that line, and puts you in insert mode. `O` does the same, but the new line is *above* the current one.

```
police inspector                         police inspector
came by and asked                        came by and asked
Quasi "who is a test          O          Quasi "who is a test
                        create line above
Quasi replied, "I         current line   Quasi replied, "I
□on't know, but his                      □
face rings a bell."                      don't know, but his
"jokes" 34 lines, 618 char                             OPEN MODE
```

(Show mode is still on.)

```
police inspector                         police inspector
came by and asked                        came by and asked
Quasi "who is a test     new text**ESC**  Quasi "who is a test
                           put text
Quasi replied, "I         on new line    Quasi replied, "I
□                                        new te□
don't know, but his                      don't know, but his
```

The D command deletes from the current cursor position to the *end* of the current line. The C command changes the text from the current cursor position to the *end* of the current line. The A command appends at the *end* of the current line, and the I command inserts at the *beginning* of the current line. To move the cursor to the beginning of the line just type in a 0 (that's a zero, not an oh), and to move the cursor to the end of the line , you type in a $.

Two commands, r and R, are sometimes very helpful in reducing keystrokes, The r command allows you to replace the current character with one of your choosing. The first character you type after an r replaces the character under the cursor:

```
police inspector                         police inspector
came by and asked                        came by and asked
Quasi "who is a test          r9         Quasi "who is a test
                        replace "t"
Quasi replied, "I        with "9"        Quasi replied, "I
new te□                                  new te□
don't know, but his                      don't know, but his
```

Note that r does not put you in insert mode. It just changes *one* character.

The R command is similar to the r command, but it places you in insert mode and allows you to change as many characters as you want. The characters you type in replace the ones already there, but they don't affect the rest of the line. The R command simply overwrites text until you hit ESC.

```
police inspector                            police inspector
came by and asked               0           came by and asked
Quasi "who is a test         move to        Quasi "who is a test
                            first column
Quasi replied, "I                           Quasi replied, "I
new tex9                                     new tex9
don't know, but his                         don't know, but his
```

```
police inspector                            police inspector
came by and asked                           came by and asked
Quasi "who is a test      R1234ESC          Quasi "who is a test
                          replace text
Quasi replied, "I                           Quasi replied, "I
new tex9                                     123 4 ex9
don't know, but his                         don't know, but his
```

The s command is equivalent to a cl command. It changes one or more characters. For example, 4s is the same as 4cl. S is the same as cc (change the whole line.)

A RETURN as a cursor motion will move the cursor to the beginning of the first *word* on the next line. It's useful for indented text or program blocks.

Some commands simply don't fall into the typical categories of moving the cursor or deleting, changing, and adding text. One of these is the ^L command, which redraws the screen. If something messes up your screen (perhaps some static on your telephone line), you can use the ^L command to have your entire screen redrawn. The ^L command doesn't change the current cursor position.

Remember the undo command (u)? vi saves deleted text and u puts it back. vi also saves the previous state of a line *before any changes were made to it.* The U command will bring back that original state:

```
police inspector                            police inspector
came by and asked               xxx         came by and asked
Quasi "who is a test       delete three     Quasi "who is a test
                           characters
Quasi replied, "I                           Quasi replied, "I
123 4 ex9                                    123 x 9
don't know, but his                         don't know, but his
```

```
police inspector
came by and asked
Quasi "who is a test

Quasi replied, "I
123⊠9
don't know, but his
```

    u

undo one
"x"

```
police inspector
came by and asked
Quasi "who is a test

Quasi replied, "I
123⊡k9
don't know, but his
```

```
police inspector
came by and asked
Quasi "who is a test

Quasi replied, "I
123⊡k9
don't know, but his
```

    U

undo whole
line

```
police inspector
came by and asked
Quasi "who is a test

Quasi replied, "I
⊡234tex9
don't know, but his
```

The p command also puts deleted text back, but it allows you to control text placement. p puts the last deleted text *after* the current cursor position. (P puts it before.)

```
police inspector
came by and asked
Quasi "who is a test

Quasi replied, "I
⊡234tex9
don't know, but his
```

    dw

delete word

```
police inspector
came by and asked
Quasi "who is a test

Quasi replied, "I
⊡
don't know, but his
```

```
police inspector
came by and asked
Quasi "who is a test

Quasi replied, "I
⊡
don't know, but his
```

    3k

up three
lines

```
police inspector
came by and asked
⊡uasi "who is a test

Quasi replied, "I

don't know, but his
```

```
police inspector
came by and asked
◻uasi "who is a test

Quasi replied, "I

don't know, but his
```

p
put text
after cursor

```
police inspector
came by and asked
Q1234tex◻uasi "who is a

Quasi replied, "I

don't know, but his
```

```
police inspector
came by and asked
Q1234tex◻uasi "who is a

Quasi replied, "I

don't know, but his
```

2dd
delete two
lines

```
police inspector
came by and asked
◻uasi replied, "I

don't know, but his
face rings a bell."
~
```

```
police inspector
came by and asked
◻uasi replied, "I

don't know, but his
face rings a bell."
~
```

p
put back
lines

```
police inspector
came by and asked
Quasi replied, "I
◻1234tex9uasi "who is a

don't know, but his
```

As you can see, p puts back whole lines as well.

The y and Y commands allow you to take (yank) the text without deleting it, so that you can later put it somewhere else with the p or P command. *yobject* yanks whatever *object* happens to be (yw, yl, ye, y$, etc.). yy yanks the current line. Y is the same as yy. You can precede y and Y with numbers to determine the number of objects or lines you want to yank. The key sequence YP is often referred to as "copy line." The Y yanks the current line, and P puts the yanked text above the current line.

```
police inspector
came by and asked
Quasi replied, "I
◻1234tex9uasi "who is a

don't know, but his
```

YP
copy line

```
police inspector
came by and asked
Quasi replied, "I
◻1234tex9uasi "who is a
Q1234tex9uasi "who is a


don't know, but his
```

The following list summarizes the vi commands we covered in this chapter:

Using vi **from UNIX:**
$ **vi** *file*   edit *file*
$ **vi** **-r** *file*   recover *file* from crash

Note: most of the following vi commands may be preceded by a number for repetition.

Basic cursor motions:
h j k l ← ↓ ↑ →
CR   Down line to first non-blank
0 (zero) Beginning of line
$ End of line (EOL)

Screen control:
^U ^D   Up or down half page
^B ^F   Up or down whole page
^L   Reprint page

Character input modes:
†a   Append after cursor
†A   Append at end of line
†i   Insert before cursor
†I   Insert before first non-blank
†o   Add lines after current line
†O   Add lines before current line

Delete and change:
dd   Delete line
†cc   Change line
D   Delete from cursor to EOL
†C   Change from cursor to EOL
x   Delete character
†s   Change character
†S   Change line
r*chr*   Replace current chr with *chr*
†R   Overprint change

Word commands:
w   Next word
b   Back word
e   End of word
dw   Delete word
†cw   Change word

Search:
/*string*CR   Search for *string*
?*string*CR   Reverse search for *string*
n   Repeat last / or ?
N   Reverse of n

Generic commands:
object **is any cursor motion:** w **for word;** b **for back word;** h, j, k, l **for left, down, up, right;** /*string* **for up to** *string* **etc.**

d*object* Delete *object*
†c*object* Change *object*

Miscellaneous:
u   Undo previous command
U   Restore entire line
y*object* Save *object* in temp buffer
Y   Save line(s) in temp buffer
p   Put saved buffer after cursor
P   Put saved buffer before cursor

Control commands:
:w   Write file
:wq   Write file and quit
:q   Quit
:q!   Quit (override checks)
:*ed-cmd* Run the ed command *ed-cmd*
:*num*   Go to line *num*
zz   Same as :**wq**
:set *mode* Turn on *mode*

---

† Note: All commands marked with † enter input mode and are exited with the escape (ESC) character.

Now that you know about vi, you can use it for just about everything you need to type. Letters, programs, electronic mail, and even recipes can be created and edited with vi without any difficulty at all, once you've learned just a few basic commands. You shouldn't consider this chapter a complete description of vi; vi is much too complex to cover in one chapter. If you want more information on vi, there are several references listed in Appendix A.

TABLE 7-3. Partial list of terminals supported for vi

TERM	Terminal	TERM	Terminal
a980	Adds Consul 980	i400	Infoton 400
regent	Adds Regent series	adm2	Lear Siegler ADM-2
viewpoint	Adds Viewpoint	adm3	Lear Siegler ADM-3
aa	Ann Arbor 4080	adm31	Lear Siegler ADM-31
aaa	Ann Arbor Ambassador	adm3a	Lear Siegler ADM-3a
c100	Concept 100	adm42	Lear Siegler ADM-42
c108	Concept 108	adm5	Lear Siegler ADM-5
dm1520	Datamedia 1520	microterm	Microterm ACT-IV
dm2500	Datamedia 2500	microterm5	Microterm ACT-V
dm3025	Datamedia 3025a	mime	Microterm Mime I, Mime II
3045	Datamedia 3045a	mime2a	Microterm Mime IIa
dt80	Datamedia dt80/I	fox	Perkin-Elmer 1100
gt40	DEC gt40	owl	Perkin-Elmer 1200
gt42	DEC gt42	bantam	Perkin-Elmer 550
vt100	DEC vt100	tek4012	Tektronix 4012
vt132	DEC vt132	tek4013	Tektronix 4013
vt50	DEC vt50	tek4014	Tektronix 4014
vt52	DEC vt52	tek4015	Tektronix 4015
ep40	Execuport 4000	tek4023	Tektronix 4023
ep48	Execuport 4080	tek4025	Tektronix 4024, 4025, 4027
h1000	Hazeltine 1000	tek4112	Tektronix 4110 series
h1420	Hazeltine 1420	t1061	Teleray 1061
h1500	Hazeltine 1500	t3700	Teleray 3700
h1510	Hazeltine 1510	t3800	Teleray 3800 series
h1520	Hazeltine 1520	tty4424	Teletype 4424M
h1552	Hazeltine 1552	tty40	Teletype Dataspeed 40/2
h2000	Hazeltine 2000	tty5620	Teletype 5620
h19	Heathkit h19	tty5420	Teletype 5420
hp2621	HP 2621a, 2621P	tvi912b	Televideo 912
hp2624	HP 2624B, 2623A	tvi920b	Televideo 920
hp2626	HP 2626A, 2626P	tvi925	Televideo 925
hp2640A	HP 2640A	tvi950	Televideo 950
hp2640B	HP 2640B, 2544A	vc303a	Volker-Craig 303a
hp2645	HP 2645	vc303	Volker-Craig 303
hp2648	HP 2648A	vc404	Volker-Craig 404
i100	Infoton 100		

UNIX in the Office

This chapter shows how useful a UNIX system can be in an office environment. We'll discuss how you can use the UNIX system to communicate to other users, set up an automatic appointment reminder service, and perform simple desk calculations. We'll also discuss how to format documents using the `nroff` program.

♦ Talking to Other Users ♦

Sometimes you may want to send a message to a user who is logged in on another terminal. That terminal may be located in another office on the floor, or even in another plant location, making it inconvenient for you to talk directly to that person. As an alternative to calling the person on the telephone, you can use the `write` command. `write` allows you to send a message to any other logged-in user. The message that you send will appear on that user's screen. The user will then have the option to send you a reply by initiating a `write` command from his or her own terminal. With this technique, two users can effectively have a "conversation" through their terminals.

The general format of the `write` command is

`write` *user tty*

where *user* is the user id of the logged-in user and *tty* is an optional tty number. This latter information is needed when there is more than one logged-in user with the same user id—the *tty* number designates the terminal that the message is to be sent to.

As an example, the command

    write pat

tells the UNIX system that you wish to start a conversation with the user `pat`.

If `pat` is not currently logged in, then the following will occur:

```
$ write pat
pat is not logged on.
$
```

If `pat` is logged in, the `write` command will print the following on `pat`'s terminal (it will also "beep" `pat`'s terminal a few times to alert him in case he fell asleep):

```
Message from bob on EEdepta (tty02) [ Fri Mar 24 14:20:35 ] ..
```

(Here we assume that the `write` command was initiated by the user `bob`.) The actual format of this line may differ slightly on your system.

After initiating the write, the system will wait for you to type your message. This message can contain as many lines as you like. Each line that you type will get displayed on `pat`'s terminal. When you have finished typing your message, enter *CTRL-d* as the first and only character on the line. This will terminate the `write` and display the line `<EOT>` on `pat`'s terminal to tell him you are finished.

If `pat` decides to answer your message, he can initiate his own `write` command from his terminal:

```
$ write bob
```

Any lines that `pat` now types will automatically be displayed on `bob`'s terminal. When `pat` has finished his message, he too must type in *CTRL-d* to terminate his `write`.

With `write` commands simultaneously active on both `pat`'s and `bob`'s terminals, you can see how these two users can effectively carry on a conversation. As a matter of convention, most UNIX users typically end their message lines with the characters −o to tell the other user that their message line is finished and that they are (possibly) awaiting a reply (as in "over"). The characters −oo are often used to signal the end of the conversation (as in "over and out").

The following sequence of screens depicts a typical conversation. On the left-hand side of the page we show `bob`'s screen, and on the right-hand side we show `pat`'s screen.

```
$ date
Fri Mar 24 14:32:30 EST 1989
$ who
mblc     tty06    Mar 24 08:53
pat      tty08    Mar 24 13:01
bob      tty02    Mar 24 13:19
$
```

bob *checks to make sure* pat *is logged in*

```
$ date
Fri Mar 24 14:32:30 EST 1989
$ who
mblc    tty06    Mar 24 08:53
pat     tty08    Mar 24 13:01
bob     tty02    Mar 24 13:19
$ write pat
```

*Now he initiates a conversation
with him*

```
$ pwd
/a1/pat/tp
$

Message from bob on EEdepta (tty02) ..
```

Here's what happens on pat's *terminal*

```
$ date
Fri Mar 24 14:32:30 EST 1989
$ who
mblc    tty06    Mar 24 08:53
pat     tty08    Mar 24 13:01
bob     tty02    Mar 24 13:19
$ write pat
Hello, Pat
I'm trying to find the file
fopen.c.  Do you know what
directory it's in?    -o
```

bob *types his question and
waits for* pat *to answer*

```
/a1/pat/tp
$

Message from bob on EEdepta (tty02) ..
Hello, pat
I'm trying to find the file
fopen.c.  Do you know what
directory it's in?    -o
write bob
Yes.  You can find it in
/usr/src/lib/libc/port/stdio  -o
```

pat gets the question and sends his response

```
$ write pat
Hello, pat
I'm trying to find the file
fopen.c.  Do you know what
directory it's in?     -o

Message from pat on EEdepta (tty08) ..
Yes. You can find it in
/usr/src/lib/libc/port/stdio  -o
Thank you  -oo
$
```

bob gets the answer, thanks pat, and then terminates the conversation from his end

Although not shown above, bob typed in a *CTRL-d* after thanking pat. This terminated the write that he initiated and returned his command prompt. Let's see what happens on pat's terminal:

Now pat terminates the conversation from his end by typing CTRL-d

```
Message from bob on EEdepta (tty02) ..
Hello, pat
I'm trying to find the file
fopen.c.  Do you know what
directory it's in?     -o
write bob
Yes.  You can find it in
/usr/src/lib/libc/port/stdio  -o
Thank you  -oo
<EOT>
$
```

```
Hello, pat
I'm trying to find the file
fopen.c.  Do you know what
directory it's in?     -o

Message from pat on EEdepta (tty08) ..
Yes.  You can find it in
/usr/src/lib/libc/port/stdio  -o
Thank you  -oo
$
<EOT>
```

The conversation has now been terminated from both ends

Inhibiting Messages with the `mesg` Command

Sometimes you may decide that you don't want to receive any messages. For example, you may be running a particular program and you don't want your screen to get all messed up when someone `writes` to you. The perfect example is when using a screen editor such as `vi`. If someone tries to write to you while you're in the middle of editing a file, the incoming text will simply overwrite information on your screen, turning your screen into a royal mess! Don't be alarmed, however, as the problem is only temporary; all you have to do to restore your screen to its previous state is type in the screen refresh command *CTRL-l*.

You can tell the UNIX system that you don't want to receive any messages by using the command `mesg`. This command takes a single argument: `n` or `y`. The former specifies that you don't want to receive any messages; the latter specifies that you do. So to inhibit incoming messages while you are editing a file, type the command:

```
mesg n
```

before you enter the editor. Then, after your edits are complete, you can tell the system that you're willing to once again receive messages by typing the command:

```
mesg y
```

If anyone tries to write to you while you have messages inhibited, they will get `Permission denied`. Printed at their terminal:

```
$ write steve
Permission denied.                    steve is not receiving messages
$
```

Incidentally, you can find out your current message-receiving status by simply typing `mesg` with no arguments:

```
$ mesg n                                No messages, please
$ mesg                                  Let's verify it
is n
$ mesg y                                I changed my mind
$ mesg
is y
$
```

◆ Electronic Mail ◆

One of the phrases you will hear most often when someone talks about office automation is *electronic mail*. Electronic mail gives you the ability to send messages, memos, or any types of documents to other users electronically—that is, without the use of paper.

The main difference between sending a message to someone using the electronic mail facility and the `write` command is that the latter requires that the person be logged in at the time that the message is sent. With electronic mail, the mail is automatically kept by the system until the user issues the necessary command to read his or her mail. Some people send electronic messages using the following approach: if the user is logged in, then they use the `write` command to talk to the user directly. If the user isn't logged in, then they instead use the `mail` command to send the message.

Under the UNIX system, either the `mail` or `mailx` command can be used to send and read electronic mail. The `mailx` command has more powerful features than the `mail` command: It allows you to quickly review your messages and to easily file them away into different *folders*. However, since the `mail` command is much simpler to use, that's the one we'll describe in this text. The fundamental principles we show here using `mail` also apply to using `mailx`. For more details on `mailx`, consult your *UNIX User's Reference Manual*.

The format of the command to send mail to a user is simple:

```
mail user
```

where *user* is the user id of the person you want to send the mail to. Once this command line has been typed, the `mail` program will then wait for you to type your message to be sent to *user*. You can then type in as many lines as you like. When you are done, type *CTRL-d* to tell the `mail` program that the message is completed. The `mail` program will then take your message and "mail" it to the specified user.

Periodically, the shell automatically checks to see if you have received any new mail. If you have, then you will get the following message displayed at your terminal:

```
you have mail
```

This check is also performed automatically every time you log in.

If you get the message telling you that you have mail, you will then want to read your mail. Reading mail is even easier than sending it—you simply type the command `mail` with *no* arguments. This causes the `mail` program to display any mail that has been sent to you. As each item of mail is displayed at your terminal the `mail` program displays a `?` and then waits for you to give a "filing disposition" for that piece of mail. Normally, after you type in your disposition, the next piece of mail will then be displayed. After reading your last piece of mail, the `mail` program will return you to the shell command level.

The most commonly used mail dispositions are summarized in Table 8-1. For more information, look under the `mail` command in section 1 of the *UNIX User's Manual*.

TABLE 8-1. Common `mail` dispositions

Option	Meaning
RETURN	No disposition on this piece of mail; it will still be there next time `mail` is read; next piece of mail is then displayed
d	Delete this piece of mail; next piece of mail is then displayed
s *file*	Save this piece of mail in *file*; next piece of mail is then displayed
*	Print a list of disposition commands
q	Quit reading mail; any unread pieces will be there next time mail is read
x	Quit reading mail; any pieces of mail that were deleted will be restored

Note that on some systems the disposition `?` is used to obtain a list of commands rather than `*` (and some systems accept both!).

Let's take a look at an example of `mail`. We'll assume here that the user `pat` wants to send some mail to `ruth`. We'll also assume that `ruth` is not logged in at the time that `pat` sends the mail. We'll show `pat`'s terminal on the left side of the page and `ruth`'s on the right side.

```
$ mail ruth
```

Send mail to ruth

After `pat` has typed the command `mail ruth`, he can then enter his message to `ruth` The `mail` command takes every line that he types in up to the *CTRL-d* as the message to be mailed.

```
$ mail ruth
ruth,
      I wanted to remind you that
we have a meeting scheduled for
Monday (3/27) at 1pm.
                            pat
CTRL-d
$
```

pat types in his message

Typing *CTRL-d* causes `pat`'s message to be mailed to `ruth`. It also returns his command prompt as an indication that the `mail` command has finished execution.

Now let's assume `ruth` arrives at work and logs in:

Upon logging in, `ruth` *is automatically told that she has mail*

```
login:ruth
Password:
you have mail

Good morning.
There are 4 users logged in.
$
```

To read her mail, all that `ruth` has to do is type in the command `mail`:

`ruth` *reads her mail; the* `mail` *program then waits for her to enter a disposition*

```
Good morning.
There are 4 users logged in.
$ mail
From pat Fri Mar 24 13:27 EST 1989
ruth,
      I wanted to remind you that
we have a meeting scheduled for
Monday (3/27) at 1pm.
                            pat

?
```

```
There are 4 users logged in.
$ mail
From pat Fri Mar 24 13:27 EST 1989
ruth,
     I wanted to remind you that
we have a meeting scheduled for
Monday (3/27) at 1pm.
          pat


? d
$
```

she decides not to save it, so she
types in a d *(for delete)*

The mail program inserts a "postmark" at the front of each piece of mail telling where the mail came from and the time and date that it was sent.

If ruth had more mail, then the next piece would have been displayed after she entered her d disposition. Since she got back her command prompt instead, she obviously had no more mail.

There are some additional points worth noting about the mail command. First, you can simply type mail at your terminal at any time to see if you have mail. If you don't have any mail, then the message No mail. will be displayed:

```
$ mail
No mail.
$
```

You can send the same piece of mail to more than one user by simply listing each user on the command line, as in:

```
$ mail tony fred leela alice
```

Since mail reads the message to be sent from standard input, you can redirect its input from a file. So to send the contents of the file reminder to ruth, the following could be used:

```
$ mail ruth < reminder
$
```

If you have to send a long message to someone, this technique comes in handy. You can first enter your message into a file using a text editor such as ed or vi, make any necessary changes, and then mail the contents of the file. That way you can even keep a copy of the message for yourself!

A final point: Unlike the write command, you can send messages to users on *other* computer systems with the mail command. This is discussed in more detail in Chapter 11.

◆ Calendar Commands ◆

Two commands are provided that help you keep track of your days. One of these is a command to display a calendar at the terminal and another to remind you of things you have to do on certain dates.

Displaying a Calendar: the `cal` Command

Type in the command `cal 1990` at your terminal. This is what you'll get:

```
$ cal 1990
```

```
                                 1990

          Jan                     Feb                     Mar
   S  M Tu  W Th  F  S     S  M Tu  W Th  F  S     S  M Tu  W Th  F  S
      1  2  3  4  5  6                 1  2  3                 1  2  3
   7  8  9 10 11 12 13     4  5  6  7  8  9 10     4  5  6  7  8  9 10
  14 15 16 17 18 19 20    11 12 13 14 15 16 17    11 12 13 14 15 16 17
  21 22 23 24 25 26 27    18 19 20 21 22 23 24    18 19 20 21 22 23 24
  28 29 30 31             25 26 27 28             25 26 27 28 29 30 31

          Apr                     May                     Jun
   S  M Tu  W Th  F  S     S  M Tu  W Th  F  S     S  M Tu  W Th  F  S
   1  2  3  4  5  6  7        1  2  3  4  5                    1  2
   8  9 10 11 12 13 14     6  7  8  9 10 11 12     3  4  5  6  7  8  9
  15 16 17 18 19 20 21    13 14 15 16 17 18 19    10 11 12 13 14 15 16
  22 23 24 25 26 27 28    20 21 22 23 24 25 26    17 18 19 20 21 22 23
  29 30                   27 28 29 30 31          24 25 26 27 28 29 30

          Jul                     Aug                     Sep
   S  M Tu  W Th  F  S     S  M Tu  W Th  F  S     S  M Tu  W Th  F  S
   1  2  3  4  5  6  7                 1  2  3  4                    1
   8  9 10 11 12 13 14     5  6  7  8  9 10 11     2  3  4  5  6  7  8
  15 16 17 18 19 20 21    12 13 14 15 16 17 18     9 10 11 12 13 14 15
  22 23 24 25 26 27 28    19 20 21 22 23 24 25    16 17 18 19 20 21 22
  29 30 31                26 27 28 29 30 31       23 24 25 26 27 28 29
                                                  30

          Oct                     Nov                     Dec
   S  M Tu  W Th  F  S     S  M Tu  W Th  F  S     S  M Tu  W Th  F  S
      1  2  3  4  5  6                 1  2  3                    1
   7  8  9 10 11 12 13     4  5  6  7  8  9 10     2  3  4  5  6  7  8
  14 15 16 17 18 19 20    11 12 13 14 15 16 17     9 10 11 12 13 14 15
  21 22 23 24 25 26 27    18 19 20 21 22 23 24    16 17 18 19 20 21 22
  28 29 30 31             25 26 27 28 29 30       23 24 25 26 27 28 29
                                                  30 31
```

As you can see, typing the command `cal 1990` resulted in the display of a calendar for the year 1990. And you can get a calendar for any year you want by typing `cal` followed by the year. So, `cal 1968` would display a calendar for the year 1968, and `cal 2000` would display one for the year 2000.

In case you're not interested in getting a full year's calendar displayed at your terminal, `cal` gives you the option to display just a single month of any given year. To do this, the format of the `cal` command is:

cal *month year*

where *month* is a numerical month number from 1 through 12 and *year* is as before.

Here are some examples:

```
$ cal 1 2001                          Calendar for January 2001
        January 2001
   S   M Tu  W Th   F   S
       1   2   3   4   5   6
   7   8   9  10  11  12  13
  14  15  16  17  18  19  20
  21  22  23  24  25  26  27
  28  29  30  31

$ cal 7 1955                          Calendar for July 1955
        July 1955
   S   M Tu  W Th   F   S
                        1   2
   3   4   5   6   7   8   9
  10  11  12  13  14  15  16
  17  18  19  20  21  22  23
  24  25  26  27  28  29  30
  31

$
```

As you can see, operation of `cal` is simple; just remember that the full year must always be spelled out (so `cal 7 55` would display a calendar for July 55 and not July 1955!)

You can also type in `cal` without any arguments to get a calendar printed for the current month:

```
$ date
Fri Mar 24 14:50:10 EST 1989
```

```
$ cal
   March 1989
 S  M Tu  W Th  F  S
             1  2  3  4
 5  6  7  8  9 10 11
12 13 14 15 16 17 18
19 20 21 22 23 24 25
26 27 28 29 30 31
$
```

Calendar Reminder Service: `calendar`

Many busy people keep track of their scheduled appointments by recording
them in a book. At the beginning of each day, they may consult their book to see
what appointments are scheduled for that day. At the end of the day, they might
also consult the book to see what's in store for the next day.

The UNIX system provides a similar type of facility that enables you to
automatically keep track of your appointments. This is done with the `calen-
dar` command. Instead of recording your appointments in a book, you write
them into a file called `calendar` instead. Along with each appointment you
must also record the date—in any suitable format as long as both the month and
the day of the appointment are recorded. Suitable date formats include Feb. 4,
February 4, 2/4, etc.

At the beginning of each day, most UNIX systems will automatically check
your `calendar` file to see if you have any appointments for that day *or* for the
following day (and if it's Friday, the following day extends through Monday).

If you do have some appointments scheduled for these days, the system
will automatically mail you a list of your appoinments.

If your system does not perform this automatic check each day, then you
can do it yourself! In fact, you can get a list of your appointments for the current
and following day at any time by simply typing the command `calendar` at
your terminal. If you want, you can add this command to your `.profile` to
cause your appointments to be checked every time you log in.

But enough talk; let's see how it works. For starters, let's assume that you
have entered a list of appointments into a file called `calendar` in your HOME
directory. Now to the example:

```
$ date
Tue Jul 17 19:38:14 EST 1990
$ cd                              Go to the HOME directory
$ cat calendar                    and look at the calendar file
7/16: 9:50am    PFS Meeting

7/17: 10:30am   Call EK&F to get estimate.
7/17: 1:30pm    Meet with Pat to discuss outline
```

```
7/18: 11:00am  Computer Center User's Meeting
7/18:              in Room 3A-108

7/18: noon    lunch with Tony
$ calendar                        See what's scheduled
7/17: 10:30am  Call EK&F to get estimate.
7/17: 1:30pm   Meet with Pat to discuss outline
7/18: 11:00am  Computer Center User's Meeting
7/18:              in Room 3A-108
$
```

Don't confuse the `calendar` command with the file of the same name. The `calendar` file must reside in your HOME directory in order to get automatic once a day processing of the file (if supported on your system). However, when you execute the `calendar` command, it looks for the file `calendar` *only in the current directory.* This means that you should be in your HOME directory whenever you execute this command.

The `calendar` command is not very intelligent about appointments. When the command is executed, it sequentially searches through the `calendar` file for lines that contain either today's or tomorrow's date (and remember, "tomorrow" extends through Monday if "today" is Friday). Whenever it finds such a line , it simply displays it at the terminal. This means that if you have an appointment that spans more than one line then you must include the date on every line. This explains why you had to write the date 7/18 on the second line of the Computer Center User's Meeting reminder.

The `calendar` file must be completely maintained by you. You have to add and remove appointments from the file; the system does not do it for you. Of course, with the help of a text editor such as `ed` or `vi`, this is not a difficult thing to do.

♦ A Desk Calculator Program ♦

The UNIX system has two programs that enable you to effectively convert your computer into a handy deskop calculator. One program is called `bc`, and the other is called `dc`. We'll only briefly describe the former here. (The latter program operates using so-called "Reverse Polish Notation." Hewlett-Packard calculator owners will be quite familiar with this, so they may wish to learn how to use that program instead.)

To start up the desk calculator program you simply type in `bc`:

```
$ bc
```

As is typical, `bc` does not display any command prompt to let you know it has started—it simply sits there and waits for you to type in your calculations.   bc continues to operate this way until you enter *CTRL-d* to terminate the program.

Once you've started up bc, it's very easy to use:

```
2 + 5                                    Add 2 and 5
7
```

bc automatically displays the result of each operation; there's no need to hit an equals key or anything like that.

The symbol recognized as the multiplication operator by bc is the asterisk *:

```
753.25 * 2
1506.50
1 + 2 * 10
21
```

Multiplication and division operations are done before addition and subtraction operations, if they appear in the same expression. You can always use parentheses if you want to change that:

```
(1 + 2)*10
30
```

The division operator is the slash /. See what happens if you try to divide 1 by 2:

```
1 / 2
0
```

Normally, bc automatically selects the number of decimal places for displaying results. However, for division operations, it won't display any decimal places unless you tell it to. This is done by setting scale to the desired number of places.

```
scale=3                              Accuracy to three decimal places
1 / 2
0.500                                That's better
```

If you want to save the result of an operation, you can temporarily store it in any one of 26 "memories," identified by the letters a-z:

```
a=1749.23 * 12                       Save the result in a
```

The value stored in a can be subsequently "recalled" by simply typing a:

```
a                                    Show me what's stored in a
20990.76
```

You can even use its value in subsequent expressions:

```
a * 30
629722.80
```

There are many other features provided by bc that we won't describe here.
There is a math library for calculating logs, sines, cosines, etc.; and the program
even has some built-in programming capabilities. For more details, read *BC—An
Arbitrary Precision Desk-Calculator Language* by L.L. Cherry and R. Morris.

♦ Word Processing ♦

Nowhere is there more evidence of the computer's influence in the office than in
the area of word processing. As a result of word processing, memos, reports,
and documents are prepared in much less time and at greatly reduced costs. This
is particularly true when dealing with documents that go through many rounds
of revisions. Formerly, these documents were either partially or fully retyped.
Now, we simply make the changes to the document and the word processor
takes care of the rest—it prints the document, paginates it, justifies it, and even
checks for spelling mistakes!

♦ Formatting Text with nroff ♦

As we mentioned, the nroff program is used to control the way a document
will look when it's printed. This is done by interspersing nroff "commands"
throughout the actual text wherever such control is desired. There are about 90
different nroff commands that enable you to specify everything from the
length of each line to the spacing to use between each line of the document. It is
our intention to give you a brief introduction to nroff in this section by
describing a dozen or so basic commands. With this small set of commands, you
will be able to use nroff to format letters, memos, and even small documents.

Setting Up the Page

One of the first things you need to learn is how to tell nroff about the page that
you want the document printed on. Specifically, you should tell nroff:

- Where to set the left margin
- Where to set the right margin
- What the length of the page is

Setting the left margin is done with the page offset command `.po` (*all* `nroff` commands start with a `.` and must be typed in the first column of the line). Immediately after the `.po` you type the distance from the left edge of the paper you want the margin to set at, followed by the letter *i* to tell `nroff` that this distance is expressed in *inches* (`nroff` can also take distances expressed in other units such as centimeters or *ems*). Thus, to set the left margin in at 1 inch, the following `nroff` command would be used:

```
.po 1i
```

To set it to $2^1/2$ inches, the following would work:

```
.po 2.5i
```

You get the picture.

Setting the right margin is a little different. Instead of specifying the distance from the right margin, you specify the total length of a line of text. This is done with the line length command `.ll`. For example, suppose you're dealing with 8 $^1/_2$-by-11-inch paper. If you want your left and right margins both to be 1 inch wide, then your line length should be set to 8 $^1/_2$ - 2 = 6 $^1/_2$ inches. So to set up both margins on the page, the following two commands would appear in your document:

```
.po 1i          1-inch margin on the left
.ll 6.5i        1-inch margin on the right
```

Now we come to the last command for specifying the physical layout of the page: the `.pl` command. This command is used to specify the length of the page. So, for 8 $^1/_2$-by-11-inch paper, you would write:

```
.pl 11i
```

Filling and Adjusting Text

In order for a document to look nice, you usually try to make each line appear as uniform as possible. That means that you try to align your right margin as precisely as you can. With the `nroff` program, there are basically three choices available to you for controlling this alignment. You can have:

1. No alignment done;

2. Each line filled with as many words as possible, taking words from the following lines if necessary; or

3. Each line filled as in 2 and also padded with blanks so that every line is aligned at the right margin.

The second option is known as *filling* the text, whereas the third is known as *adjusting* the text. You can't have the latter without the former; that is, if you select the adjust option, then filling is included.

Let's take a small sample of text to see the difference between the three options. Here's the sample:

```
$ cat sample
Here is some sample text.
In the first case,
we'll show the default:
adjust and fill on.
Then, we'll see what happens
when both adjust and
fill are turned off.
$
```

Before we can proceed with our example, we must digress slightly to discuss the mechanisms for processing a document through nroff.

The general format of the nroff command is:

$$\texttt{nroff} \quad \texttt{-T}dev \; file$$

where *dev* is an abbreviation for a terminal or printer that the output from nroff is to be sent to (see Table 8-2), and *file* is the name of the document to be printed.

TABLE 8-2. Device abbreviations for nroff

Abbreviation	Used for
37	Teletype® Model 37 terminal
tn300	GE TermiNet 300
300	DASI 300
382	DTC-382
450	DASI 450
832	Anderson Jacobsen 832
2631	Hewlett-Packard 2631
4000A	Trendata 4000A
lp	ASCII line printer
X	EBCDIC line printer

In the remaining examples in this section, we'll assume that the output is going to a standard ASCII line printer; therefore, we'll use the -Tlp option. (In fact, if you can't figure out what abbreviation to use from Table 8-2, try lp—it's a good guess.)

nroff writes its output to standard output. This means that if you want to get a document printed on the printer, then you should pipe nroff's output into a line printer like lp:

```
nroff -Tlp sample | lp
```

This represents the complete command sequence to get the contents of the file sample formatted and then printed on the line printer.

If you don't pipe nroff's output anywhere, then it will get displayed at the terminal by default. This is how you can check out your format requests before they get printed. However, we do recommend that you use one of the "paging" programs such as pg or more to prevent your document from "flying" off the screen. Therefore, the command sequence

```
nroff -Tlp sample | pg
```

would enable you to view the results of the nroff at the terminal one screenful at a time. Then once you're satisfied with the results, you can pipe the output to lp instead.

Now back to the example. For the first case we'll see what happens by default; that is, if we don't explicitly insert any line adjust or fill commands. For purposes of this example, we'll assume that we have set the line length to $3^1/2$ inches, and the page length to $1^1/2$ inches. We won't bother setting the left margin.

```
$ cat sample
.ll 3.5i                          Set the line length to 3¹/₂ inches
.pl 1.5i                          and the page length to 1¹/₂ inches
Here is some sample text.
In the first case,
we'll show the default:
adjust and fill on.
Then, we'll turn
adjust off.  Finally,
we'll see what happens
when both adjust and
fill are turned off.
$ nroff -Tlp sample               Process the file through nroff
Here is some sample text.  In the first case, we'll show
the default:  adjust and fill on.  Then, we'll turn
adjust off.  Finally, we'll see what happens when both
adjust and fill are turned off.



$
```

We had the ouput of `nroff` go directly to the terminal, without feeding it through a paging program first since we're only dealing with a very small file. You'll notice that `nroff` printed three blank lines at the end. This was done to "fill up" the lines on our $1^1/_2$-inch page (most printers print six lines per inch, so $1^1/_2$-inches would represent nine lines of text).

As you can see, `nroff` filled and adjusted the lines in `sample`. Now let's see what happens if we use the `.na` command to turn off line adjusting.

```
$ cat sample
.ll 3.5i
.pl 1.5i
.na                              No line adjusting
Here is some sample text.
In the first case,
we'll show the default:
adjust and fill on.
Then, we'll turn
adjust off.  Finally,
we'll see what happens
when both adjust and
fill are turned off.
$ nroff -Tlp sample
Here is some sample text.  In the
first case, we'll show the default:
adjust and fill on.  Then, we'll
turn adjust off.  Finally, we'll
see what happens when both adjust
and fill are turned off.



$
```

`nroff` still tries to fit as many words on a line as possible; however, with adjust turned off, the lines are not padded with spaces.

To turn off line fill mode, the `nroff` "no fill" command `.nf` is used. Since adjusting can only be done with filling, lines that are not filled will not be adjusted.

The next example shows what happens when fill mode is turned off with the `.nf` command.

```
$ cat sample
.ll 3.5i
.pl 1.5i
.nf                    No fill (that also means no adjust)
```

```
Here is some sample text.
In the first case,
we'll show the default:
adjust and fill on.
Then, we'll turn
adjust off.  Finally,
we'll see what happens
when both adjust and
fill are turned off.
$ nroff -Tlp sample
Here is some sample text.
In the first case,
we'll show the default:
adjust and fill on.
Then, we'll turn
adjust off.  Finally,
we'll see what happens
when both adjust and
fill are turned off.
$
```

As you can see, nroff really did nothing at all to the text. The .nf command is useful when you want nroff to leave a portion of your text alone. It simply "writes it as it sees it."

After you've turned off fill mode, you may later decide to turn it back on again. This is readily accomplished with the fill command .fi. And if you turned adjust mode off with a .na command and wanted to turn it back on, the command to use is .ad. Of course, turning adjust back on automatically turns fill back on.

Related to the notion of filling and adjusting text is hyphenation of words at the end of lines. Normally, nroff does not do this for you. However, you can use the .hy command to have nroff automatically hyphenate your text. This can improve the appearance of your formatted text. (This book was produced using the automatic hyphenation feature.)

Skipping Lines

To skip a line in your text, you can simply insert a blank line at the appropriate point in your file:

```
$ cat sample
.pl 1.5i
Skip a line

here
$ nroff -Tlp sample
```

```
Skip a line

here




$
```

To skip more lines, you simply insert more blank lines in the file:

```
$ cat sample
.pl 1.5i
Skip 4 lines




here
$ nroff -Tlp sample
Skip 4 lines




here




$
```

Alternatively, you can use the `nroff` command designed specifically for skip-ping lines: `.sp`. The number of lines to skip is typed right after the `.sp` or may be omitted if you just want to skip a single line. The following shows how a `.sp 4` command is used to skip four lines.

```
$ cat sample
.pl 1.5i
Skip 4 lines
.sp 4
here
```

```
$ nroff -Tlp sample
Skip 4 lines



here



$
```

Centering Text

It's very easy to center text on the page with `nroff`. To center a single line, you simply place the `.ce` command before the line to be centered:

```
$ cat sample
.ll 3.5i
.pl 1.5i
 .ce                                    Center the line that follows
Center this line
xxxxxxxxxxxxxxxxxxxxxxxxxxxxxxxxxxx
$ nroff -Tlp sample
            Center this line
xxxxxxxxxxxxxxxxxxxxxxxxxxxxxxxxxxx




$
```

To center more than one consecutive line of text, it is not necessary to include separate `.ce` commands before each line. Instead, you can use a single `.ce` immediately before the group of lines to be centered. In that case, the `.ce` takes the form:

$$.ce\ n$$

where *n* is the number of lines to be centered.

```
$ cat sample
.ll 3.5i
.pl 1.5i
```

```
.ce 4                               Center the next four lines
Stephen Kochan & Patrick Wood
Pipeline Associates, Inc.
239 Main Street
West Orange, New Jersey 07052
$ nroff -Tlp sample
        Stephen Kochan & Patrick Wood
           Pipeline Associates, Inc.
              239 Main Street
        West Orange, New Jersey 07079



$
```

Underlining Text

To underline some text in `nroff`, you simply use the `.ul` command. On the next line after this command, you type the word or words that are to be underlined. It's that simple.

```
$ cat text
.ll 3.5i
.pl 1.51
Underlining a
.ul
word
in the middle of a sentence is easy.
.ul
Underlining an entire sentence is just as easy.
$ nroff -Tlp text
Underlining a word in the middle of
a sentence is easy.  Underlining an
entire sentence is just as easy.
$
```

Whatever text gets typed on the line following the `.ul` will get underlined by `nroff`. Beware that some printers may not directly support this capability You may have to use a special filter program to get your text printed properly. See your system administrator if you run into problems.

Getting Double-Spaced Output

To get double-spaced output, you can place the command

```
.ls 2
```

at the beginning of your text. You can actually supply any number you desire after the `.ls`. So `.ls 3` would give you triple-spaced output, whereas `.ls 1` would produce single-spaced output (this is what you get by default).

Indenting Text

The `.in` command makes it easy to indent text. The number that immediately follows the `.in` specifies the distance to indent from the left margin. The indentation remains in effect until another `.in` command is issued.

```
$ cat sample
.ll 3.5i
.pl 1.5i
Indentation is useful for setting off
certain portions of text.
.in .5i
Here we indent in a half-inch from the
left margin.
.in 0i
And then we go back
$ nroff -Tlp sample
Indentation is useful for setting off
certain portions of text.
    Here we indent in a half-inch
    from the left margin.
And then we go back



$
```

Going to a New Page

Sometimes you may want to start some text at the top of a new page. To force this situation, use the `.bp` command, which stands for *break page*.

Give Me a Break

Normally, when `nroff` is operating in fill mode, it tries to fit as many words on a line as it can by bringing in words from the subsequent lines. However, there are times when `nroff` will not do this, even while operating in fill mode. Certain commands cause this; in `nroff` terminology, these commands are said to cause a *break*. For example, the line space command `.sp` causes a break.

`nroff` will not use words that follow the `.sp` to fill the line before the break. And since this line will not be filled, it won't be adjusted either. Let's look at an example.

```
$ cat sample
.ll 3.5i
.pl 1.5i
Here is some text to show the effect
of causing a break.
.sp
Notice that words from this line were
not used to fill in the previous line.
Also notice that the line before
the .sp was not filled or adjusted.
$ nroff -Tlp sample
Here is some text to show the
effect of causing a break.

Notice that words from this line were not used to fill
in the previous line.  Also notice that the line before
the .sp was not filled or adjusted.


$
```

Breaks can also be caused in other ways: A blank line in your text causes a break, as does any line that *begins* with a blank space (but *not* a tab).

Sometimes you may want to force a break. To do this you can use the `.br` command. This command causes a break but otherwise has no effect.

Command Summary

To refresh your memory, we have summarized each of the `nroff` commands described in this section in the following table. In the third column we have identified whether the command causes a break.

TABLE 8-3. Basic `nroff` commands

Command	Description	Breaks?
`.ad`	Adjust text (provided fill mode hasn't been turned off)	*no*
`.bp`	Go to top of next page	*yes*
`.br`	Cause a break	*yes*
`.fi`	Fill text (and also adjust it provided adjust hasn't been turned off with a `.na` command)	*yes*
`.ce n`	Center next *n* lines of text (or just next line if *n* is omitted)	*yes*
`.hy`	Hyphenate text	*no*
`.in ni`	Indent *n* inches from the left margin	
`.ll ni`	Set line length to *n* inches	*no*
`.ls n`	Set line spacing to *n*; *n* = 2 for double-spaced output	*no*
`.na`	Don't adjust text	*no*
`.nf`	Don't fill or adjust text	*yes*
`.pl ni`	Set page length to *n* inches	*no*
`.po ni`	Set left margin to *n* inches	*no*
`.sp n`	Skip *n* lines (or just 1 if *n* is omitted)	*yes*
`.ul n`	Underline next *n* lines of text (or just next line if *n* is omitted)	*no*

A Small Example

Now we are ready to take a look at a small, complete example. We'll show how a letter can be formatted using the `nroff` commands covered in this section.

Let's assume that we have letterhead that is only 5 inches wide and 5 inches long. We'll leave 1/2-inch margin on both sides of the page.

The `nroff` input for the sample letter is shown on the following page:

```
.po .5i                          ½-inch left margin
.ll 4i                           ½-inch right margin
.pl 5i                           Length of page is 5 inches
.hy                              Hyphenate words
.nf                              Don't fill lines
.in 2.5i                         Indent in 2.5 inches
January 9, 1989
.in 0i                           Indent back
.sp 3                            Skip three lines
Herb Feltner
Howard W. Sams & Company
4300 W. 62nd Street
Indianapolis, IN  46268
.sp 2                            Skip two more
Dear Herb:
.sp 2                            And two more
.fi                              Now fill and adjust
Enclosed is the second edition of our book.
As soon as we receive the corrections from
your copy and production editors we will
incorporate them into the text and then
start work on the index.
.sp
Please call me if you have any questions.
.sp 3                            Skip 3 lines
Sincerely yours,
.sp 2                            Skip 2 lines
Steve Kochan
```

We entered "no-fill" mode at the start so that the address lines weren't filled by `nroff`. Later, when we were about to start the text of the letter, we turned fill mode back on. And since we never explicitly turned off adjust mode, all subsequent lines were filled *and* adjusted. (Remember, lines can only be adjusted if they are also filled. As long as adjust mode isn't turned off with a `.na` command, lines will always be adjusted whenever fill mode is enabled.)

Running this text through `nroff` produces the following result:

```
                                     January 9, 1989



      Herb Feltner
      Howard W. Sams & Company
      4300 W. 62nd Street
      Indianapolis, IN  46268


      Dear Herb:


      Enclosed is the second  edition  of  our
      book.  As soon as we receive the correc-
      tions from your copy and production edi-
      tors  we  will incorporate them into the
      text and then start work on the index.

      Please call me if  you  have  any  ques-
      tions.



      Sincerely yours,


      Steve Kochan
```

Formatting Larger Documents

The last example shows how easy it is to format small documents with `nroff`. Actually, it's just as easy to format larger documents, except when dealing with such documents you'll need some features not provided by the commands we have presented. The most obvious feature is page numbering; `nroff` does not number your pages for you. In fact, it does nothing special at all at the start of a new page. This can be annoying if you have to format multipage documents. Also, `nroff` does nothing special at the bottom of a page. It will just keep on printing all the way to the bottom without leaving a margin.

In case you want to format multipage documents, you can insert the following lines at the start of the document:

```
.lt 6.5i                      Change this to your line length
.de hd
.if \\n%>1 \{\
```

```
'sp .5i
.tl ''-%-'' \}
'sp |1i
.ns
..
.de fo
'bp
..
.wh 0 hd
.wh -1i fo
```

These nroff commands will cause each page after the first to be numbered using the format -*n*-, where *n* is the page number. This will appear centered on the page, $1/2$ inch down from the top. These commands will also cause 1 inch to be left at the bottom of each page.

nroff Add-On Packages

If you find that you still need more text-processing features, such as automatic footnote processing, the ability to define a block of text that can't be split across two pages, automatically numbered lists, and so on, then you will have to use the special nroff add-on package known as mm— which stands for Memorandum Macros. As the name implies, this add-on package was developed for the express purpose of formatting technical documents, in particular memoranda.[†] To find out how to use the MM formatting package, read *UNIX Text Processing*.

There are also special packages designed to work with nroff to format tables (like those used in this book) and mathematical equations. The name of the former program is tbl and the latter neqn.

Typesetting Text: troff

This entire book was typeset by a program that is nearly identical to nroff. This program is called troff and it differs from nroff primarily in that it produces its output for higher resolution devices such as laser printers and phototypesetters. Since the commands for nroff and troff are highly compatible, the former can be used to debug text before it is sent off to the laser printer or phototypesetter for printing.

Among the programs that work with troff are the following:

- tbl—allows you to format tables for troff (as well as for nroff).

- eqn—allows you to describe complex equations using a simple language.

---

† If the MM package is not available on your system, then you may instead have an older add-on package called MS.

- `pic`—allows you to include figures in your document. The figures are described in a special language and then run through the `pic` program.

- `cip`—allows you to interactively draw figures on a Teletype 5620 terminal. The output from `cip` is actually a `pic` description of the figure.

- `grap`—allows you to include graphs inside your documents. Graphs are described in a special language and then run through the `grap` program.

Initially, `troff` was designed with a specific phototypesetter in mind: the Wang Laboratories, Inc C/A/T phototypesetter. However, now `troff` is "device independent," i.e., it can be used to produce high-quality output on a variety of devices provided they have the necessary hardware capabilities and support software. For example, with the proper software filters, `troff` output can be previewed on terminal screens and can be printed on laser printers such as Hewlett-Packard's LaserJet and Apple's LaserWriter.

The DOCUMENTER'S WORKBENCH System

As of System V, the programs related to formatting text have been grouped into a package known as the DOCUMENTER'S WORKBENCH system. These programs include `nroff`, `troff`, device-independent `troff`, `pic` and `sroff` (a faster version of `nroff`). Also included is the MM memorandum macros package.

This concludes this introduction to the UNIX text processing tools. If you are interested in more information about these tools, you should read *UNIX Text Processing*.

CHAPTER
◆ ◆ ◆ ◆ ◆

9

Program Development

We noted in the introduction to this book that the UNIX system was designed with ease of program development as a primary goal. The system provides a wide assortment of programming languages and development tools. The inherent power and flexibility of the UNIX system allows the programmer to use these tools easily and creatively. The net result is the development of programs in less time than would be required under other operating systems.

We don't have enough space here to go into detail about all of the development tools that are available. We hope, though, that we will be able to point you in the right direction. Table 9-1 shows the languages used most by UNIX programmers. It also gives a brief description of what they're used for. Each language has its own place in the sun. However, you will find that there are usually several choices of programming languages for solving a particular problem. Many times, a combination is the best choice. For example, it's not uncommon to see shell programs that execute programs developed in other languages (such as awk and C) to solve a part of the problem. The shell itself may simply control the execution of the other programs, or it may even do a lot of the processing itself.

Only experience will tell you which programming language is best suited for solving a particular problem. In many cases it may be a trade-off of development time versus execution speed. For example, for many applications you can usually develop a shell program in less time than an equivalent C program. However, the former usually takes *much* longer to execute than an equivalent program developed with the latter, largely due to the fact that the shell is an interpretive programming language.

TABLE 9-1. Programming languages

Program	Primarily used for
awk	String processing; file editing
C	General purpose and system programs; fast-executing programs
f77 (Fortran 77)	Number-crunching; engineering, statistical and mathematical applications; fast executing programs
ksh and sh	General purpose programs; file manipulation; process control
lex and yacc	Writing language processors (compilers)

In the next section of this chapter, we'll show you how to compile C programs under the UNIX system. Then, we'll introduce you to a program called make that allows for automatic program generation. This will be followed by a description of the *Source Code Control System* (SCCS) that enables you to automatically track and regenerate different versions of a program system.

◆ C Program Development ◆

C is the most popular programming language used under the UNIX system, and not without reason. As we mentioned, the operating system itself is primarily written in C with just a few assembly language routines added. The C programming language was developed with systems program development in mind. However, it has proven to be such a flexible and powerful programming language that it is now widely used for general purpose programming applications as well.

It is not our intention to teach you how to program in C here. Consult Appendix A for a list of books on the C programming language.

Compiling C Programs

A file that contains a program written in the C language must have .c as the last two characters of its name in order for it to be compiled. So, for example, monitor.c would be a valid name for a file that contained a C program.

The cc command is used to compile a C program, and its format is rather straightforward:

cc *files*

where *files* is a list of files to be compiled. So the cc command

```
cc monitor.c
```

would be used to compile the program contained in `monitor.c`. If the compiler finds any errors in your program, it will proceed to list them at the terminal, together with a number that locates the line in the file that caused the error (to the best of the compiler's ability).

If no errors are discovered by the C compiler, then it will create an object file with the same name as the source file, except the last two characters will be `.o` instead of `.c`.

The final phase of compilation involves *linking* (or *loading*) the object file to create an *executable object*. In this phase, the compiler tries to resolve external references against the standard C library `libc`. This library contains the *standard I/O library* routines such as `printf` and `fopen`, as well as other functions such as `strcat`, `malloc`, and so on.

If all external references are satisfied, then an executable object file called `a.out` will be created. To execute that file, all you have to do is type its name to the shell:

```
$ a.out
```

If only one file is compiled with the `cc` command, then the `.o` object file will be automatically removed by the compiler. However, if you compile more than one file at once, these separate `.o` files will be kept. This enables you to work efficiently with C programs that span more than one source file. For example, suppose you have a C program that is contained in four source files called `main.c`, `init.c`, `process.c`, and `cleanup.c`. Well, you can proceed to compile all four files at once by simply typing the `cc` command:

```
cc main.c init.c process.c cleanup.c
```

The C compiler will then proceed to separately compile `main.c`, `init.c`, `process.c`, and `cleanup.c` and to link them together if no error is found in any source program.

If an error is found in one or more of the files, then the compiler will not attempt to link the program. It is now up to you to reedit the files that contained errors and then recompile them. This time, however, you have to recompile only the files that you made changes to.

Let's assume that after issuing the above `cc` command, the compiler came back and reported an error in `init.c` and `cleanup.c`. After making your changes to `init.c` and `cleanup.c`, you can again try to compile the program by typing the command:

```
cc main.o init.c process.o cleanup.c
```

This time you specify the files `main.o` and `process.o` instead of `main.c` and `process.c`, respectively, to tell the C compiler that these two files don't have to be recompiled. The compiler will use the object files it wrote the last time these files were compiled.

There are many options that can be specified to the C compiler. The -c option specifies that you don't want to have the program linked and forces creation of a .o file. For example,

```
cc -c main.c
```

causes main.c to be compiled but not linked. It also forces creation of the file main.o (even though only one file is being compiled).

The -O option causes a special optimization program to be run to try to improve the efficiency of your object code. So the command

```
cc -O main.c init.o process.o cleanup.o
```

causes the file main.c to be compiled and linked with init.o, process.o, and cleanup.o and also causes the special optimization program to be run.

The -o option enables you to designate a file name to place the final executable object code in, rather than a.out. So the command

```
cc main.c init.c process.c cleanup.c -o dact
```

will compile the four indicated .c files, placing the resulting executable program in the file dact. The contents of this file can subsequently be executed by simply typing the file name to the shell:

```
$ dact
```

The final option to be described here, -l, is particularly useful if you are using a function from a library other than the standard C library (see Section 3 of your *UNIX Programmer's Reference Manual*). For example, if you use a function from the UNIX math library, such as sqrt, then you must specify the -lm option to the C compiler when your program is linked:

```
cc stats.c -lm
```

You should note that the -lm must be placed *after* the names of the files that are being compiled/linked.

The letter m that immediately follows the -l indicates that you want to reference a function from the math library. Other libraries are available. As we mentioned earlier, the standard C library *libc* is automatically linked with your program by the C compiler.

For a description of all options that are available with the cc command, look up the cc and ld commands in Section 1 of your *UNIX User's Reference Manual*.

C Programming Tools

There is a wide variety of tools that are available to help you develop and debug your C programs. These programs are summarized in Table 9-2. For more information about a specific tool, consult your manual.

TABLE 9-2. C programming tools

Tool	Used for
adb	Debugging C programs (better to use sdb or ctrace if available)
cb	Automatically formatting C programs
cflow	Generating a flow graph of external references
ctrace	Tracing execution of a C program statement by statement
cxref	Generating a cross-reference listing of a C program
lint	Checking a C program (that may span many files) for bugs or nonportable uses of the language
make	Regenerating a program system by automatically tracking files that have changed since system was last made
prof	Obtaining performance data such as the number of times a function is called and the amount of time spent in each function
SCCS	Maintaining and updating source programs; automatic version tracking
sdb	Debugging C programs; symbolic debugger that knows about C data types and expressions

◆ The make Program ◆

The UNIX system provides a very powerful program called make. This program is particularly useful for the development of program systems that comprise more than one file. make automatically keeps track of files that have changed and causes their recompilation when necessary. It also automatically relinks your program if required.

The make program takes a file, known as the *makefile*, as its input. This file describes the following to make:

- the names of the files that make up the program system
- their interdependencies
- how to regenerate the program system

This makefile is typically called makefile or Makefile by convention, although any file name will do. However, if you do use a different name, then you must supply the name as an argument whenever you execute the make command.

Once this information has been described to make, make takes over and does the rest. Simply typing the command make causes the program to examine your makefile and regenerate the system according to the *rules* you have laid out in the file. Typically, this will include recompiling any source program that you changed since the last time it was compiled and subsequently relinking the program system if no compilation errors are reported.

This automated method of program generation saves you from the bother of having to keep track of the files you change and also from recompiling each one yourself. Furthermore, it is not uncommon for several source files to depend on another source file (a .h header file in C is a prime example). If you change that file then you may need to recompile all of the files that depend on it. By specifying this dependency in the makefile, make will take care of recompiling the necessary files whenever that particular file is changed.

Let's take a simple example to see how make works. Here assume that you have a program called dact that is contained in four C source files called main.c, init.c, process.c, and cleanup.c. Also suppose that the file process.c needs a file of definitions called process.h. The file dependencies are depicted in Fig. 9-1.

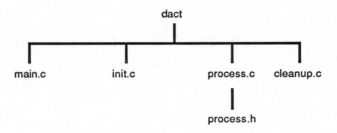

Fig. 9-1. File dependencies for dact program

Making a change to any source file (.c file) will necessitate recompiling that program and also relinking the dact program. Making a change to process.h will require recompiling process.c and relinking dact.

Suppose you have created the following Makefile to describe your program system to make:

```
$ cat Makefile
#
#   Makefile to create the dact system
#

dact : main.o init.o process.o cleanup.o
    cc -o dact main.o init.o process.o cleanup.o

main.o : main.c

init.o : init.c
```

```
process.o : process.c process.h

cleanup.o : cleanup.c
$
```

The first three lines are merely comment lines that are ignored by `make`. The next nonblank line tells the `make` program that the file `dact` depends on the object files `main.o`, `init.o`, `process.o`, and `cleanup.o`. That is, `dact` (the item on the left of the `:`) needs to be *remade* if a change is made to any of the files to the right of the `:`. The line that follows tells the `make` program how to remake `dact`. It will automatically be executed any time a change is made to any of the four `.o` files. This line executes the `cc` command to link together the four `.o` files. This line executes the `cc` command to link together the four indicated object files and place the resulting executable object in the file `dact`. Note that this file must begin with a tab character. If more commands were needed to remake `dact`, then thay would be included here as well, each one preceded by a tab.

The next nonblank line

```
main.o  :  main.c
```

specifies that the file `main.o` needs to be remade if a change is made to the file `main.c`. Notice that there's no line that follows to tell `make` how to remake `main.o`. This is because `make` "knows" how to make a `.o` file from a `.c` file.

The line in the makefile that reads

```
process.o : process.c process.h
```

indicates that the file `process.o` must be remade if a change is made to either `process.c` or `process.h`.

Let's assume the current directory contains the `Makefile` shown previously as well as the source files previously mentioned:

```
$ ls
Makefile
cleanup.c
init.c
main.c
process.c
process.h
$
```

Now let's see what happens if you try to make the `dact` system. This is done by simply typing `make dact`:

```
$ make dact
    cc -O -c main.c
    cc -O -c init.c
"init.c", line 4: syntax error
***Error code 1

Stop.
$
```

Typing in the command make dact initiates execution of the make program. The first thing make does is look for a file called either Makefile or makefile in your current directory. If either is found, then it is taken as the file that tells it what it's supposed to do. make then scans Makefile, looking for a line containing dact (the argument you gave to make) followed by a colon. When it finds the line

```
dact : main.o init.o process.o cleanup.o
```

it then looks to the right of the colon to see what files dact depends upon. Here, we specified that dact needs main.o, init.o, process.o, and cleanup.o. So make then starts with the first file in the list, main.o, and scans Makefile to see if a line containing main.o to the left of a colon exists in the file. The line

```
main .o : main.c
```

tells make that main.o depends on main.c. Since main.c does not appear to the left of a colon in the Makefile, make then proceeds to make main.o. But no commands immediately follow in the Makefile on how to make main.o. Luckily, make knows how to do this itself. So it issues the necessary C compiler command to compile the file main.c and place the output in the file main.o:

```
cc -O -c main.c
```

After main.c has been successfully compiled, make goes to the next file in the list, init.o and proceeds to make that file. Once again, the necessary C compiler command is issued to compile init.c and place the result of the compilation in init.o. As the output shown indicates, the C compiler found a syntax error at line 4 in init.c. Whenever an error occurs while making a file, make just quits right there. You've got to resolve the error in init.c before make will continue its work. Let's see what the file directory looks like now:

```
$ ls
Makefile
cleanup.c
```

```
init.c
main.c
main.o
process.c
$
```

Let's assume you edited `init.c` to correct the syntax error. Now you can reissue the `make` command:

```
$ make dact
    cc -O -c init.c
    cc -O -c process.c
    cc -O -c cleanup.c
    cc -o dact main.o init.o process.o cleanup.o
$
```

This time `make` picked up right where it left off. It didn't recompile `main.c` because that file was not changed since the last time `main.o` was created. So it proceeded to compile `init.c`, `process.c`, and then `cleanup.c`. After having satisfied all of `dact`'s dependencies, it then proceeded to make `dact` by linking together the four `.o` files (recall that you specified in `Makefile` how to do this). Here's the files that you now have in your current directory:

```
$ ls
Makefile
cleanup.c
cleanup.o
dact
init.c
init.o
main.c
main.o
process.c
process.o
$
```

After using the `dact` program for a while, let's suppose you had to make a change to the file `process.h`. So assume you edited this file and made the necessary changes. Now all you have to do to generate a new version of `dact` is issue the same `make` command you've used all along:

```
$ make dact
    cc -O -c process.c
    cc -o dact main.o init.o process.o cleanup.o
$
```

Isn't that nice? make recognized that dact depended upon the four .o files main.o, init.o, process.o, and cleanup.o, and that process.o in turn depended upon process.c and process.h. Realizing that process.h had been changed more recently than process.o, it automatically remade process.o. Then, it realized that process.o was changed more recently than dact, so it remade dact.

Don't worry if you run make without having made any changes to your files, as no harm will be done. make will simply tell you that your program is up to date and do nothing else:

```
$ make dact
'dact' is up to date.
$
```

You can use this feature to ensure that your program is in fact up to date. If not, then make will automatically remedy the situation.

We noted that make automatically knows how to make a .o file from a .c file. make also knows that a .o file depends upon a corresponding .c file. This makes specification of that dependency in your makefile unnecessary. So the makefile from the example we have shown can be more concisely specified as follows:

```
#
#    Makefile to create the dact system
#
dact : main.o init.o process.o cleanup.o
    cc -o dact main.o init.o process.o cleanup.o

process.o : process.c process.h
```

We hope this small example has shown how useful the make program can be. When developing large program systems that span many files, make is invaluable. Read the document *Make—A Program for Maintaining Computer Programs* by S.I. Feldman, Bell Laboratories, Inc., for a thorough description of all its features.

◆ SCCS ◆

A package of programs called SCCS is available to help you manage the development and maintenance of your programs. SCCS stands for Source Code Control System and is of value mainly to developers and maintainers of large programs.

Suppose you are responsible for the support of a large programming system and that the current release version of this system is Version 3.5. Also suppose that you have customers out there who have earlier versions. Imagine now that a customer having Version 1.6 calls in with a problem. After diligently getting a detailed description of the problem you attempt to recreate it on your current version, Version 3.5. As you might expect, the problem does not appear in your version. What you really have to do is try to duplicate the problem on the same version the customer has, Version 1.6.

If your programming system was developed using SCCS, then recreating Version 1.6 of your system is easy. You simply tell the SCCS system the version number you're interested in, and it does the rest. The main purpose of the SCCS system is to automatically track changes between different versions of a program. The system automatically maintains a list of these changes and has the ability to quickly recreate a particular version on request.

SCCS only keeps track of the changes between versions and not the actual complete versions themselves. Thus, it does not waste much disk space.

A program system that has already been developed without using SCCS can easily be placed under the SCCS system. In this section we'll describe how to work with SCCS. This includes discussions on how to create files under SCCS and how to extract and update them.

Placing Your Program Under SCCS

To place a system of programs under the SCCS system you use the `admin` command. This command tells the SCCS system which files to keep track of for you. (It also serves another purpose that won't be described here.) The basic format of the `admin` command to perform this function is:

admin −n −i*file* s.*sccsname*

This command will have the effect of placing *file* under SCCS, giving it the name s.*sccsname*. *sccsname* and *file* are usually one and the same. Just note that *all* SCCS files must begin with the characters s..

The `admin` command must be run separately for each file you want to place under SCCS. As an example, the command

```
admin −n −imain.c s.main.c
```

would place the file main.c under SCCS, calling it s.main.c.

If you have many source files that you want to place under SCCS, then you can use a for statement as taught in Chapter 6:

```
for f in *.c
do
    admin −n −i$f s.$f
done
```

This would place all your .c files contained in the current directory under SCCS.

Every SCCS file has a number associated with it known as its *version number*. This number starts at 1.1, which means *release* 1, *level* 1. As you'll see, whenever a change is made to an SCCS file, 1 gets automatically added to its level number.

The `help` Command

If you run the `admin` command on some files in your directory, you may get some messages displayed at the terminal. Unless you did something wrong, it's probably just a warning message such as the one that follows. Anyway, a command called `help` is available in case you need more explanation about a particular message. It takes as its argument the message number that appears in parentheses at the end of the message. For example, this is the sort of result you might get when placing a file under SCCS:

```
$ admin -n -imain.c s.main.c
No id keywords (cm7)
$
```

The message number in parentheses is `cm7`. Let's get some help:

```
$ help cm7
```

```
cm7:
"No id keywords"
No SCCS identification keywords were substituted for.
You may not have any keywords in the file,
in which case you can ignore this warning.
If this message came from delta then you just made a
delta without any keywords.
If this message came from get the
the last time you made a delta you changed the lines
on which they appeared.
It's a little late to be
telling you that you messed up the last time you made
a delta, but this is the best we can do for now, and
it's better than nothing.

This isn't an error, only a warning
$
```

Better than nothing? Well, we'll leave it for you to decide. Just know that this form of help is available when you need it.

Extracting Files from SCCS

Once you have placed your source files under SCCS, you should remove the original source files, leaving only the "s." versions. From that point on, any access to your source files must be done through the SCCS system. This includes displaying your files as well.

To retrieve an SCCS file, use the get command. This command takes several different options, but to just examine the file, use the -p option. So the command

```
get -p s.main.c
```

would write the latest version of the source file stored in s.main.c to your terminal. (It actually goes to standard output in case you want to redirect or pipe it somewhere.)

If you want to extract a copy of the file for editing, then use the -e option instead. The file that is extracted will have the same name as the SCCS file, except without leading s. characters. So, for example, the command

```
get -e s.main.c
```

would extract the latest version from s.main.c and place it in the file main.c.

If you just want to extract a file and not edit it (perhaps you just want to compile it), then use the get command without any option:

```
get s.main.c
```

This works like the -e option, except you won't be given write permission on the file, meaning you won't be allowed to change it.

You can specify more than one file to get. For example, to extract the latest version from all your SCCS files, you could type:

```
get s.*
```

You can also supply the name of a directory to get, and get will look in the directory and extract only the SCCS files (ie., files beginning with s.) from the directory.

get takes other options that we won't describe here. One of these allows you to specify a specific version to extract. This is what makes it so easy to recreate an earlier version of a programming system. You simply use get to extract all of the files from the specific version; then you "remake" the program system.

Recording Your Editing Changes

Once you have finished making your editing changes to a file that you extracted from SCCS, you will want to put the new copy of the file back under SCCS. This is done with the delta command. This command takes as its argument the name of the SCCS file—that is, with the leading s.. The delta program will then look for the file of the same name without the leading s. and will record the changes that you made to that file. It will also automatically update the current level number on the file. delta prompts you to enter an optional comment to be recorded with this version of the file. After this has been done, the delta program will remove the file you edited.

Here is an example of the use of the delta command.

```
$ delta s.main.c                Record changes
comments?fix timing bug         Comments are entered
No id keywords (cm7)
1.2
1 inserted                      New version and changes displayed
0 deleted
4 changed
$
```

Getting Information on SCCS Files

The prs command enables you to obtain information about your SCCS files. Without any options other than an SCCS file name, a revision history is displayed.

```
$ prs s.main.c
s.main.c:

D 1.2 89/04/15 17:59:21 steve 2 100001/00000/00004
MRs:
COMMENTS:
fix timing bug

D 1.1 89/04/15 17:58:36 steve 1 00004/00000/00000
MRs:
COMMENTS:
date and time created 89/04/15 17:58:36 by steve

$
```

Here you see that SCCS file was last updated on 4/15/89 at 5:59 P.M. You also see the comment that you entered when you did the delta on the file.

The four basic SCCS commands described in this section are summarized in the following table.

TABLE 9-3. Basic SCCS commands

Command	Used to
admin	create new SCCS files
delta	make a change to an SCCS file
get	extract SCCS files
prs	print information about an SCCS file

It is worth noting that SCCS and `make` work together quite well. If the `make` program doesn't find a particular file *f*, then it will automatically look for the file `s`.*f*. If it finds it, then it will assume it is an SCCS file and will issue the necessary `get` command to extract it. After `make` is finished with the extracted SCCS file, it will automatically remove it.

If you're interested in learning more about SCCS, then read the document *Source Code Control System User's Guide* by L.E. Bonanni and C.A. Salemi, Bell Laboratories, Inc.

10

Security

I n recent years, information and computer time have become valuable resources that require protection; security is now a very important part of multiuser systems. One need for security is to keep unauthorized people from gaining access to a computer system; another is to keep an authorized user from tampering with other users' (or the system's) files; still another is to allow some users certain privileges that others aren't allowed. Ideally, this should all be done with as little bother to the users as possible—security should be available when needed but unobtrusive when not.

Security on UNIX systems is made available through a few simple commands and features that form the basis for a complete security system that can be as lax or tight as desired. This chapter divides UNIX security into four major parts:

- Password security
- File security
- The su and newgrp commands
- File encryption

◆ Password Security ◆

There's a file on UNIX systems called /etc/passwd that contains all the information the system needs to know about each user, *including the password*. Believe it or not, this file can be printed out by *anyone* on the system. Why is the system so trusting? Well, the passwords are *encrypted* (more on this later) using an encoding scheme that makes deciphering someone's password very difficult. A typical excerpt from /etc/passwd looks like this:

```
$ cat /etc/passwd
root:xyDfccTrt18Ox,m.y8:0:0:admin:/:/bin/sh
console:lo1ndT0ee0Mzp,M.y8:1:1:admin:/:/bin/sh
pat:XmotTvoyUmjls:10:10:p wood:/usr/pat:/bin/sh
steve:J9exPd97Ftlbn,M.z8:15:10:s kochan:/usr/steve:/bin/sh
restrict:PomJklO9JkY41,./:16:16::/usr/restrict:/bin/rsh
$
```

The user id is listed first, then a colon (:), then the encrypted password, then another colon, and then more information that is discussed in Chapter 12.

Whenever you log in, the password you type in at the terminal is encrypted and checked against the encrypted password for your id in /etc/passwd. If they match, you are allowed on the system; if they don't, you are given the message Login incorrect, and you must try again.

If you want to change your password, you can't modify /etc/passwd - that's not allowed on a UNIX system. If it were, sooner or later someone would go in and change all the passwords; then nobody would be able to log in. Instead, you use the passwd command. All you have to do is type in passwd, and it prompts you for the rest:

```
$ passwd
Changing password for pat
Old password: wizzard1                   Not printed
New password: wom2bat                    Not printed
Re-enter new password: wom2bat           Not printed
$
```

Before allowing you to change a password, the passwd command requests that you type in the old password. This is just to make sure it's really you and not someone else using your terminal while you're away. If you make a mistake typing in the old password, the system responds with sorry, meaning that no change was made and that you should try again. If the old password is correct, the passwd command then asks you to enter the new password. Since the passwords are not printed, the command makes sure you don't unwittingly make a mistake by asking you to enter your new password a second time. If the two entries don't match, the passwd command will ask you to enter the *new* password twice:

```
$ passwd
Changing password for pat
Old password: wom2bat                    Not printed
New password: wizzard1                   Not printed
Re-enter new password: wizrd1            Not printed
They don't match; try again.
New password: wizzard1                   Not printed
Re-enter new password: wizzard1          Not printed
$
```

The `passwd` command is like many other UNIX commands in that it prints nothing when your password has been successfully altered. It simply finishes and goes back to the shell.

System V Release 3.2

As of System V Release 3.2, the encrypted passwords in `/etc/passwd` were moved into the file `/etc/shadow` which is *not* readable by ordinary users. The password field in `/etc/passwd` is ignored. The `passwd` command was also modified to take this change into account.

Note that although this change improves the security of passwords on UNIX systems, it shouldn't stop you from selecting good ones!

Choosing Good Passwords

Although many UNIX systems don't put restrictions on passwords (some don't require them at all), if you want to keep your user id secure, you should use non-obvious passwords. First and last names, initials, birth dates, and the like are poor passwords. Even passwords from ordinary English words can be cracked given a weekend or two of computer time and an on-line dictionary. "Good" passwords are those that are at least six characters long, aren't based on personal information, and have some nonalphabetic characters in them: `4score`, `adv8ance`, `my_name`, `bon1jour`, and `a1b2c3` are unique enough to make discovery difficult but not impossible. Misspelled words and two-word combinations make good passwords.

Even better passwords are `dg71m33ex` and `z_1_y_2_x`. These are almost impossible to crack. Unfortunately, the former is almost impossible to remember. If a password is so weird that you have to write it down, its not a good password—writing down passwords is not a good security procedure. Many computer systems require paswords like `dg71m33ex`. This just causes everyone to write down their passwords and tape them to their terminals!

You should change your password periodically, so that even if someone has discovered it, any unauthorized use would be cut off. The interval for changing a password depends on how secure an id has to be; however you should change it at least every six months. Chapter 12 discusses how to have the UNIX system *require* users to change their passwords periodically.

The only times a password is typed in are when you log in and when you change your password. The password isn't printed at these times in order to keep prying eyes from seeing it. However, someone with sharp eyes and a good memory can get your password just by watching your fingers at the keyboard. When you type in your password, you should make sure no one is nearby.

◆ File Security ◆

File security has to do with who can access a file, and what they can do with the file once they have accessed it. For example, you might want a file containing some sensitive information to be unreadable by other users (perhaps your secret recipe for baked basilisk). But you might want another file readable by everyone (your list of recipes and their prices). The UNIX system allows you to change the access *permissions* of a file to suit your needs. These permissions determine who can read a file, who can write to it, and who can execute it, if it happens to be a program.

File Attributes

If you use the `ls` command with the `-l` option, it prints out some cryptic information along with the size of the file, the last time it was modified, and the file name.

```
$ ls -l zombie
-rwxrwxrwx 1 pat group1 70 jul 28 21:12 zombie
$
```

Skipping the `-rwxrwxrwx` and the number following it for now, you can see there are two words listed before the file size (which is 70 bytes). These words tell the name of the *owner* and *group* associated with the file. Every file has an owner and group associated with it. The owner of the file is a user, usually the one who created the file; the group is a label for several users who have been logically *grouped* together and given a name. For example, several people working on the same project are usually put in one group so they can have free access to each other's files while restricting access to outsiders (i.e., users not in that group). Every user id is in a group, even if it's the only one in it. It's also possible for you to belong to more than one group (for example, suppose you're simultaneously working on different projects).

In the previous example, `pat` is the owner of `zombie`, which is associated with `group1`.

Going back to the `-rwxrwxrwx`, you see the beginning `-`. This means that this is a regular file and not a directory (recall from Chapter 4 that a directory will have a `d` instead). After the `-` there is the `rwxrwxrwx`, which is called the *mode* or *permissions* of the file. It tells us who can do what with `zombie`. You'll notice that here the pattern `rwx` is repeated three times. Each of these three patterns tells us what a particular type of user can do with the file. The first `rwx` tells us that the owner of `zombie` (in this case `pat`) can read (`r`) from, write (`w`) to, and execute (`x`) the file. The second `rwx` tells us that any user who is a member of the group `group1` can also do these things with the file. The third `rwx` says that *any* user can (Fig. 10-1).

If one of the permissions is denied, a `-` shows up in the place of the appropriate letter. For example, `rw-` means read and write, but no execute (good for plain text files that you have no need to execute as programs); `r-x` means read and execute, but no write (good for the permission of a program that you don't want someone to overwrite).

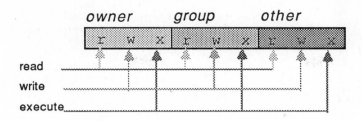

Fig. 10-1. File modes

Changing File Permissions

So now you have a way to control the accessability of your files for each of the three types of users: owner, group, and others. Let's say, for example that you're pat, the owner of the file zombie, and you don't want any user other than pat to be able to write into (and thereby alter or destroy) zombie. On the other hand, since you feel zombie is a useful program, you want it to be available to all users to examine and execute. So you want the new mode of zombie to be rwxr-xr-x, thus allowing users in your group and others to read (or copy) and execute the file, but not to tamper with it.

To alter the mode of zombie, you must use the chmod command with the new mode and the file name as arguments. The new mode is not specified to chmod as rwxr-xr-x, but as a *three digit number* that is computed by adding together the numeric equivalents of the desired permissions (Fig. 10-2).

owner			group			other		
r	w	x	r	w	x	r	w	x
4			4			4		
+	2			2			2	
+		1			1			1
digit			*digit*			*digit*		

Fig. 10-2. Computing new permissions

In this case, the new mode is 755, where the 7 is rwx for the owner, the first 5 is r-x for the group, and the second 5 is r-x for others (Fig. 10-3).

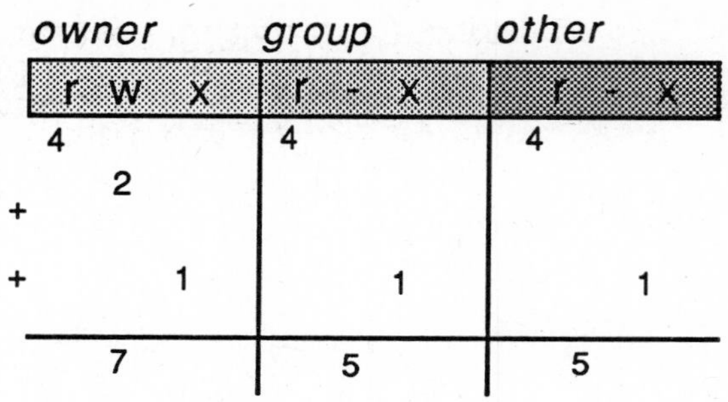

Fig. 10-3. Computing `rwxr-xr-x`

To change the mode of `zombie` to `rwxr-xr-x`, you use the `chmod` command (see Chapters 5 and 6) with the three digit number:

```
$ chmod 755 zombie
$
```

And if you look at the mode of `zombie` now, you can see it has indeed changed.

```
$ ls -l zombie
-rwxr-xr-x  1 pat   group1  70 Jul 28 21:12 zombie
$
```

Some other examples of `chmod` are shown here with the resultant modes. Note that only the owner or the system administrator can change the mode of a particular file; thus, if other users can't access the file, they cannot use `chmod` to gain access.

```
$ chmod 700 zombie
$ ls -l zombie
-rwx------  1 pat   group1  70 Jul 28 21:12 zombie
$
```

Now only `pat` is allowed any kind of access to `zombie`.

```
$ chmod 711 zombie
$ ls -l zombie
-rwx--x--x  1 pat   group1  70 Jul 28 21:12 zombie
$
```

Now group members and others are allowed to execute `zombie`, but not to copy or examine it.

```
$ chmod 771 zombie
$ ls -l zombie
-rwxrwx--x  1 pat   group1   70 Jul 28 21:12 zombie
$
```

Now users in `group1` are allowed the same privileges as `pat`, but others can still only execute `zombie`.

There is another way to change the modes of a file with `chmod`. It allows you to specify a *symbolic* mode instead of a numeric one. The format of the symbolic mode is:

[who] op permission

where *who* is a combination of the letters `u` for the owner's permissions (think of this as the "user"), `g` for the group's permissions, and `o` for others' permissions. `a` can be used to specify all of these (`ugo`) and is the default. *op* can be a `+` to add *permission* to the mode, a `-` to remove *permission* from the mode, or an `=` to assign *permission* to the mode. *permission* is a combination of the letters `r`, `w`, and `x`, meaning read, write, and execute, respectively.

So to change the mode of `zombie` to `-rw-rw-rw-`, you would type in:

```
$ chmod a=rw zombie
$ ls -l zombie
-rw-rw-rw-  1 pat   group1   70 Jul 28 21:12 zombie
$
```

Note that the `a` may be omitted. To add execute permission you can type in:

```
$ chmod +x zombie
$ ls -l zombie
-rwxrwxrwx  1 pat   group1   70 Jul 28 21:12 zombie
$
```

Finally, to remove write permission from others, you would use `o-w`:

```
$ chmod o-w zombie
$ ls -l zombie
-rwxrwxr-x  1 pat   group1   70 Jul 28 21:12 zombie
$
```

One of the main advantages of the symbolic mode is that you can add or remove permissions without knowing what the old ones are. For example, when you first create a shell program, the permissions don't include execute. This can be added with a quick `chmod +x` command without knowing what the original read/write permissions are.

The permissions can be used to prevent accidental overwriting or removal of an important file. All you have to do is change the mode to `-r-xr-xr-x` and you can't change the file even though you are the owner. You have to change the mode to give yourself write permission before you can alter the file.

```
$ chmod 555 zombie
$ ls -l zombie
-r-xr-xr-x  1 pat  group1  70 Mar 18 16:57 zombie
$ echo hi there > zombie
zombie: cannot create
$
```

Here the shell cannot redirect the output of the echo command into the file zombie because the write permission isn't set.

Even rm will not immediately remove the file; it will ask for confirmation first:

```
$ ls -l zombie
-r-xr-xr-x  1 pat  group1  70 Mar 18 16:57 zombie
$ rm zombie
zombie: 555 mode ?              Do you really want to remove it?
```

If you type a y when rm asks for confirmation, the file will be removed *regardless of the mode*; any other input will cause rm to quit without removing the file.

```
$ rm zombie
zombie: 555 mode ? n            I don't want to remove it
$
```

Changing Group and Owner

As the owner of zombie, you can change the group associated with it with the chgrp command:

```
$ chgrp group2 zombie
$ ls -l zombie
-rwxrwxr-x  1 pat  group2  70 Jul 28 21:12 zombie
$
```

Now group2 has full read, write, and execute permission, and group1 no longer does. (Members of group1 now fall into the "others" category.)

You can even change the owner, although that is a little chancy, since once you change the owner, you cannot change it back—the new owner would have to do that. To change ownership of zombie, you use the chown command:[†]

```
$ chown steve zombie
$ ls -l zombie
-rwxrwxr-x  1 steve group2  70 Jul 28 21:12 zombie
$
```

---

† Berkeley UNIX systems allow only the administrator to use chown.

As you can see, `steve` is now the owner of `zombie`. To change the group, owner, or permissions, you would have to log in as `steve`.

For the commands `chmod`, `chgrp`, and `chown`, you can specify more than one file name, and appropriate file attributes of all of the files specified will be changed, provided you own the files to begin with:

```
$ chmod 666 *.c
$
```

This makes all C programs in this directory readable and writeable by all users.

```
$ chmod 700 x y zzz
$
```

This denies access to files `x`, `y`, and `zzz` to all users but the owner, who can read, write, and execute the file.

```
$ chown steve *
$
```

This makes `steve` the owner of all files in this directory.

Directory Permissions

Directories also have modes that work in ways similar to ordinary files. You need read (`r`) permission to use `ls` on a directory, you need write (`w`) permission to add or remove files from a directory, and you need execute (`x`) permission to `cd` into a directory or use it as part of a path. Note that to use any file, you must have the proper access permissions for the file *and all the directories* in the path of that file.

If you don't have execute permission in all directories along the path to a file, you cannot use the file, no matter what the file's permissions are. If you don't have read permission to a directory, an `echo *` will not work. You can still access a file in such a directory if the execute permission of the directory is set, but you must use its full name; file name expansion will not work. If you don't have write permission in a directory, you can't create files in that directory, nor can you move or remove them. The opposite is also true: If you do have write permission in a directory, you can remove a file, no matter what the file's permissions are or who the owner is.[†]

Let's look at some possible directory modes:

[†] As of System V Release 3.2, a directory can be set up so that only the owner of a file can remove or rename it, even if the directory is writable by all. Refer to Chapter 12 for more information.

```
$ ls -l
total 5
drwxrwxrwx   2 pat   group1   32 Aug 4 18:03 anyone
drwxrwxr-x   2 pat   group1   32 Aug 4 18:03 group
drwxr-xr-x   2 pat   group1   32 Aug 4 18:03 me
drwx------   2 pat   group1   32 Aug 4 18:03 just_me
d--x--x--x   2 pat   group1   32 Aug 4 18:03 nobody
$
```

The directory anyone is available to all users—anyone can create and remove files from this directory. The directory group is open to the owner and members of group1 for creating and removing; other users can list its contents and read from or write to *existing* files (if the permissions on those files allow access), but may not create new files. In the directory me, only the owner can create or remove files. The directory just_me is accessible only to the owner. No other user can access any of the files in it. The last directory nobody is only searchable; nobody can create or remove files, nor can anyone use ls on it; however, if you know the name of a file in nobody, you can access that file because you can search (execute) the directory.

Changing the access modes of a directory is the same as for a file. If you want to change the mode of nobody to rwx for all classes of users, you type in:

```
$ chmod 777 nobody
$ ls -ld nobody
drwxrwxrwx   2 pat   group1   32 Aug  4 18:03 nobody
$
```

As you can see, it's now open to all users. The -d option to ls tells ls that information about the *directory* should be listed, rather than information about its *contents*.

♦ The su and newgrp Commands ♦

The su command is helpful when you use more then one user id on a system and you want to do things with the files owned by a different id without logging off and logging in under that id. su changes the *effective* user-id to that of someone else's. For example, if you're logged on as pat and want to *become* for all intent and purposes the user steve, you would type in:

```
$ su steve
enter password:zaq123                    Not printed
$
```

If the password isn't the correct one for the user steve, your effective user-id isn't changed and the message `sorry` is displayed. If you do type in the right password, however, you'll be granted all the privileges associated with the user `steve`. In the meantime, you'll lose all the privileges associated with the id `pat`. When you're finished being the other user and you want to go back to being yourself, you just press *CTRL-d*. This puts you back to the privileges you had before running `su`.

The `su` command has one other important feature. If used without a user-id, `su` attempts to change to the user `root`, which is an administrative id that has access to the entire system. `root` is often referred to as the "super-user" (`su` stands for "super-user"). `root` has access to all files and all devices on the system and can make any changes to the system. Needless to say, the password for `root` should be a well kept secret, for use only by system administrators. Chapter 12 goes into greater detail about `root`.

Similar to the `su` command is the `newgrp` command. At any given time, you belong to only one group, so to change groups the `newgrp` command is used along with the new group name:

```
$ newgrp group2
$
```

This changes your current group to `group2`. Now you can access files as if you were in `group2`. As with `su`, you now have none of the privileges associated with `group1`.

Of course, having groups at all is rather silly without a mechanism for controlling which groups you can `newgrp` to. The file `/etc/group` contains a list of groups and eligible members.

```
$ cat /etc/group
root::0:root
console::1:root,console
bin::2:root,bin
sys::3:root,bin,sys
group1::10:pat,steve
group2::11:pat,steve
restrict::16:restrict
anyone:JuklOk08KjllK:17:pat,steve
$
```

Like the `/etc/passwd` file, the information is separated by colons, with the group name first, an optional password next, a number that identifies the group next (this is described in Chapter 12), and a comma-separated list of the members of that group last.

You must be listed among the members of a group to change to it unless an encrypted password is associated with the group. If an encrypted password is given, then any user can `newgrp` to that group if he knows the password. As you can see, one group, `anyone`, has an encryted password. In order to change to this group, `newgrp` will request any user except `pat` and `steve` to enter the correct password for the group.

```
$ newgrp anyone
enter password:a1b2c3                    Not printed
$
```

Of course, if the correct password isn't typed in, the change isn't allowed. Unlike `su`, you don't press *CTRL-d* when you want to get back to your previous group; `newgrp` without a group name changes you back to the default group.

♦ File Encryption ♦

As we said before, the passwords in `/etc/passwd` are *encrypted*— encoded in such a way so as to make reading them very difficult. An encryption program is available to users—the `crypt` command.[†] `crypt` uses a key to scramble its standard input into an unreadable mess that is sent to standard output:

```
$ cat names
Pat
Tony
Ruth
Bill
$ crypt xyzzy < names
>.TCcb2@jedG0^K
$
```

As you can see, the encrypted form of a file is quite unreadable. In this example, `xyzzy` is the key used to encrypt the file.

The nice thing about `crypt` is that it also performs the *decryption* of the text. In fact, the same key is used both for encryption and decryption. First you create an encrypted version of the file `names`:

```
$ crypt xyzzy < names > names.crypt
$ cat names.crypt
>.TCcb2@jedG0^K
$
```

Now you have a file called `names.crypt` that is the encrypted version of `names`. To reproduce the contents of `names`, you use the `crypt` command again, *specifying the same key that you used when encrypting the file.*

---

† Due to export restrictions on "encryption technology," some versions of UNIX distributed outside of the United States do not have the `crypt` command.

```
$ crypt xyzzy < names.crypt
Pat
Tony
Ruth
Bill
$
```

As you can see, the crypt command decrypted the file names.crypt.

If you don't give crypt a key as an argument, it will prompt you for one:

```
$ crypt < names
Enter key:xyzzy                          Not printed
>.TCcb2@jedG0^K
$
```

This usage of crypt is preferred over typing the key on the command line. First, when the key is typed in on the command line, it is printed on your terminal for everyone to see; when you are prompted for it, crypt prevents it from being printed. Also, when the key is typed in on the command line, it is possible that other users can see it by using the ps -f command (which prints the status of a process along with the command name *and any arguments*). crypt wipes out this information once it starts up, but there is a short period when it is available.

Normally, after you encrypt a file you should remove the original copy of the file, leaving yourself with only the encrypted version. In this way, the information in the file can be accessed only by someone who knows the key. Note that after removing the original, you can't forget the key! If you do, the information in the file is, for all intents and purposes, lost.

In order to make crypt security better and make life easier for users, most editors on the UNIX system have crypt built-in. The -x option to ed and vi tells them you are editing an encrypted file:

```
$ ed -x names.crypt
Enter file encryption key: xyzzy      Not printed
19
1,$P
Pat
Tony
Ruth
Bill
*1a
Bob
*w
23
*q
```

```
$ crypt < names.crypt
Enter key:xyzzy
Pat
Bob
Tony
Ruth
Bill
$
```

The editor automatically reencrypts the file (using the same key) when it is written.

Without the -x option, you'd have to decrypt the file before running the editor and reencrypt it after quitting. The disadvantage of this is that the decrypted version of the file would be left sitting around while it was being edited. With the -x option, a decrypted version of the file never exists: the editor works directly on the encrypted file. To further increase the security of your encrypted files, you can create the file using the -x option to the editor; then the file never exists in the file system in its unencrypted form.

What was said about good and bad passwords for logins applies here to keys, too. Simple keys allow a decrypter to try various possibilities until the correct one is found. Nontrivial keys make trial and error decryption almost impossible. Of course, you should use something you can remember, otherwise, you might have some trouble decrypting your own files!

File encryption is a helpful way of hiding information from other users, administrators, and casual intruders. The crypt command shouldn't be considered unbreakable, however, since the methods it uses to encrypt text is not kept secret, and decryption methods are known. Anyone who is determined enough and has the time, patience, and computer facilities can crack the encrypted text. Because of this and other reasons, you should never use your password for the encryption key.

One simple and effective technique that vastly increases the security of crypt is to compress a file with the pack[†] command before encrypting it. pack compresses a file with a sophisticated technique that decreases redundancy and causes character information to cross byte boundaries in the packed output. pack appends a .z to the input file name and puts the packed version in that file. After packing, the original is removed:

```
$ pack salaries
pack: salaries: 37.8% Compression
$ ls -l salaries*          pack creates packed file salaries.z
-rw-r--r--  1 pat  group1  4718 May  3 21:12 salaries.z
$ crypt < salaries.z > encrypted
Enter key:xyz1y0
$ rm salaries.z
$
```

---

† Berkeley UNIX systems supply the compact command instead of pack. compact tacks a .C onto the end of the file name instead of .z.

To restore the original, you first run `crypt` and then `unpack`:

```
$ crypt < encrypted > salaries.z
Enter key:xyz1y0
$ unpack salaries
unpack: salaries: unpacked
$
```

There is presently no known way of decrypting a packed file without knowing the key. Unfortunately, the `-x` option to `ed` and `vi` won't work with these files; they must be decrypted and unpacked to be edited.

For more information on UNIX security, refer to *UNIX System Security*.

C H A P T E R

11

Communications

This chapter discusses how to communicate between UNIX systems, how to send mail and files to users on other UNIX systems, and how to use some of the communication equipment hooked up to your system.

◆ Telephone Communications ◆

Some UNIX systems have communication equipment that allows them to be used *remotely*. Typically, this involves having a telephone line and a device called a *modem* hooked up to one of the ports that a terminal normally uses. The modem (short for *modulator-demodulator*) is a converter that changes the binary codes that go between the computer and the terminal into sounds that can be transmitted over telephone lines.

By connecting a terminal to another modem, a user can then

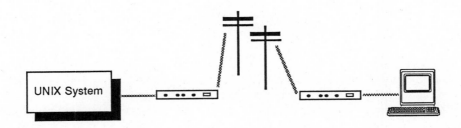

Fig. 11-1. Fig 11-1

access a system from almost anywhere (Fig. 11-1). Most modems are fairly slow compared to directly connected lines. The most popular modems operate at 1200 or 2400 bits per second (*baud*), which translates into about 120 or 240 characters per second, respectively. Directly connected lines run up to 19,200 baud on some UNIX systems.

Your UNIX system may have *dial-out* capability—the ability to make calls as well as receive them The modem, or a device attached to it, generates touch-tone® or rotary dial pulses under program control (referred to as *automatic calling*), thus allowing your system to call other systems and exchange data.

Inter System `mail`

One way to access this feature is with the `mail` command. In Chapter 8, the `mail` command was used to send mail from one user to another *on the same system*. You can also use it to send mail to a user *on another system*. First, you need to know what system the other user is on and what his user id is. Then you need to determine if your system can send mail to the other system. This can be done by typing in the `uuname` command, which prints out a list of systems known to your own:

```
$ uuname
remote1
remote2
vortex
$
```

If the system you want to send mail to is in the list, you're in business. If there are no systems printed out, then your system probably doesn't have any dial-out capability. Even so, you should check with your system administrator just to be sure.

Let's say the system you want to send mail to is in the `uuname` list. To send mail to a user `john` on the system named `remote1`, you type

```
$ mail remote1!john
```

and proceed to type in your mail just as you did in Chapter 8. Note that there can be no spaces before or after the exclamation point (!). This is because the *system!user* string is considered to be a single argument by `mail`. In general, mail can be sent to any user on any system in the `uuname` list. Just remember, the user id must exist on the system you are mailing to; otherwise, the mail will be returned to you with a `User Unknown` message.

Sending mail to a system that is not in your `uuname` list is a lot trickier. This can only be done if you know that one of the systems on the list communicates with the system you want to mail to. If so, you can use that system as a *link* between your system and the final destination. You simply mail to the known system followed by the final destination system:

```
$ mail known!final!user
```

Only the first system in the list must be known to your system; that system must then forward the mail to the final destination. Again, if the forwarding system doesn't know the final destination system, the mail will be returned.

As you might guess, you can have as many forwarding systems in the route as you want. You simply separate the system names with exclamation points:

```
$ mail system1!system2!...!system_last!user
```

Only `system1` must be in your `uuname` list; each system along the line need only know about the next system in the list.

UUCP

Sending mail to remote systems is merely one function of a number of commands grouped under the label *UUCP* (UNIX-to-UNIX copy).

The UUCP commands, of which `uuname` is one, do the actual call-ups and file transfers between systems, maintain usage statistics, and ensure security. One of the UUCP commands is `uucp`. It is similar in form to the `cp` command, only `uucp` allows you to copy files between systems. The general format of the command is:

uucp *source_file destination*

source_file is usually (but doesn't have to be) on your system, and *destination* is usually a file or directory on *another* system. *destination* is specified in the form *system!filename* or *system!directory*.

For example, use this command to copy the file `names` to the directory `/usr/tmp` on system `remote1`:

```
$ uucp names remote1!/usr/tmp
$
```

This will copy `names` to `/usr/tmp/names` on `remote1`, as will the command:

```
$ uucp names remote1!/usr/tmp/names
$
```

We said before that the `uucp` system ensures security. It does this by giving system administrators the option to restrict incoming and outgoing `uucp` file transfers to a single directory structure, usually headed by `/usr/spool/uucppublic`. Under this restriction, files can only be copied to a directory under `/usr/spool/uucppublic`. If you send a file to such a system, it must be directed to someplace in `/usr/spool/uucppublic` or you will get mail back saying `remote access to path/file denied`. `uucp` does give you some help with this: It allows you to use the construct ~/*user id*, which is replaced with /usr/spool/uucppublic/*user id*. For example,

```
$ uucp names remote1!~/john/names
$
```

is interpreted by uucp as:

```
$ uucp names remote1!/usr/spool/uucppublic/john/names
$
```

~/ is simply a convenient shorthand for /usr/spool/uucppublic.

uucp can also be used to copy files *from* another system *to* your system. You simply specify the file you want (using the *system!file* notation) as the source file:

```
$ uucp remote1!~/file1 ~/file1
$
```

This copies /usr/spool/uucppublic/file1 on remote1 to the file /usr/spool/uucppublic/file1 on your system. Of course, this requires that file1 be in /usr/spool/uucppublic on remote1. If file transfers are restricted for the remote system, you won't get the file. In this case, you will probably need to have a user on the remote system send you the file by running uucp on that system.

When you send files via uucp, they will be readable and writable by everyone on the receiving system. If you're sending files that shouldn't be accessible by everyone, you should pack and encrypt them using pack and crypt as discussed in Chapter 10. Not only does this prevent others from reading your files, it also reduces the size of the files and subsequently the amount of time required to transmit them. Even if you don't need to encrypt your files, you should consider packing them to reduce transmission overhead (particularly if you're sending files over a long-distance telephone connection).

After you run the uucp command to send a file to another system, you may have to wait several minutes for the file transfer to actually take place. When you get a $ after running uucp, you are being informed that the file transfer has been *queued* or placed in line to be sent. (There may be other file transfers waiting to be performed before yours.) To find out whether the file has been sent, the command uulog can be used. The status of all uucp transfers for the system remote1 can be determined by using the uulog command with remote1 as an argument:

```
$ uulog remote1
uucp remote1   (12/7-19:19:30,3524,0) SUCCEEDED (call to remote1 )
uucp remote1   (12/7-19:19:32,3524,0) OK (startup)
uucp remote1   (12/7-19:19:33,3524,0) REMOTE REQUESTED
     (remote1!/usr/users/pw/sources/xfer.c --> local!~/test/ (pat))
```

```
uucp remote1  (12/7-19:19:49,3524,1) REMOTE REQUESTED
     (remote1!/usr/users/pw/sources/xfer.c --> local!~/test/ (pat))
uucp remote1  (12/7-19:20:02,3524,2) OK (conversation complete tty0 39)
uucp remote1  (12/8-10:27:08,214,0) FAILED (LOGIN FAILED)
uucp remote1  (12/8-10:27:08,214,0) CONN FAILED (LOGIN FAILED)
uucp remote1  (12/8-10:27:42,223,0) SUCCEEDED (call to remote1 )
uucp remote1  (12/8-10:27:45,223,0) OK (startup)
uucp remote1  (12/8-10:27:46,223,0) REMOTE REQUESTED
     (remote1!/usr/journal/v2n1/color.inset --> local!~/journal/ (pat))
uucp remote1  (12/8-10:28:12,223,1) OK (conversation complete tty0 37)
uucp remote1  (12/8-11:13:39,247,0) SUCCEEDED (call to remote1 )
uucp remote1  (12/8-11:13:41,247,0) OK (startup)
uucp remote1  (12/8-11:13:42,247,0) REMOTE REQUESTED
     (remote1!/usr/journal/v2n1/tips.figs/figs.ps --> local!~/journal/ (pat))
uucp remote1  (12/8-11:13:53,247,1) OK (conversation complete tty0 22)
uucp remote1  (12/8-18:40:16,976,0) SUCCEEDED (call to remote1 )
uucp remote1  (12/8-18:40:19,976,0) OK (startup)
pat remote1 remote1N3a5e (12/8-18:40:20,976,0) REQUEST
     (local!/tmp/names --> remote1!~/john (pat))
uucp remote1  (12/8-18:40:57,976,1) OK (conversation complete tty0 49)
$
```

The last four lines of output from uulog shows the transfer of the file /tmp/names from the local system to remote1. The SUCCEEDED line says that the call (dialing) from the local system to remote1 succeeded. The OK (startup) line says that uucp managed to successfully log into and start communications with remote1. The REQUEST line says that the system has requested permission to start copying /tmp/names to ~/john. The OK (conversation complete... line says that the send was successful and that uucp is done.

A REMOTE REQUESTED line signifies that the remote system is sending a file to the local one, whereas a REQUEST line signifies that the local system is sending a file to the remote one. A FAILED line means that the transfer somehow failed. This is usually because uucp wasn't able to log into the remote system, e.g., the system was down or all its telephone lines were busy.

Left to its own devices, uulog will print the entire log for the specified system. This can amount to hundreds or thousands of lines for a busy system. In order to get just the most recent log entries from uulog, use the *-num* option. The option will be passed to tail along with the output of uulog:

```
$ uulog -5 remote1
uucp remote1  (12/8-11:13:53,247,1) OK (conversation complete tty0 22)
uucp remote1  (12/8-18:40:16,976,0) SUCCEEDED (call to remote1 )
uucp remote1  (12/8-18:40:19,976,0) OK (startup)
pat remote1 remote1N3a5e (12/8-18:40:20,976,0) REQUEST
     (local!/tmp/names --> remote1!~/john (pat))
uucp remote1  (12/8-18:40:57,976,1) OK (conversation complete tty0 49)
$
```

Chapter 12 contains information on installing and maintaining the uucp system.

cu

cu is a command that allows you to call another UNIX system, log in, and use it *while you are still logged into your original system*. It works by using your UNIX system's dial-out ability and connecting your terminal to the outgoing modem; all you have to do is tell it what system or telephone number to call:

```
$ cu 3865850
Connected
login:
```

or

```
$ cu remote1
Connected
login:
```

At this point, you can log in and use the system that you called. Note that you have not logged off of the system you were on before typing in cu. Let's try logging into another system and doing some work:

```
$ cu remote1                          Call up remote system
Connected
login: john                           Log in as john
Password: byelbye
The Plant Dept. will be working on an air-
conditioning problem Sat. Dec. 3 and Sunday Dec. 4.

$ who am i                            Are we really john?
john   tty08 Dec 3 13:22
$ pwd                                 Enter a few commands
/usr/john
$ ls
file1
names
uucpfiles
$ CTRL-d                              Log off
login:
```

After having done some work on the other system, you'll want to log off and continue working on your original system. Logging off is not enough, however, since the terminal is still hooked up to the outgoing modem, which is still dialed into the other system. You have to tell the cu command to disconnect you from the other system. This is done by typing in ~ . at the beginning of a line, followed by a *RETURN*:

```
$ cu remote1                        Call up remote system
Connected
login: john                         Log in as john
Password:byelbye
The Plant Dept. will be working on an air-
conditioning problem Sat. Dec. 3 and Sunday Dec. 4.

$ ls
file1
names
uucpfiles
$ CTRL-d
login: ~[local].                    Disconnect
Disconnected
$
```

The [local] is printed by cu to indicate that the command you're typing in will affect you on the local system. Note that you should always log off of the remote system before disconnecting. Some systems will not log you off automatically when you disconnect, so the next user who comes along on that line may be given access to your login.

cu is useful if you regularly use more than one UNIX system since it lets you use another system without logging off the system you're using. cu is also useful when you want to transfer small *text* files between your UNIX system and another. It has some built-in commands that use the communications link established when you call another system to transfer the files. The commands are ~%take and ~%put, which take files from and put files onto the other system, respectively. To take a file (i.e., copy it) from the other system, you call it up, log in, and then type in:

~%take *from to*

where *from* is the name of the file on the other system and *to* is the name you want for the file on your regular system. The *to* file name is optional; cu will use the *from* file name if the *to* file name isn't given. For example, let's say you want to copy the file file1 from another system:

```
$ cu remote1
Connected
login: john
Password: byelbye
The Plant Dept. will be working on an air-
conditioning problem Sat. Dec. 3 and Sunday Dec. 4.
```

```
$~[local]%take file1                    Copy file1 from another system
stty -echo;mesg n;echo '~>':file1;cat file1;echo '~>';
mesg y;stty echo
~>:file1
123+
128 lines/2088 characters
$ CTRL-d
login: ~[local].
Disconnected
$ ls
abc
file1                                   It's been copied
test
$
```

The three lines following the ~%take are the control lines that go to the other UNIX system to transfer file1. As cu transmits the file, it prints a number when it starts to send each block of 1,024 bytes, so the numbers in the line 123+ are printed out one at a time as the transfer proceeds. The last line is printed out when the transfer is complete; it tells you the number of lines and characters transferred.

Similarly, if you wanted to copy the file test to another system, you would use the ~%put command:

```
login: john
Password: bye1bye
The Plant Dept. will be working on an air-
conditioning problem Sat. Dec. 3 and Sunday Dec. 4.

$~[local]%put test                      Copy test to remote system
stty -echo; cat - > test; stty echo
1+
5 lines/30 characters
$
```

This method of transferring files is really only useful for small files since the terminal is locked during the transfer, and a 50,000-byte file transferred at the rate of 120 characters per second takes around seven minutes to send across. Also, there is no checking performed for errors in transmission, so there is a greater probability that large files may be garbled. uucp, however, has error checking and recovery built in, making it more reliable for transferring large files. Also, cu can only be used to send and receive text files. uucp can handle both text and binary files.

♦ Networking ♦

A *network* is just a method of hooking two or more systems together to exchange information. The UUCP commands create what is known as the *dial-up UNIX network* (Fig.11-2).

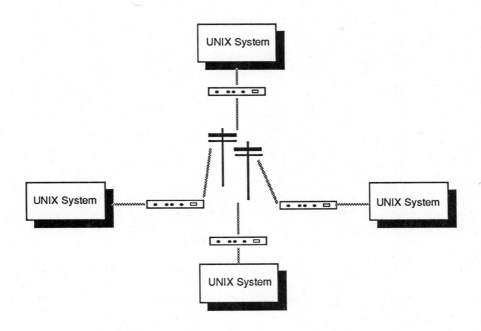

Fig. 11-2. UUCP dial-up network

This network is rather simple, due to the limited scope of the UUCP commands, and is used mainly for exchanging mail and news messages between member systems. The dial-up UNIX network currently consists of several thousand UNIX systems throughout the world.

Sometimes, other networking arrangements are used in large companies and universities that have UNIX systems. Usually, the number of file transmissions between systems is so great that the method of transfer the UUCP network uses is not fast enough to keep up with the traffic. So the UNIX systems are hooked together in a network that allows faster (50,000+ characters/second) data transmission.

The network may be as simple as a connection between the terminal ports on two UNIX systems, or as complex as several systems all tied into a large (and expensive) network manager that may handle millions of characters per second over specially designed communication links. Fig. 11-3 through Fig 11-5 show some typical networking arrangements:

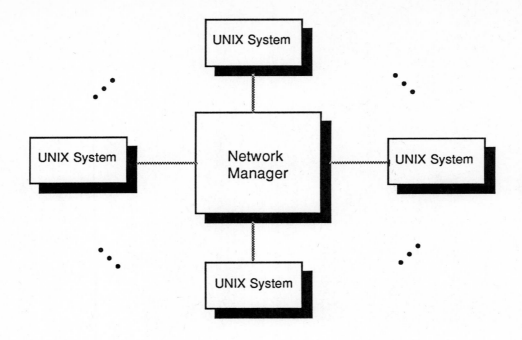

Fig. 11-3. Star network

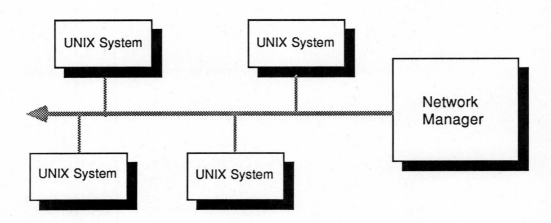

Fig. 11-4. Multidrop network

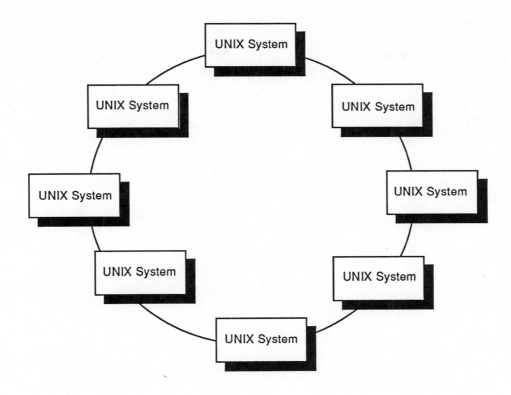

Fig. 11-5. Ring network

Quite often large networks are hybrids composed of several different types of smaller networks.

Commands to access a network can be as simple as ordinary UNIX commands (with the underlying UNIX system modified to use the network hardware) or as complex as a whole new set of commands for file transfer, remote command execution, interdepartmental mail, etc.

Two networking systems have recently gained wide acceptance in the UNIX community: the Networked File System (NFS) from Sun Microsystems which runs on most Berkeley UNIX systems as well as many System V-based UNIX systems, and the Remote File Sharing (RFS) which AT&T licenses as a part of the System V, Release 3, distribution. Both of these networking systems are transparent, in that the user doesn't have to know the network is there to use it: the files on a remote system are made available to the users on the local system in such a way that the files appear to be regular files on the local system. Users can look at, edit, execute, and use the files as if they were stored locally, and the UNIX system takes care of the hard work of communicating all this to the remote system. Chapter 12 discusses how these networks work in a little more detail, but general users of these networks don't have to concern themselves with the networks at all, except when the network or the remote systems go down.

Before NFS and RFS were available, some UNIX systems implemented remote versions of the `cp`, `login`, and `sh` commands. These are `rcp`, `rlogin`, and `rsh` (on some systems called `rshl` or something like this to distinguish it from the restricted shell, also named `rsh`). We'll discuss the `rlogin` and `rcp` commands here.

The `rlogin` command allows you to log into a remote system over the network. It works similarly to the `cu` command, except that on some networks the system administrator can choose to allow a user on one system to log into another without entering a login name or password, as long as the user's name appears in the remote system's `/etc/passwd` file. If the user's name isn't listed on the remote system or if the systems aren't set up to allow equivalency of login names between systems, the user is required to give the login name and password in the same manner as `cu`. When the session on the remote system is over, the user simply types `~.` as before with `cu` to disconnect:

```
$ rlogin remote1                    Log into remote1
login: john                         remote1 doesn't know john
Password: bye1bye
The Plant Dept. will be working on an air-
conditioning problem Sat. Dec. 3 and Sunday Dec. 4.

$ pwd
/usr/john
$ ls
file1
names
uucpfiles
$ ~.
Closed connection.
$ rlogin remote2                    Log into remote2
login: john                         remote2 knows john
The Plant Dept. will be working on an air-
conditioning problem Sat. Dec. 3 and Sunday Dec. 4.

$ pwd                               remote2 knows john
/usr/john
$ ls
bin
memos
sources
$ ~.
Closed connection.
$
```

If you want to set up your user id on a remote system so that you don't have to enter your password when you use `rlogin` (like `john` on `remote2`), you can create the file `.rhosts` on the remote system that lists the systems and users allowed to `rlogin` without a password:

```
$ rlogin remote1                    Log into remote1
login: john                         remote1 still doesn't know john
Password:byelbye
The Plant Dept. will be working on an air-
conditioning problem Sat. Dec. 3 and Sunday Dec. 4.

$ ed .rhosts
?
a
local john
.
w
11
q
$ ~.
Closed connection.
$ rlogin remote1                    Log into remote1
The Plant Dept. will be working on an air-
conditioning problem Sat. Dec. 3 and Sunday Dec. 4.

$                                   Now remote1 knows about john
```

The `.rhosts` file must be in the HOME directory of the user on the remote system. Each line contains a system name and a user name separated by a space or tab. These specify which users on which systems are allowed to use this login without specifying a password. Chapter 12 gives more information on setting this up on a system-wide basis.

`rcp` is used to copy files remotely. It works the same as the `cp` command, except that a path name can begin with *system*: to specify that the file or directory is on the remote system *system*:

```
$ rcp remote1:/usr/john/file1 file1
$
```

This copies `file1` from the directory `/usr/john` on the system `remote1` to `file1` in the current directory. Similarly,

```
$ rcp file2 remote1:/usr/john/file2
$
```

copies `file2` from the current directory to `/usr/john` on the system `remote1`. `rcp` will only work if your user id exists on the remote system and if the remote system allows equivalency of login names.

You should ask your system administrator for information about networks that your UNIX system may be connected to.

Refer to *UNIX System Networking* and the suggested readings in Appendix A for more information on UNIX networking.

12

Administrating Your System

T his chapter should be named, "So You Just Bought a UNIX System—Now What?" It is meant to help you get started as an administrator. We'll tell you about what administrative commands are available and what can be done with them, as well as information about the overall functions of a UNIX system administrator.

Why does a UNIX system need an administrator? Ideally, a well designed system should require no attention under normal conditions. UNIX systems normally don't need much attention. Most of the time, the administrator's duties fall into the areas of adding new users and removing old ones, backing up and restoring files, installing new software, and starting up and shutting down the system. These are things that can't be totally automated because of security reasons or because a human must be at the machine to mount disks or tapes and push buttons. All these functions are straightforward and require little to moderate effort. They occur so frequently that there are many administrative commands to perform them.

There are some administrative functions that come about due to abnormal conditions such as system crashes, faulty hardware, runaway user programs, and overloaded or faulty disk systems. In these cases, the administrator's duties are less clearly defined. Often the problem is obscure or the external manifestation of another, hidden problem. Some administrative commands are available to aid the administrator, but often fixing the problem requires a little floundering around at first.

This chapter is by no means complete, as it cannot cover problems that are specific to particular types of hardware. Instead we try to give you information about the various *functions* of an administrator and *solutions* to the more common problems you may encounter. For a more thorough discussion of UNIX administration, see *UNIX System Administration*.

This chapter is divided into two parts; the first describes what every administrator should know, whether your system is a single-user home computer or a large multiuser commercial system. It is subdivided into the following sections:

- Getting to know your system
- UNIX system startup and shutdown
- The `cron`
- File systems
- Adding and removing users

The second half is devoted to topics that will interest only some administrators. It is broken down into the following sections:

- System security
- Accounting
- `uucp`
- The line printer spooler

If you've just purchased a UNIX system, you may want to read the section on UNIX system startup and shutdown first. It describes some of the steps involved in getting your system running.

su

Some administrative commands can be run only by the *super-user*. The super-user is the user `root`. It has privileges other users don't have. It can read and write *any* file, regardless of permissions and can run *any* program. To become the super-user, you need to use the command `su`:

```
$ su
password:sys_1_yz
#
```

The `#` prompt tells you that you are the super-user. Be extremely careful when you're the super-user (i.e.,you have a `#` as your prompt) as it's very easy to remove important files. Use `su` only when necessary and do everything you can as a "normal" user.

We'll use `#` for all commands that *must* be run by the super-user and `$` for all others. You'll see that you can read most of the system files we'll mention as a normal user, but you must be the super-user to change them.

The `sysadm` Command

Starting with System V, Release 2, UNIX systems were shipped with the `sysadm` command. This command allows you to perform simple administration tasks such as adding users, adding modems, backing up files, and managing networks from a simple, menu-based environment. It's very easy to use, and the documentation that comes with your system describes how to use it. Instead of going into it here, we'll discuss the underlying work that `sysadm` does when it adds users, backs up files, etc. You shouldn't hesitate to use `sysadm` to manage your system, but if something goes wrong, you need to know what's been going on.

♦ Getting to Know Your System ♦

All UNIX systems are equipped with a certain minimum amount of hardware. This usually includes a hard disk of around 20 million (M) bytes of storage, a tape drive or floppy disk for backups, 4M bytes of memory, a terminal, and a printer. Additional equipment may include more terminals, communications equipment, such as modems or automatic call units (ACUs), larger disks, and more memory. As a system administrator, you should look at your UNIX system, see what is attached to it, and understand the functions of the various devices. The above devices have been described in previous chapters. This section shows you how to access them through the UNIX system.

Files, Files, and More Files

The first thing you should know about the way the UNIX operating system communicates with the various devices is that everything is treated as a file. As far as any program is concerned, disks are files, modems are files, even memory is a file. All the devices attached to your system have files in the directory `/dev` associated with them. When I/O is performed on these files, the actions are translated by the UNIX operating system into actions on the actual devices. For example, the file `/dev/mem` is the computer's memory. If you `cat` this file you will actually be displaying the system's memory at your terminal. For security reasons, this file is not readable by an ordinary user; however, as an administrator, you can look at it when you're the super-user.

These files (in `/dev`) are usually referred to as *device files*. To look at some of the devices on your system, change your directory to `/dev` and do an `ls`:

```
$ cd /dev              Change to device directory
$ ls                   Look at device files
console                System console
diskette               Floppy disk
dsk                    Disks
lp                     Printer
mem                    Memory
mt                     Tapes
net                    Network
rdiskette              "Raw" floppy
```

```
rdsk                                    "Raw" disks
rmt                                     "Raw" tapes
swap                                    Swap disk
syscon                                  System console, different name
systty                                  System console, yet another name
tty00                                   ⎫
tty01                                   ⎬ Terminal ports
tty01                                   ⎭
$
```

This example gives you a partial list of the devices usually found in /dev. Your ls will give a different list of files, probably more than shown here, but the ones shown here will be found on most UNIX systems. These are the devices we'll be talking about throughout the chapter.

The console, syscon, and systty files are used to communicate with the console of your UNIX system. (They are one and the same.) If your system is a single-user system, then you're probably using the console when you use the system (suprise!).

diskette and rdiskette refer to the floppy disk. The rdiskette file differs from the diskette file in the manner that I/O is performed on the diskette.

dsk, mt, rdsk, and rmt are directories that we'll look at in a moment.

The lp file refers to a line printer and the kmem and mem files refer to memory. The swap file refers to the area on the disk where processes are swapped. (Remember swapping from Chapter 2?)

The net file is used to communicate with a network, and the files tty*nn* are the ports for terminals (*nn* is the number of the port). For a multiuser UNIX system, there will be one tty*nn* file for each terminal or modem attached to the system.

dsk and rdsk are directories that contain files that correspond to disk drives. Usually the file names in each directory are the same, and the only difference between the two is that the rdsk directory contains "raw" disk devices, which are used by some system utilities for faster access to the disks. A typical dsk directory contains the following:

```
$ ls dsk
0s0
0s1
0s2
0s3
0s4
0s5
0s6
0s7
1s0
1s1
```

```
1s2
1s3
1s4
1s5
1s6
1s7
$
```

Under the UNIX system, disk drives are logically divided into *sections* (see Fig. 12-1). The files `0s0`, `0s1`, `0s2`, etc., correspond to sections one, two, three, etc., of disk number zero. The files `1s0`, `1s1`, `1s2`, etc., correspond to sections one, two, three, etc., of disk number one.

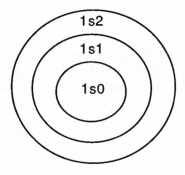

Fig. 12-1. Three section disk drive

If there were more disks attached to the system, the sections would be numbered *n*`s0`, *n*`s1`, etc., for each disk *n*. Sometimes, systems with many disk drives will have a naming scheme as follows:

$$c\textit{controller}\,d\textit{disk}\,s\textit{section}$$

Where *controller* is the number of the disk controller (a piece of electronic hardware that sits between the system and the disk and controls the operation of several disks), *disk* is the number of the disk, and *section* is the number of the disk section. `c1d1s0` refers to the first section on the second disk on the second controller. `0s0` is usually equivalent to `c0d0s0` and `0s1` to `c0d0s1`, so the three-character section names are simply shorthand for disks on controller zero.

The `mt` and `rmt` directories contain device files that correspond to tape drives:

```
$ ls mt
0h
0hn
0m
```

```
0mn
1h
1hn
1m
1mn
```

The files `0m` and `0h` refer to the first tape drive, high and medium density, respectively, and `1m` and `1h` to the second one. The files ending with `n` refer to the same drives, except the tape isn't rewound after it's used, whereas using the other files causes the tape to be rewound when the program using it finishes. The files in `rmt` refer to the raw interfaces of same tape drives.

If you don't see all of these files in the `/dev` directory, don't panic. Not all UNIX systems have tape drives, terminal lines, networks, or line printers. Also, some UNIX systems have device files for devices that aren't there now but may be added later. So don't be concerned if you see an `lp` file but don't have a printer attached to your system. Some UNIX systems have renamed some of the files to be more meaningful: `tape` or `tp` instead of `mt`, and so forth. The important thing is that you know that there are files in `/dev` corresponding to your disks, tapes, memory, and other devices. Usually a manual that comes with your system will describe the device associated with each file.

What's Going on Here

The UNIX system provides all users with several commands that print information about the system. In previous chapters, we talked about one of them, the who command. Remember when we discussed processes in Chapter 2? Well, there's a command that will give you information about the ones that are running on your system. It is the `ps` (process status) command. `ps` without any options prints the status of all processes for a particular user. If you type in `ps` at your terminal, you'll get a few lines back describing the processes you have running:

```
$ ps
   PID TTY      TIME COMMAND
   195 01       0:21 sh           The shell
   253 01       0:00 ps           This ps command
$
```

The `ps` command prints out four columns of information: `PID`, the "process id," which is a unique number assigned to each process; `TTY`, the terminal number that the process was run from; `TIME`, the amount of computer time in minutes and seconds that process has used; and `COMMAND`, the name of the process. (The `sh` process in the above example is the shell that we got when we logged in, and it's used 21 seconds of computer time.) Almost every command you type in at your terminal creates a new process. Until the command is finished, it shows up in the output of the `ps` command as a running process.

Process number 253 in the above example is the ps command that was typed in.

The ps command with the -e option lists information about *every* process running on the system:

```
$ ps -e
    PID TTY         TIME COMMAND
      0 ?          0:08 sched           Process scheduler
      1 ?          7:19 init            UNIX state control
      2 ?          0:00 vhand           UNIX "housekeeping"
      3 ?          0:02 bdflush         UNIX "housekeeping"
    129 ?          0:00 lpsched         Printer queue program
    181 ?          0:28 cron            Alarm clock
     72 tty00      0:00 getty           Terminal program
    195 tty01      0:21 sh              Your shell
     51 console    1:33 sh              Console's shell
    197 tty02      0:00 getty           Terminal program
    302 tty08      0:00 ps              This ps
$
```

sched performs a familiar operation: It's the scheduling process that gives each process a slice of the CPU. It has a ? in the TTY column because it was started automatically, not from a terminal. (We'll see how that's done later.) vhand and bdflush are processes that manage memory and log messages. The init and getty processes we'll get to shortly. The lpsched process coordinates the printing of files on the printer /dev/lp. The cron process is described in a separate section. sh showed up in the last ps; it's the shell on this terminal. The second sh belongs to the system's console, indicated by the console in the TTY column, and ps is the command that produced the list.

When there are several users logged into a system, the output of the ps -e command is much longer. There is usually a sh for each user, as well as a line for each command they may happen to be running at the time.

The getty Process

When you log in, several things take place. First you get a login: prompt, and you type in your user id. You then get a Password: prompt, and you type in your password. If the password is correct, messages are printed at your terminal, your .profile file is executed to set up your shell environment, and finally you get a $ prompt from the shell.

There's a lot of stuff going on behind the scenes here; let's see what really happens when you log in. Each terminal port that *doesn't* have someone logged in on it has a getty process associated with it. The getty process does nothing until a terminal is connected to the port or someone dials up the port. When you call up and are connected, getty sends the string login: to the terminal. Then it waits for your response. After you type in your user id, the getty process starts up a new process called login, tells it what your user id is, and goes away. The `login` process prompts you for your password, checks the response and either starts a shell for you if the password is correct or goes back to asking for your user id if it's not.

When your shell is started by the `login` process, it does two things before printing out your `$`. The first thing it does is run a shell program `/etc/profile`. `/etc/profile` is like your `.profile` but it is for everyone on the system, not just you. It performs operations the administrator wants to be done when a user logs in. For example, `/etc/profile` prints out the file `/etc/motd`. This is the message of the day that we referred to at the beginning of Chapter 4. The `/etc/profile` may print out the time and date, system name, number of users, and other information of interest to users logging in. As an administrator, you can edit this file and put messages in it that you want everyone logging into your system to see. Also, `/etc/profile` might change the `PATH` shell variable to include a directory that contains commands local to your system. You should `cat` the `/etc/profile` file on your system and see what it contains.

After running the `/etc/profile` program, your shell process runs the `.profile` program in your `HOME` directory. After that your shell is ready for use, so it prints out your familiar `$`.

Here's a summary of the steps involved, from initiating the `getty` to obtaining the command prompt:

```
getty→login→sh→/etc/profile→$HOME/.profile→$
```

◆ System Startup and Shutdown ◆

After hooking your system together and plugging it in, you must start it up. This involves something called *booting the system*. Put simply, this is the procedure of loading the UNIX kernal from disk into the system's memory. In the dark ages, this entailed a lot of switch setting, button pushing, typing, and praying. Newer UNIX systems *boot* automatically when turned on. Some systems may prompt you for some input; however, if you hit *RETURN*, this will usually load UNIX. Just to be sure, you should check the manuals that came with your system for a section entitled "Powering On," "Startup," "Booting Procedures," or some such nonsense. That section should tell you what you have to do to get your system started.

When a UNIX system is started, it may run in what's known as *single-user* mode. In this mode, there are no `getty`s running, no other users, and the only processes are `init`, `sched`, and those run by the administrator from the console. UNIX systems start up in single-user mode to allow you to check the system's operation and make sure everything is OK before allowing other users onto the system. When the system is in single user mode, the console runs as super-user, and `#` is the prompt. No passwords are requested; the system simply makes the console `root` and gives you a `#`. As we'll see later, some things having to do with file systems are best done in single-user mode.

The `init` Process

UNIX systems always run in one of several *modes* or *levels*. These levels are controlled by the `init` process. For example, when a UNIX system is started, it might run in single-user mode.

Of course, for other users to log in, the UNIX system must have at least one other level in which `gettys` run so that logins can occur. This level is called *multiuser* mode. The `init` process controls the level the system is in. It reads the file `/etc/inittab` which details the processes to be run in the various levels. When `init` *n* is typed in by `root`, the UNIX system goes into level *n*, and `init` reads `/etc/inittab` to decide what processes to kill and start up. For example, `init` 2 causes the system to enter multiuser mode. `/etc/inittab` has a list of `gettys` (one for each port) that `init` starts up when mode 2 is entered. Valid levels for `init` are numbers from 0 to 6 and the letter s.[†] s is single-user mode, 2 is multiuser mode, and 0 is for shutting down.

If you look at `/etc/inittab`, you'll see something like this:

```
$ cat /etc/inittab
bchk::bootwait:/etc/bcheckrc </dev/console >/dev/console 2>&1
brc::bootwait:/etc/brc > /dev/console 2>&1
mt:23:bootwait:/etc/brc </dev/console >/dev/console 2>&1
is:2:initdefault:
r0:0:wait:/etc/rc0  > /dev/console 2>&1 </dev/console
r1:1:wait:/etc/rc1  > /dev/console 2>&1 </dev/console
r2:23:wait:/etc/rc2 > /dev/console 2>&1 </dev/console
r3:3:wait:/etc/rc3  > /dev/console 2>&1 </dev/console
co:s12345:respawn:/etc/getty console console
00:2:respawn:/etc/getty tty00 1200
00:23:respawn:/etc/getty tty00 9600
01:23:off:/etc/getty tty01 9600
$
```

The format of each line is

$$id:level:action:process$$

id is a word that uniquely identifies a line.

level is one or more numbers (0 through 6) or the letter s that determines what level(s) *action* is to take place in.

---

† Prior to System V, the levels range from 0 to 7, where 0 is single-user mode.

action can be one of the following:*

initdefault—when init starts, it will enter *level*; the *process* field for this *action* has no meaning.

sysinit—run *process* before init sends anything to the system console.

bootwait—run *process* at system startup time and wait until it's finished before running anything else (init doesn't wait by default).

respawn—if *process* doesn't exist, start it, wait for it to finish, and then start another, e.g.,

getty→login→sh→log off→respawn getty

wait—when going to *level*, start *process* and wait until it's finished.

off—when going to *level*, kill *process*.

process is any executable program, including shell programs.

When changing levels, init kills (forces finishing) all processes not specified for that level. The following example illustrates going to single-user mode:

```
# init s
INIT: New run level: S

INIT: SINGLE USER MODE
#
```

Going Multiuser

To go to multiuser mode, all you have to do is type init 2.† This will initiate a series of events that ends with the gettys being started, allowing other users to log in. If you look at the /etc/inittab on your system, you'll see definitions for gettys under level 2, and at the very least, two shell programs /etc/bcheckrc, and /etc/rc2.‡ These are run before the gettys are started. If your inittab file has the line is:2:initdefault: like the one shown previously, then your system will come up in multiuser mode automatically.

---

* Prior to System V, use c and k as *action* instead of respawn and off.
† On some UNIX systems, to enter multiuser mode you log off from the single-user shell.
‡ Prior to system V, /etc/rc is used.

`/etc/bcheckrc` prompts you for the correct time and date or may read them from a battery-powered system clock, if one's available, and it asks you whether you want to check the file systems (usually a good idea before going multiuser). If you do, it will run the `fsck` command (see the section on file systems).

`/etc/rc2` simply runs the shell programs in the directory `/etc/rc2.d`. The programs in `/etc/rc2.d` start up the processes (except `gettys`) that you want running in multiuser mode, such as the `cron` (next section), printer controllers, and network stuff. They mount the file systems and may also start system accounting, error logging, and system activity logging. When you install a software package that requires some action to be taken when the system goes into multiuser mode, a program is usually put in `/etc/rc2.d`. We'll take a look at adding programs in `/etc/rc2.d` in the section titled **The Line Printer Spooler**.

Shutdown

When you want to turn off your UNIX system, you shouldn't just unplug it. First, if you have users logged in, they'll be just a little bit unhappy with you (tar and feathers are not uncommon). Second, when you start back up again, you may find that some of the files were scrambled at random. To avoid all this, the UNIX system provides you with the `shutdown` command. It performs all necessary actions before putting the system in single-user mode.

If you just type in `shutdown`, it sends a warning to the users to get off the system, makes sure you really want to shut down the system, and then goes about killing processes, logging off users, and unmounting the file systems. `shutdown` sends a couple of messages to the users requesting them to log off and gives them some time between messages to get off the system. The last thing `shutdown` does is run `init` to change the run level to single-user mode. Once in single-user mode, all `gettys` are turned off, and no users can log in. At this point, you can turn off (power down) your system without fear. If you have disks in other cabinets, it is usually wise to turn them off first. `shutdown` *must be run from the system console and you must be logged in as* `root`. You cannot use `su` and then run `shutdown`. If `root` is not logged into the system console, *you must log off the console and log in as* `root`.

There are three options to `shutdown`:

`-y` forces `shutdown` to assume a "yes" answer to all its querys whether you're sure you want to shut down.

`-gn` sets the *grace period*, or the amount of time `shutdown` waits between sending warnings to the users, to *n* seconds. The default is 60.

`-in` causes `shutdown` to go to `init` level *n*. The default is `s`.

If you want to shut down the system immediately, you can type

```
# shutdown -y -g0
```

which forces shutdown to shut down the system without asking for confirmation and with no grace period for the users to finish up what they're doing and log off.

The cron

The cron is a process that runs when the UNIX system is in multiuser mode. It runs commands on a regularly scheduled basis.[†] When it starts, it reads the files in the directory /usr/spool/cron/crontabs. (These files are known as cron tables, or *crontabs*.[‡])

```
# cat /usr/spool/cron/crontabs/sample
# sample crontab
# everything on a line is separated by blanks or tabs.
#min    hour   day   month   day-of-week   command
#0-59   0-23   1-31  1-12       0-6
#                              (Sunday=0)
#-------------------------------------------------------------
0        7      *      *        1-5         /morn/alarm
55       6      *      *        1-5         /morn/coffee
10       7      *      *        1-5         /morn/shower
15       7      *      *        1           /morn/leftovers
15       7      *      *        2,4         /morn/eggs
15       7      *      *        3           /morn/waffles
15       7      *      *        5           /morn/pancakes
45       7      *      *        1,3,5       /work/drive
45       7      *      *        2,4         /work/car_pool
0       10      *      *        0,6         /morn/alarm
1       10      *      *        0,6         /bin/sleep 600
0       13      *      5-9      6           /house/mow_lawn
0       12     15      4        *           /taxes/1040
#
```

An asterisk (*) means do it every time, a *number,number,number* means do it only when one of the *numbers* matches the appropriate time or date, and a *number—number* means do it when any number in the range matches the appropriate time or date.

The first entry in the crontab is

```
0        7      *      *        1-5         /morn/alarm
```

This says that the program /morn/alarm is to be run at 7:00 A.M. every Monday through Friday (1-5). The next entry starts the coffee at 6:55 so it's ready when you wake up. At 7:15 you get breakfast. On Monday it's leftovers, Tuesday and Thursday it's eggs, Wednesday it's waffles, and Friday it's pancakes.

[†] The at command can be used to run commands *once* at specified times and dates.
[‡] Prior to System V Release 2, the cron read the file /usr/lib/crontab, which is equivalent to /usr/spool/cron/crontabs/root.

You car pool on Tuesday and Thursday, and you drive yourself on Monday, Wednesday, and Friday. On Saturday and Sunday the alarm goes off at 10:00 and at 10:01 you go back to sleep for 10 minutes (600 seconds). On Saturday at one o'clock in the afternoon, during the months from May to September, you mow the lawn. At noon on April 15, you fill out your 1040 form.

Of course, this is merely a sample crontab. You might want to replace the `/house/mow_lawn` program with `/usr/pay/local_kid`.

On a real UNIX system, the `cron` is used to run programs periodically that you don't want to be bothered with typing in several times per day. It is also used to run programs at night that you don't want running during the day for fear of slowing down other users. Programs typically run via the `cron` are things like accounting and file saves. Each crontab belongs to the user corresponding to the name of the file. The `root` crontab contains commands that have to be run with super-user capabilities. Other crontabs don't run with super-user privileges, but any crontabs named after system users run with the privileges of those users. For example, a `uucp` crontab would run with `uucp`'s privileges (presumably because it performs duties that require access to `uucp`'s files and directories).

The `cron` is usually started from `/etc/rc2` (above) when the system goes multiuser. It's stopped by `shutdown`. If you want to change a crontab, you cannot just edit it. The `cron` reads all the crontabs when it starts. In order to make it reread the crontabs, you must use the `crontab` command. The `crontab` command copies its standard input to the crontab file of the invoking user. For example,

```
# crontab
0    0    *    *    *    /etc/zap
CTRL-d
#
```

installs that line as `root`'s crontab. Any existing crontab entries are lost. You can use the `-l` option to `crontab` to get the contents of the crontab for editing:

```
# crontab -l > root.crontab
# ed root.crontab
586
a
0    0    *    *    *    /etc/zap
.
w
616
q
# crontab < root.crontab
#
```

If you specify a file name to `crontab`, it will use that file instead of standard input. So the above example could have used `crontab root.crontab` instead of `crontab < root.crontab`.

If you need to change or install a crontab for a user other than `root`, you can `su` to that user and run the `crontab` command. It will then operate on the crontab for that user.

♦ File Systems ♦

The UNIX file system is one of the key parts of the UNIX system. It's what provides you with hierarchically-organized directories and files. The file system divides each disk drive into 1024—byte[†] portions called *blocks* numbered from zero to the number of blocks that can fit on that disk (Fig. 12-2).

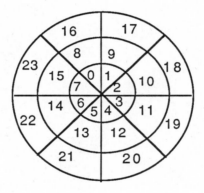

Fig. 12-2. Disk block numbering

For example, a 40 million (40M) byte disk will have blocks numbered from zero to around 39,000. The blocks are grouped into four sections: block zero is called the *boot block*. It is not used by the file system. Block one is called the *super block*. This block contains, among other things, the size of the disk and the sizes of the other two sections. Next comes the *i-list*. This is a variable number of blocks that contains *i-nodes*. We'll discuss i-nodes shortly. The rest of the disk is devoted to free storage (data) blocks that are available to store the contents of files (Fig. 12-3).

The logical representation of a file is very different from its *physical* representation. The logical representation is the file that you see when you type in `cat`. You get a stream of characters representing the contents of the file. The physical representation is how the file is actually organized on the disk. A file that is longer than one block will usually have its contents scattered about the

_____

† Prior to System V blocks were 512 bytes long.

disk. When you access your file, however, the UNIX file system fetches the blocks in the proper order and gives you the logical representation of your file.

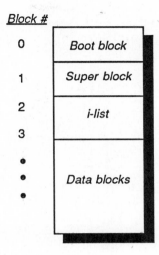

Fig. 12-3. Four sections of a file system

Of course, there must be a list somewhere in the UNIX system that tells the file system how to convert the physical representation to the logical. This is where the *i-node* comes in. An i-node is a 64-byte table that contains information about a file. Some of the things in an i-node are the file's size, its owner and permissions, and whether it's an ordinary file, a directory, or a special file. The most important item in the i-node is the *disk address list*. This is a list of 13 block numbers. The first ten block numbers are the first ten blocks of the file. So to give you the logical representation of a file up to ten blocks long, the file system will fetch the blocks in the order that appear in the disk address list.

What if you have a file larger than ten blocks? The eleventh block number in the disk address list gives the number of a block that contains up to 256 more block numbers. So for files of sizes up to 10+256 blocks (272,384 bytes) this method suffices. If your file is even larger than 266 blocks, the twelfth block number in the disk address list gives the number of a block that contains up to 256 more block numbers, and each of those blocks contains up to 256 block numbers that are used to fetch the file's contents. The thirteenth block number in the disk address list works similarly, only it goes one level further than the twelfth.

If you sat down and figured it out, you'd find that the maximum size of a file on a UNIX system is 16,842,762 blocks or 17,246,988,288 bytes! Fortunately, the UNIX file system imposes more practical limits on the maximum size of files (usually 1 to 2 million bytes) so that users can't inadvertantly create a file that uses up all the blocks on an entire disk.

The way the file system translates file names to i-nodes is really quite simple. A directory is actually a file containing a table of information; for each file in the directory, there's an entry in the table that has the file's name and the i-node number associated with the file. When you type `cat xxx`, the file system looks for the entry named `xxx` in the current directory's table, gets the i-node number associated with it, and then starts fetching the blocks that contain the information in `xxx` (Fig. 12-4).

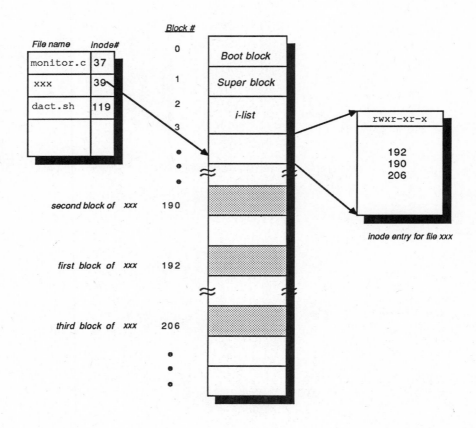

Fig. 12-4. Accessing the contents of `xxx`

Creating a File System

The administrator of a UNIX system can create a file system on a disk with the command `/etc/mkfs` (make file system).

```
# /etc/mkfs /dev/dsk/1s1 2400    make a 2,400 block file system
```

```
Mkfs: /dev/dsk/1s1?
(DEL if wrong)
bytes per logical block = 1024
total logical blocks = 1200
total inodes = 288
gap (physical blocks) = 7
cylinder size (physical blocks) = 400
mkfs: Available blocks = 1179
#
```

The file `/dev/dsk/1s1`, you'll remember, refers to the first section of the second disk. The `2400` is the size of the file system in blocks. Although you can use an entire disk for a single file system, the UNIX system allows you to create several *separate* file systems on one disk. Many UNIX systems run one file system per disk. Many others run with several per disk. The reasons for this difference seem to be more philosophical than practical.

When `mkfs` runs, it gives you the opportunity to abort it before it continues. After printing

```
Mkfs: /dev/dsk/1s1?
(DEL if wrong)
```

it waits ten seconds before actually making the file system, allowing you to abort it during this period by typing *DELETE*. When it continues, it prints out information about the file system, including the number of logical 1024-byte blocks, the number of i-nodes, and the number of blocks on the file system available for data storage.

You can optionally give the second argument as *number:number*, where the first *number* is again the size in blocks, and the second *number* is the number of i-nodes (that is, the maximum number of files that can be stored in the file system). By default, the number of i-nodes is the number of blocks divided by four. The maximum number of i-nodes per file system is 65,500. If for some reason you need more than 65,500 i-nodes on a disk, you must create two or more file systems on that disk.

There are other values you can specify to `/etc/mkfs`, but the defaults are usually just fine. If you get instructions with your UNIX system that tell you to use `/etc/mkfs` in a particular way, then follow those instructions.

Mounting and Unmounting File Systems

A very nice feature of UNIX file systems is that they are *mountable*, meaning that each file system can be attached to the overall directory tree *at any point*. For example, the directory `/` is the *root* directory of the system. It is also the top of the root file system, which is always mounted. The directory `/usr` is in the directory `/`, but usually it's a separate file system from the root file system, with all the files in it residing on a separate portion of the disk or another disk entirely. The /usr file system is simply mounted onto the root file system at the point where the directory /usr exists in the overall hierarchy (Figs. 12-5 and 12-6).

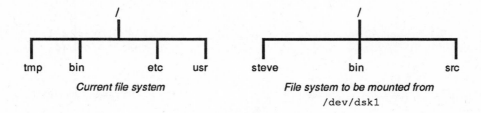

Fig. 12-5. File system before mounting /dev/dsk/0s1

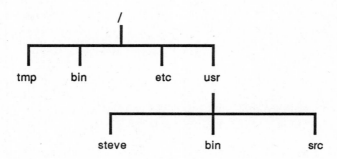

Fig. 12-6. File system after mounting /dev/dsk/0s1 as /usr

To mount a file system, you use the /etc/mount command. This command lets you place a file system anywhere within the existing directory structure:

```
# /etc/mount /dev/dsk/0s1 /usr      Mount /dev/dsk/0s1 on /usr
# /etc/mount /dev/dsk/0s2 /usr/src  Mount /dev/dsk/0s2 on /usr/src
#
```

You can put a −r at the end of the /etc/mount command if the file system should be mounted read-only. Disks that are *write-protected* must be mounted this way.

When you mount a file system, you should make sure the directory you're mounting it on is empty, as its contents are not accessible while the file system is mounted.

To get information about the file systems mounted on your UNIX system, you can use the `/etc/mount` command without any arguments.

```
# /etc/mount
/ on /dev/dsk/0s0 read/write on Wed Dec 14 06:55:23 1988
/tmp on /dev/dsk/0s3 read/write on Wed Dec 14 07:18:41 1988
/usr on /dev/dsk/0s1 read/write on Wed Dec 14 09:44:22 1988
/usr/src on /dev/dsk/0s2 read/write on Wed Dec 14 09:44:45 1988
#
```

The `/etc/mount` command printed the directory where the file system is mounted (e.g., `usr`), the device in `/dev` it's on, whether it's readable only or readable and writable, and the time and date it was mounted.

To unmount a file system, you use the `/etc/umount` command. This command is simply the reverse of the `/etc/mount` command. It removes a file system from the directory structure.

```
# /etc/umount /dev/dsk/0s3        Unmount /dev/dsk/0s3
# /etc/mount                      List mounted file systems
/ on /dev/dsk/0s0 read/write on Wed Dec 14 06:55:23 1988
/usr on /dev/dsk/0s1 read/write on Wed Dec 14 09:44:22 1988
/usr/src on /dev/dsk/0s2 read/write on Wed Dec 14 09:44:45 1988
#
```

You should note that the root file system cannot be unmounted.[†] Also note that `/etc/umount` will not work if a user is using any file in the file system you're trying to unmount. This includes being `cd`ed to a directory in that file system. Unmounting file systems should be done only after going to single-user mode (via `/etc/shutdown`).

File System Status Commands

There are many commands that give information about file systems. A few of the more useful ones are given here.

The `df` command prints out the number of free i-nodes and blocks on the mounted file system:

```
$ df
/usr    (/dev/dsk/0s1 ):     138126 blocks     11675 i-nodes
/tmp    (/dev/dsk/0s3 ):      19184 blocks      2437 i-nodes
/       (/dev/dsk/0s0 ):       3066 blocks       670 i-nodes
$ df -t
```

---

† Some UNIX systems may allow you to unmount the root file system. Don't!
Unpredictable things may happen.

```
/usr     (/dev/dsk/0s1 ):       138126 blocks       11675 i-nodes
                   total:    209792 blocks     25216 i-nodes
/tmp     (/dev/dsk/0s3 ):        19184 blocks        2437 i-nodes
                   total:     20000 blocks      2496 i-nodes
/        (/dev/dsk/0s0 ):         3066 blocks         670 i-nodes
                   total:      4000 blocks      2864 i-nodes
$
```

df with the −t option prints the total number of i-nodes and blocks as well. This command is used most often to see if a file system is getting filled up. We'll talk later about what you can do if you run low on i-nodes or blocks.

du prints a list of each directory in a file system along with the number of blocks used by the files in that directory and its subdirectories. The du command is not file system specific; it can be used on any directory structure. It is useful when you want to find *how* the space on a file system is being used:

```
$ du /usr                                    Print disk usage on /usr
1762  /usr/bin/graf
5622  /usr/bin
453   /usr/lib/acct
2325  /usr/lib/spell
797   /usr/lib/uucp
16583 /usr/lib
695   /usr/mail
334   /usr/man/a_man/man7
594   /usr/man/a_man/man1
204   /usr/man/a_man/man8
457   /usr/man/a_man/man0
1677  /usr/man/a_man
1713  /usr/man/u_man/man1
722   /usr/man/u_man/man3
366   /usr/man/u_man/man2
158   /usr/man/u_man/man5
237   /usr/man/u_man/man4
51    /usr/man/u_man/man6
426   /usr/man/u_man/man0
5153  /usr/man/u_man
9644  /usr/man
32    /usr/spool/lp
1     /usr/spool/uucppublic/oko
6     /usr/spool/uucppublic/weather
1     /usr/spool/uucppublic/tgd
10    /usr/spool/uucppublic
316   /usr/spool/uucp
455   /usr/spool
50794 /usr
$
```

du can point out where your file system is being used up by large files. The -a
option to du causes it to print out the sizes of ordinary files as well as the totals
for each directory.

Saving and Restoring File Systems

Due to the frailties of all things mechanical (and human), it's good to have backups of your files. That way if your disk decides to take a vacation, you have the
information stored somewhere else. UNIX systems provide several mechanisms
for backing up file systems, and for each, a corresponding method for restoring
the saved files. As luck would have it, these methods vary from one UNIX version to the next and even from system to system within the same version. We
will discuss tar, a method of file system backup that is available on most UNIX
systems.

tar

tar stands for tape archiver. It takes as its arguments a command and a directory to be archived onto a tape or another disk. The commands used for saving a
directory structure are c and r. The command c causes tar to create a new
archive on the tape or disk. The command r causes tar to add a new archive
to the end of the one that's already there. There is also an optional number you
can specify to tell it which tape drive to use (it's probably best to use the default).

```
# tar c /usr          Archive /usr to the default tape drive
# tar c2 /            Archive / to tape drive 2
# tar r2 /            Add new archive of / to existing archive on drive 2
#
```

If you want to archive to a file, you can do so by using the f option to tar. It
tells tar that the next argument is the name of a file it should send its output to:

```
# tar cf /bck/1 /usr          Archive /usr to /bck/1
#
```

tar is also used to read an archive back in. You just use the x option,
which causes files to be extracted from the archive:

```
# tar xf /bck/1          Extract files from /bck/1
# tar x                  Extract files from the default tape drive
#
```

tar places the extracted files and directories in the current directory.

If you just want to see what's in the archive, you can use the t command to
get a table of contents:

```
# tar tf /bck/1                 List the files in /bck/1
                    . . .
# tar t                         List the files on the default tape drive
                    . . .
#
```

Again, you can specify a number after the x or t command to tell it which tape drive to use.

If you have a floppy drive instead of a tape, you can still use tar1. Simply specify the floppy device to tar1 as you would a file:

```
# tar cf /dev/diskette /usr/pat   Backup /usr/pat
#
```

Here, /dev/diskette represents the floppy drive. Note that different UNIX vendors often use different names for the floppy drive. Xenix uses fd0 for the PC floppy drive, and System V Release 3 on 386-based systems uses f0d9dt and f0q15dt in /dev/dsk for low and high density floppies, respectively.

What To Do When a File System Gets Full

Sooner or later, a file system will get filled up with too many files, causing you to run low on blocks, or i-nodes, or both. There are several things you can do at this point. You can go through and remove old, unnecessary files (perhaps saving them on tape or floppy disk first). You can ask users to get rid of their unnecessary files by putting a message in /etc/motd. You can move some of the files to a different file system; this usually entails moving users to another file system along with their files. You can buy a new disk and move the old file system (or parts of it) to a file system on the new disk.

To move a user to another file system, you have to do three things (in single-user mode):

1. Move the user's files and directories to the other file system.

2. Change the user's HOME in /etc/passwd to reflect the change. (We'll discuss this in the section on adding and removing users.)

3. Send the user mail telling him you've moved him.

tar is the easiest way to move a directory structure from one file system to another. To move the entire structure in /usr/pat to /usr1/pat, you would type in the following lines:

```
# cd /usr                        Change to the old directory
# tar cf - pat | (cd /usr1; tar xf -) Copy the structure
# rm -r /usr/pat                 Remove the old directory
#
```

The first `tar` runs in the directory `/usr` and sends an archive of the directory `pat` to its standard output. This is piped to another `tar` that runs in `/usr1` (`cd /usr1`). That `tar` reads the first `tar`'s output and creates a new directory structure. The command `rm -r /usr/pat` removes `/usr/pat` and all files and directories under it.

After you get a new disk and run `mkfs` on it, you can move users from the old disk to the new using the previous method. If you buy a larger disk than the old one, you can simply move the entire file system using the same method. You simply run the previous `tar` sequence once on the entire file system.

You might note that you can move a user's directory structure in multiuser mode by telling the user to log off, disabling the user id by changing the mode of the user's HOME to 000 or temporarily removing his entry in `/etc/passwd` (see the next section), and then proceeding to copy the user's files.

/etc/fsck

Before going to multiuser mode, it's best to check the file systems before mounting them. Also, if the system goes down without going through proper shutdown procedures (e.g., a power failure), the file systems should be checked. The UNIX system provides you with a tool to check file systems—/etc/fsck. /etc/fsck scans a file system and checks it for inconsistencies. Usually, /etc/fsck is run automatically at startup time whenever the system wasn't shut down properly. Sometimes, however, you'll have to run /etc/fsck yourself. To use it, all you have to do is type /etc/fsck and the file system in /dev that you want checked:

```
# /etc/fsck /dev/rdsk/0s1

/dev/rdsk/0s1
File System: usr Volume: pwb01

** Phase 1 - Check Blocks and Sizes
** Phase 2 - Check Pathnames
** Phase 3 - Check Connectivity
** Phase 4 - Check Reference Counts
** Phase 5 - Check Free List
2193 files 19572 blocks 3066 free
#
```

/etc/fsck normally goes through the five phases shown in the previous example. Phase 1 scans through the i-node list looking for inconsistencies in the block numbers and file sizes and i-node formats. Phase 2 removes files whose corresponding i-nodes were flagged in phase 1. Phase 3 checks directory connectivity by making sure all directories exist somewhere in the overall hierarchical structure. Phase 4 checks the number of *links* for all files and directories. The number of links for a file or directory is simply the number of times it is listed in a directory. The number is usually one, but can vary widely, particularly for directories. Phase 5 checks the *free-block list,* which is the list of empty blocks that are free to be used for new files or to grow old files. If an error in the free-block list is found in phase 5, phase 6 is performed. Phase 6 reconstructs the free-block list:

```
# /etc/fsck /dev/rdsk/0s1

/dev/rdsk/0s1
File System: usr Volume: pwb01

** Phase 1 - Check Blocks and Sizes
** Phase 2 - Check Pathnames
** Phase 3 - Check Connectivity
** Phase 4 - Check Reference Counts
** Phase 5 - Check Free List
1 DUP BLKS IN FREE LIST
BAD FREE LIST
SALVAGE? y

** Phase 6 - Salvage Free List
2193 files 19572 blocks 3066 free

**** FILE SYSTEM WAS MODIFIED ****
#
```

The SALVAGE? message is a request for you to input a y or n to determine whether the free-block list should be reconstructed. /etc/fsck will ask lots of questions like this when a file system has been corrupted. It's usually best to answer y to all questions, as /etc/fsck is fairly smart about repairing file systems. Note that most corrective actions will result in some loss of data.

The following is an example of /etc/fsck with a file system that has been corrupted by a power failure:

```
# /etc/fsck /dev/rdsk/0s1

/dev/rdsk/0s1
File System: usr Volume: pwb01

** Phase 1 - Check Blocks and Sizes
** Phase 2 - Check Pathnames
** Phase 3 - Check Connectivity
** Phase 4 - Check Reference Counts
UNREF FILE I=615  OWNER=uucp MODE=100400
SIZE=0 MTIME=Dec 10 16:23 1988
```

```
CLEAR? y
** Phase 5 - Check Free List
2193 files 19572 blocks 3066 free

***** FILE SYSTEM WAS MODIFIED *****
#
```

Here, /etc/fsck found an inconsistency in i-node number 615. It asked if it should clear the i-node and when it received a y, did so. After making any changes to the file system, /etc/fsck will print the message FILE SYSTEM WAS MODIFIED.

Another common message from /etc/fsck is a request to "reconnect" an unreferenced file. If a system crashes when the disk is very active, files sometimes end up "stranded"—they exist on the disk but don't have a directory entry. When /etc/fsck finds one of these files, it asks you if it should reconnect the file. Since it doesn't know where the file originally came from, /etc/fsck reconnects it in the directory lost+found at the top of that file system's directory hierarchy:

```
# /etc/fsck /dev/rdsk/0s1

/dev/rdsk/0s1
File System: usr Volume: pwb01

** Phase 1 - Check Blocks and Sizes
POSSIBLE FILE SIZE ERROR I=615
** Phase 2 - Check Pathnames
** Phase 3 - Check Connectivity
** Phase 4 - Check Reference Counts
UNREF FILE I=921  OWNER=pat MODE=100644
SIZE=10240 MTIME=Dec 10 17:32 1988
RECONNECT? y
** Phase 5 - Check Free List
2193 files 19572 blocks 3066 free

***** FILE SYSTEM WAS MODIFIED *****
# mount /dev/dsk/0s1 /usr
# ls -l /usr/lost+found
-rw-rw-r-- 1 pat    group1  10240 Dec 10 17:32 000921
#
```

Note that if you create a file system with mkfs, it won't have a lost+found directory. You have to create one, and also fill it with files and then remove them. (This creates "slots" in the directory file that /etc/fsck uses.)

```
# /etc/mkfs /dev/dsk/1s1 10000    Make a new file system
# /etc/mount /dev/dsk/1s1 /mnt    Mount it on /mnt
# cd /mnt
```

```
# mkdir lost+found                    Create lost+found
# cd lost+found
# for name1 in 1 2 3 4 5 6 7 8        Create 64 directory slots
> do
> for name2 in 1 2 3 4 5 6 7 8
> do
> echo > $name1$name2
> done
> done
# rm *                                Remove the files
#
```

The different messages that can come from /etc/fsck are much too numerous to mention the rest of them here; however, just remember that you can usually respond to any message that ends with a ? with a y with confidence. If you find that /etc/fsck has lost too much of its data when you mount the file system and look at it, you may have to restore the file system from a backup.

If /etc/fsck is typed in without a file system, it will use the file /etc/checklist as the list of file systems to check.

If you really want to go into a file system and repair it yourself, you should read more about the organization of UNIX file systems and about fsck and fsdb in *UNIX System Administration*. Extensive information on the UNIX file system can be found in the suggested readings for UNIX internals found in Appendix A. /etc/fsdb is an interactive file system editor that allows you to patch up damaged file systems. Don't use it until you become very familiar with the UNIX file system structure.

Table 12-1 lists the file system commands covered in this section.

TABLE 12-1. File system commands

Command	Description
df	Print number of free i-nodes and blocks for each file system
du	Print number of blocks for each directory in a hierarchy
/etc/mkfs	Make a file system
/etc/mount	Mount a file system
/etc/umount	Unmount a file system
/bin/tar	Tape archiver
/etc/fsck	Check file system for inconsistencies
/etc/fsdb	Interactive file system editor

◆ Administrating Remote File Systems ◆

This section discusses administration of the two most common remote file systems: Networked File System (NFS) and Remote File Sharing (RFS). Both of these systems allow users to access files on remote systems transparently, without even knowing that a network is involved. Although these systems vary considerably in their implementation, the day-to-day administrative procedures are very similar.

In order for your users to access files over the network, two things must be done. First, the remote system must make some of its directory structures available to other systems on the network. Second, you must mount the remote system's directory structure on your system. In other words, there must be some agreement between both machines that certain files and directories will be available across the network. The system that makes its files available to others on the network will be called a *server*, and the system that uses a remote file system will be called a *client*.

NFS

Systems using NFS *export* their directories to the network, making them available for mounting to other systems. Any directory may be exported, not just mount points for file systems; however, exported directory structures do *not* cross file system boundaries, meaning that if you export / to NFS, other file systems under it, such as usr or tmp, are not exported along with it. An NFS server exports its directories to the network by putting the directories in the file /etc/exports and running the exportfs command. /etc/exports should contain on each line a directory to be exported and an optional list of systems that are allowed to remotely mount the directory. If no system list is specified, all systems on the network will be able to mount the directory.

```
# cat /etc/exports
/usr/src        remote1 remote2
/usr/mail
#
```

In this example, the directory structure /usr/src is exported to remote1 and remote2, and /usr/mail to all systems on the network. When used with the -a option, the exportfs command reads this file and exports all the directories listed to the network. This is usually done at system startup time.

The NFS server programs, portmap, mountd, nfsd, and biod perform the actual network management of the directories. These must be running at all times for NFS to work. Although you can start them by hand whenever you want to have your system to run NFS, it's better to put entries in your /etc/rc2.d directory[†]:

```
# cat /etc/rc2.d/Snfs
/etc/exportfs -a
/etc/portmap
```

[†] Many System V machines use run level 3 to designate "network" mode and run level 2 "unnetwork" mode, so you may want to put the Snfs file in /etc/rc3.d.

```
/etc/mountd
/etc/nfsd 2 &
/etc/biod 2 &
#
```

Note that the file name must begin with an S. Files that begin with S or K are executed when init changes state. The S files are for starting processes that should run in the new state, and the K files are for killing processes that shouldn't run in the new state. The files in /etc/rc2.d are run when the system goes into multiuser mode.

The number specified to nfsd and biod determine the number of copies of these programs to run at once. Small systems can get away with one of each; larger systems, particularly those that normally act as servers, should have two to four each.

On the client system, you can mount any remote file system that's been exported to your system or the entire network with the mount command. Instead of a disk partition, you specify the server's name followed by a colon and the directory to be mounted:

```
# mount -t nfs server1:/usr/src /src
#
```

Here, the directory structure /usr/src on the remote system server1 is mounted onto the /src directory on the local system. The -t nfs specifies that the file system type is a remote NFS directory.

When your system is finished with a remote file system, it should unmount it with the umount command with the server name and directory name:

```
# umount server1:/usr/src
#
```

mount and df both give you information about the local and remote file systems:

```
# df
/         (/dev/dsk/0s0      ):      3066 blocks       670 i-nodes
/tmp      (/dev/dsk/0s3      ):     19184 blocks      2437 i-nodes
/usr      (/dev/dsk/0s1      ):    138126 blocks     11675 i-nodes
/src      (server1:/usr/src  ):     23962 blocks      2433 i-nodes
# /etc/mount
/ on /dev/dsk/0s0 read/write on Wed Dec 14 06:55:23 1988
/tmp on /dev/dsk/0s3 read/write on Wed Dec 14 07:18:41 1988
/usr on /dev/dsk/0s1 read/write on Wed Dec 14 09:44:22 1988
/src on server1:/usr/src read/write on Wed Dec 14 14:25:09 1988
#
```

RFS

Systems using RFS *advertise* their directories to the network, making them available for mounting to other systems. Any directory may be advertised, not just mount points for file systems. An RFS server advertises its directories by running the `adv` command. It has the following syntax:

adv *resource directory [clients]*

where *resource* is the name that remote systems will use to identify this directory, *directory* is the directory to advertise, and *[clients]* is an optional list of clients that may use the resource. By default, all clients that can connect to the server.

```
# adv sources /usr/src remote1 remote2
# adv mail /usr/mail
#
```

In this example, the directory structure `/usr/src` is advertised to `remote1` and `remote2`, and `/usr/mail` to all systems on the network. The `adv` commands can also be put in the file `/etc/rstab` and will be run whenever the system enters `init` level 3.

If you want to make an advertised resource unavailable to the network, use the `unadv` command with the resource name:

```
# unadv mail
#
```

On the client system, you can mount any remote resource that's been advertised to your system or the entire network with the `mount` command. Instead of a disk partition, you specify `-d` and the resource specified to the `adv` command:

```
# mount -d sources /src
#
```

You can put the resources you want to have mounted automatically at startup time in `/etc/fstab`. These will be mounted whenever the system enters `init` level 3. The format of `/etc/fstab` is:

resource directory -d

Where *resource* and *directory* are the two arguments that you would normally specify to `mount`.

When your system is finished with a remote resource, it should unmount it with the `umount` command followed by the resource to unmount:

```
# umount sources
#
```

If the umount fails because one or more remote users are using the resource, you can force an unmount with the fumount:

```
# fumount sources
#
```

mount and df both give you information about the local and remote file systems:

```
# df
/            (/dev/dsk/0s0     ):       3066 blocks        670 i-nodes
/tmp         (/dev/dsk/0s3     ):      19184 blocks       2437 i-nodes
/usr         (/dev/dsk/0s1     ):     138126 blocks      11675 i-nodes
/src         (sources          ):      23962 blocks       2433 i-nodes
# /etc/mount
/ on /dev/dsk/0s0 read/write on Wed Dec 14 06:55:23 1988
/tmp on /dev/dsk/0s3 read/write on Wed Dec 14 07:18:41 1988
/usr on /dev/dsk/0s1 read/write on Wed Dec 14 09:44:22 1988
/src on sources read/write on Wed Dec 14 14:25:09 1988
#
```

This has been a brief overview of network administration. You should know that there's a lot more to managing networks than can be discussed in a single chapter. For more information on setting up and administrating your networks, see *UNIX System Networking* and your UNIX documentation.

◆ Adding and Removing Users ◆

Even if you have a single-user UNIX system, you will want to know how to add and remove users. Single-user simply means that only one user can use the system at a time; there can be many user id's, but there is only one terminal for them to log into. Right now, you might be saying to yourself, "I'm the only one using this system, so I don't need more than one user id." That may be true now, but what happens when your kids decide they want to use the system for their homework, or you want to show off your new system to your friends? Do you want them logging into your HOME directory, where all your valuable files are? Probably not. What you'll have to do is add a new user id, say kids, and let them use that. This is a lot simpler than you might think. It requires two steps:

1. enter a line for the user id in /etc/passwd

2. create a HOME directory for that user id

To add a user to your system you will have to edit the /etc/passwd file and add a line for the new user id. Let's take a look at the /etc/passwd file and see what's in it now:

```
$ cat /etc/passwd
root:xyDfccTrt18ox,M.y8:0:0:admin:/:bin/sh
console:lo1ndT0Mzp,M.y8:1:1:admin:/:/bin/sh
pat:XmotTvoyUmjls:10:10:p wood:/usr/pat:/bin/sh
steve:J9exPd97Ftlbn,M.z8:15:10:s kochan:/usr/steve:/bin/sh
restrict:PomJkl09JkY41,./:16:16::/usr/restrict:/bin/rsh
$
```

Before you can add a new user id to the file, you need to know what goes on the line. The general format of each line in the file is:

id:password:uid:gid:user info:home:shell

As you remember from Chapter 10, the first two items on each line are the user id and the encrypted password. The two numbers following are the *user id number (uid)* and the *group id number (gid)*. The uid is a unique number that is assigned to each user id. This is used by the system to distinguish one user from another. Every process has a uid associated with it; this determines what privileges and permissions that process has with respect to other processes and files (discussed in Chapter 10). The gid's purpose is to distinguish between the members of various groups.

The next item in /etc/passwd is any information about the user you want to put in, such as name or telephone number. The last two items on the line are two PATHs. The first is the HOME directory assigned to the user, and the second is the shell the user gets when he logs in (in most cases it is /bin/sh, /bin/rsh, or /bin/csh). If this field is blank, the user gets /bin/sh by default.

Now let's see what you have to do to add a new user to the /etc/passwd file. The user id is kids. You can ignore the password for now. The uid must be unique, so let's pick 17. The gid can be the same as one of the others, or it can be different; let's use a different one, 17. The HOME directory can be any name (remember, you're going to create it later), but it's a good idea to use the same name as the user id. So if users are put in the /usr file system (as they often are on most small UNIX systems), the HOME will be /usr/kids. If you use this method for all users, you can easily figure out any user's HOME directory. The shell can be the standard shell, /bin/sh. Now let's see what this line looks like:

```
kids::17:17:my kids:/usr/kids:/bin/sh
```

Now all you have to do is add this line to /etc/passwd:

```
# ed /etc/passwd                    Note:running as root
270
$a                                  Add kids at end of file
kids::17:17:my kids:/usr/kids:/bin/sh
.
w
```

```
308
q
# cat /etc/passwd
root:xyDfccTrt18Ox,M.y8:0:0:admin:/:/bin/sh
console:lo1ndT0ee0Mzp,M.y8:1:1:admin:/:/bin/sh
pat:XmotTvoyUmjls:10:10:p wood:/usr/pat:/bin/sh
steve:J9exPd97Ftlbn,M.z8:15:10:s kochan:/usr/steve:/bin/sh
restrict:PomJkl09JkY4l,./:16:16::/usr/restrict:/bin/rsh
kids::17:17:my kids:/usr/kids:/bin/sh
#
```

The password is blank in the file above, so you should change it and tell the kids what the password for their user id is:

```
# passwd kids
New password:new_pwrd
Re-enter new password:new_pwrd              Make sure it's right
#
```

Note that if the password isn't set in /etc/passwd, a user logging in on the user id kids will not be required to enter a password.

After creating an entry in the /etc/passwd for kids, you need to create the HOME directory for kids. This is simple; you've already created plenty of directories!

```
# mkdir /usr/kids                    Make /usr/kids
# chown kids /usr/kids               Make kids the owner
# chgrp 17 /usr/kids                 Make 17 the group
#
```

The sysadm command has a menu for adding and removing users and groups.

Removing Users

Removing users is simply the opposite of adding them. First you delete the user's entry in /etc/passwd. Then you remove the user's HOME and all of his files:

```
# rm -r /usr/kids                    Remove entire directory tree
#
```

It might be a good idea to back up the user's files to tape before removing them, just in case the user decides he wants his files later on.

System V Release 3.2

As of System V Release 3.2, the encryted passwords in `/etc/passwd` were moved to the `/etc/shadow` file. Since `/etc/shadow` is readable only by `root`, this can improve password security. The `pwconv` command is used to create and update the `/etc/shadow` file from the `/etc/passwd` file.

If the `/etc/shadow` file doesn't already exist on your system, simply run `pwconv`, and the `/etc/shadow` file will be created with the correct information in it. After you add or remove a user from your system, you should run the `pwconv` again to update the `/etc/shadow` file.

◆ System Security ◆

In Chapter 10 we talked about what users can do with UNIX security. Now we're going to say a few words about what a system administrator can do with the tools provided by UNIX. For detailed information on UNIX security for administrators, refer to Chapter 5 of *UNIX System Security*. The first thing we'll look at is passwords. The format of the `/etc/passwd` file allows you to *require* users to change their passwords periodically. If you look at the `/etc/passwd` file again, you will see that some of the encrypted passwords have a comma (`,`) in them followed by a few more characters and a colon (`:`):

```
$ cat /etc/passwd
root:xyDfccTrt18ox,M.y8:0:0:admin:/:/bin/sh
console:lo1ndT0ee0Mzp,M.y8:1:1:admin:/:/bin/sh
pat:XmotTvoyUmjls:10:10:p wood:/usr/pat:/bin/sh
steve:J9exPd97Ftlbn,M.z8:15:10:s kochan:/usr/steve:/bin/sh
restrict:PomJkl09JkY4l,./:16:16::/usr/restrict:/bin/rsh
kids::17:17:my kids:/usr/kids:/bin/sh
#
```

The user ids `root`, `console`, and `steve` have four characters after the comma in the password, `restrict` has two, and `pat` and `kids` don't have commas at all.

The first character after the comma determines the *maximum* number of weeks the password is valid. The second character determines the *minimum* number of weeks that must transpire before the password may be changed again by the user. (This is to keep users from changing their passwords to a new one and then immediately back to the old one.) The remaining characters tell when the password was most recently changed.

To read the information you must first know how to count in password-*ese*. The way you count is `.=0`, `/=1`, `0-9=2-11`, `A-Z=12-37`, and `a-z=38-63`. (Table 12-2 gives an interpretation of password-*ese*.)

TABLE 12-2. Counting in password-*ese*

Password-ese	Number it represents	Password-ese	Number it represents
.	0	B	13
/	1	C	14
0	2	D	15
1	3	E	16
2	4	. . .	. . .
3	5	Y	36
4	6	Z	37
5	7	a	38
6	8	b	39
7	9	c	40
8	10	. . .	. . .
9	11	y	62
A	12	z	63

Let's take a look at one of the user ids above. The user id steve has an M after the comma. This says that the password must be changed at least every 25 weeks. The period that follows the M says that the password may be changed as often as steve likes. Anything else would require some time to elapse before the password could be changed again. The z8 tells the passwd command when the password was last changed. This field is also checked when the user logs in, and if the password has expired, the user is required to change it before he can log in.

You must put the first two characters in the /etc/passwd file (immediately after the encrypted password) in order to require periodic changing of passwords. The other two characters are put there by the passwd command when a user changes his password. Note that if you want to have a user change his password you can put two periods as the last time the password was changed (so the password entry looks something like *xxxxxxxxxx*,M...), and the user will be required to change his password the next time he logs in.

There are two special cases of this format that the system recognizes. The first is when the maximum number of weeks (first character) is less than the minimum (second character). In this case, the user is not allowed to change his password. Only the super-user can change this user's password. The user id restricted above is an example of this (.=0, /=1, first < second).

The second special case is when both the first and second character are periods (so the minimum and maximum are zero). In this case, the user is required to change his password the next time he logs in. After doing so, the periods are removed by the passwd command, and the user is never again required to change his password. Appendix F of *UNIX System Security* has the listing of a C program for modifying password aging information.

System V Release 3.2

Along with the addition of the `/etc/shadow` file in System V Release 3.2, the password aging fields were moved from `/etc/passwd` to `/etc/shadow`. The format of the `/etc/shadow` file is:

login : password : lastchanged : min : max

where *login* is the user's login name, *password* is the user's encrypted password, *lastchanged* is the number of days since January 1, 1970 that the password has been modified, *min* is the minimum number of days that must pass before the password may be changed again, and *max* is the maximum number of days the password is valid. All of these values are stored as normal decimal numbers, so none of the base-64 computations need to be used any more.

As of System V Release 3.2, the `passwd` command may be used to modify the aging information in the `/etc/shadow` file. The `-n` option to `passwd` changes the *min* field, and the `-x` option changes the *max* field. The `-f` option may be used to force a user to change his password the next time he logs in. Note that only the super-user can change these attributes.

```
# passwd -x 100 pat          Set max for pat to 100 days
# passwd -n 7 steve          Set min for steve to one week
# passwd -f kids             Force kids to change password on next login
#
```

The `-s` option can be used to show password attributes for a given user:

```
# passwd -s steve
steve  PS  03/01/89  7  175
#
```

The `PS` says that the login `steve` has a password (`NP` means the login doesn't have a password, and `LK` meas the login is locked so the user can't log in); the date is the last time the password was changed; the `7` is the *min* field, and the `175` is the *max* field.

Note that the `pwconv` command can be used to convert an old password file into a new `/etc/passwd` and `/etc/shadow` file with the encrypted password and aging information put into the new format in `/etc/shadow`.

umask

The `umask` command can be used to set the default creation modes of users' files and directories. If you put `umask` in the `/etc/profile`, you can control the permissions of files that users create. The way it works is the opposite of the `chmod` command: the mode you give it tells the system which permissions should *not* be given when a file is created. For example, umask 002 means that files and directories will be created *without* write permission to others (recall that chmod 002 *gives* write permission to others), and umask 022 means that files and directories will be created without write permission to the group or others. Typical modes for umask are given in Table 12-3.

TABLE 12-3. Typical umask modes

Command	Description
umask 002	Create files without write permission for others
umask 022	Create files without write for group or others
umask 006	Create files without read or write for others
umask 026	Create files without read or write for others and without write for group
umask 007	Create files without read, write, or execute for others
umask 077	Create files without read, write, or execute for anyone but the owner

Putting umask in the /etc/profile will change only the *default* creation modes. It will not prevent users from changing the modes of their file (with chmod) to something of their own choosing, nor will it keep them from putting umask in their own .profile to override the one in /etc/profile.

Sticky Directories

As of System V Release 3.2, if a directory is writable and the "sticky bit" is turned on (with chmod +t), a user can only remove a file in that directory if one of the following is true:

- The user owns the file.

- The user owns the directory.

- The file is writable by the user.

- The user is the super-user.

Previous versions of UNIX allowed any user to rename or remove a file from a directory that was writable by the user. The sticky directory feature prevents this. Note that the public directories /tmp and /usr/tmp both have the sticky bit set in the standard distribution of System V Release 3.2.

To see if the sticky bit is set on a directory, simply use ls -ld on the directory:

```
# ls -ld /tmp
drwxrwxrwt  5 sys        sys          1024 Mar  7 10:27 /tmp
#
```

If the last character of the modes is a "t", then the sticky bit is set.

You can make any other directory "sticky" by using chmod +t on it:

```
# chmod +t /usr/spool/uucppublic
#
```

chmod will allow the owner of any directory to make it sticky, i.e., super-user privileges are not required to make use of this feature.

The Restricted Shell (rsh)

You may have noticed something odd about the user-id restrict (besides the fact that he's not allowed to change his password). The shell for restrict isn't /bin/sh; it's /bin/rsh. This is the *restricted shell*. The restricted shell is almost the same as the regular shell, but it's designed to *restrict* a user's capabilities by disallowing certain actions that the standard shell (/bin/sh) allows. The list of actions disallowed is very short:

- cannot change directory (cd)

- cannot change PATH shell variable

- cannot use a command containing /

- cannot redirect output (> and >>)

These restrictions are enforced *after* the .profile is executed when logging in.

These simple restrictions allow the writer of a restricted user's .profile to have complete control over what commands that user can use. The example that follows shows a simple setup for a restricted environment.

```
$ cat .profile                    User restrict's .profile
PATH=/usr/rbin:$HOME/bin
export PATH
SHELL=/bin/rsh                    Some commands use SHELL variable
export SHELL
cd /usr/restrict/restdir          Don't leave user in HOME directory
$ ls -l .profile                  Restricted user shouldn't own his .profile
-rw-r--r-- 1 pat   group1  179 Dec 14 17:50 .profile
$ ls /usr/rbin                    Directory of restricted commands
cat                               Harmless commands
echo
mail                              Let them send us mail
red                               Restricted editor
write
```

```
$ ls /usr/restrict/bin          restrict's command directory
adventure                       Lots of games
backgammon
chess
hearts
poker
rogue
$
```

Here we have a restricted environment for the user `restrict`. When `res-trict` logs in, his PATH is changed to search just the directories `/usr/rbin` and `usr/restrict/bin`. The user `restrict` can run only the commands contained in these two directories. Any other command will get a *command*: not found response. The user is effectively bottled up in the directory `/usr/restrict/restdir` and cannot `cd` out of it. The `.profile` is owned by `pat`, not `restrict`, and the permissions are such that only `pat` can change the file. (Don't let a restricted user alter his `.profile`; that defeats the purpose of the restricted shell.)

One quick note about the commands in `/usr/rbin`: they were simply copied from the `/bin` and `/usr/bin` directories. You can put almost any command from `/bin` and `/usr/bin` in `/usr/rbin`; just use common sense in choosing the commands you allow restricted users to use. For example, don't give them access to the shell, a compiler, or `chmod`, as these may be used to bypass the restricted shell. Note that the restricted shell on many systems isn't very restricted. Although newer versions of the restricted shell have better security features, you shouldn't assume that it's foolproof. If you want to have a truly restricted environment for possibly hostile users, you should use `chroot`. Refer to *UNIX System Security* for more information on `chroot`.

System Directories and Files

There are many files on a UNIX system that users should not be allowed to write. These include all commands in `/bin`, `/usr/bin`, and `/usr/lbin`; files such as `/etc/passwd`, `/usr/lib/crontab`, `/unix`, `/etc/rc0`, `/etc/rc2`, and `/etc/inittab`; and most system directories, particularly `/`, `/dev`, `/etc`, `/usr`, and `/usr/lib`.

Some files shouldn't even be *readable* by users. These include the disk-special files in `/dev/dsk` and `/dev/rdsk`. When a disk is readable, anyone can write a program that can read any file on the disk. Also, `mem` and `kmem` in the device directory shouldn't be user-readable. A talented programmer can pick out a lot of passwords by scanning memory.

It's probably easier to say what users *can* access than what they *can't*. On a standard "out-of-the-box" UNIX system, only the system directories `/tmp`, `/usr/tmp`, and `/usr/spool/uucppublic` should be writable by all users. There may be a few system log files that are writable by all users, otherwise, the only other system files that should be writable by all users are `tty` and `sxt` devices in `/dev` and possibly the tape and floppy devices.

◆ The UNIX Accounting System ◆

The UNIX accounting system is a sophisticated collection of programs that collects data on system usage by process and disk usage and connect time (the amount of time logged in) by user. Accounting can be used to charge various users for their use of the system, or it can be used to keep track of system usage and performance.

Whenever a process finishes, the accounting system stores information about it in the file /usr/adm/pacct. This information includes the command name of the process, the computer time used, the total elapsed time, the uid and gid of the user who ran the process, the amount of memory used, and the amount of I/O performed. When a user logs in or off, his action is recorded in the file /etc/wtmp. This information can later be processed to determine the amount of time the user was logged into the system.

When a UNIX system first starts up, accounting is not automatically started. The steps in starting up the accounting package are fairly simple, though.

Setting Up the Accounting System

First you must make sure there is a user id named adm on your system. It's uid must be 4, and its HOME directory must be /usr/adm. To do this, just put this line in your /etc/passwd file:

```
adm:np:4:4:Admin:/usr/adm:
```

Since all valid encrypted passwords are 13 characters long, the np in adm's /etc/passwd entry means that no one can log in or su to adm. Only the super-user can become adm by using su (the su command doesn't ask the super-user for a password).

The second thing you must do is create the following directory structure, making sure that all the files are owned by the user adm:

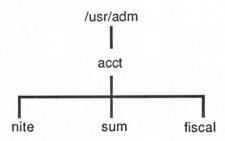

Fig. 12-7. Accounting directory

The following commands will create this directory structure with the proper ownership and permissions:

```
# mkdir /usr/adm
# cd /usr/adm
# mkdir acct
# mkdir acct/nite acct/sum
# mkdir acct/fiscal acct/fee
# chmod 755 . acct acct/*
# chown adm . acct acct/*
# chgrp 4 . acct acct/*
#
```

The third thing you must do is put these lines in the `.profile` in /usr/adm:

```
PATH=/usr/lib/acct:$PATH
export PATH
```

Next you put this line in the file /etc/rc2.d/Sacct:

```
/bin/su - adm -c /usr/lib/acct/startup
```

This starts up the accounting when the system goes into multiuser mode. You also need to put this line in the file /etc/shutdown so that accounting is turned off before the system is shut down:

```
/usr/lib/acct/shutacct
```

You may already have a file called S22acct in /etc/rc2.d. If you do, you don't have to add an Sacct file or change your shutdown command. The last thing to do is add these lines to adm's crontab:

```
0  4  *  *  1-6      /usr/lib/acct/runacct
5  *  *  *  *        /usr/lib/acct/ckpacct
15 5  1  *  *        /usr/lib/acct/monacct
```

and the following line to root crontab:

```
0  2  *  *  4     /usr/lib/acct/dodisk
```

runacct is the main daily accounting shell program. It produces daily and cumulative summary files for printing with the prdaily command (more on that later). ckpacct checks on the file /usr/adm/paact and makes sure it doesn't grow to big. It also checks the size of the /usr file system and turns off accounting if the number of free blocks falls below 500. monacct produces monthly accounting summaries. `dodisk` produces disk usage summary files that are later merged with the cumulative summary files by `runacct`.

The Accounting Summary Files

Once the accounting system has run for a few days, your UNIX system will have some files in the directory `/usr/adm/acct/sum`. The accounting summary for a particular day is stored in the file `/usr/adm/acct/sum/rprt`*mmdd* where *mmdd* is the month and day of the report. The most recent report can be printed by typing in `/usr/lib/acct/prdaily`:

```
$ /usr/lib/acct/prdaily

Dec 14 19:25 1988  DAILY REPORT FOR pipeline Page 1

from     Mon Dec 12 07:31:25 1988
to       Tue Dec 13 07:30:25 1988
1        acctg off
1        run-level S
1        system boot
2        run-level 2
1        acctg on
1        runacct
1        acctcon1


TOTAL DURATION IS 1439 MINUTES
LINE       MINUTES PERCENT # SESS  # ON     # OFF
tty00      778      54      166     166      543
console 1404        98      3       3        4
tty02      0        0       0       0        3
tty01      705      49      1       1        6

TOTALS  2887        --      170     170      561


Dec 14 19:25 1988 DAILY USAGE REPORT FOR pipeline Page 1
```

UID	LOGIN NAME	CPU (MINS) PRIME	NPRIME	KCORE-MINS PRIME	NPRIME	CONNECT(MINS) PRIME	NPRIME	DISK BLOCKS	# OF PROCS	# OF SESS	# DISK SAMPLES	FEE
0	TOTAL	275	186	19008	11362	7022	4115	538687	59681	484	200	0
0	root	8	48	193	2907	114	96	2	3502	1	1	0
2	bin	0	0	0	0	0	0	3419	0	0	1	0
4	adm	1	15	24	877	23	0	8514	786	2	1	0
5	uucp	1	1	30	47	0	0	414	376	0	1	0
6	mail	0	0	0	0	0	0	780	0	0	1	0
71	lp	0	0	0	0	0	0	32	0	0	1	0

112	jeff	2	0	124	0	36	64	6276	149	1	1	0
115	ruth	18	0	700	0	42	48	4401	5685	1	1	0
124	blb	0	0	9	3	0	0	1141	103	0	1	0
125	ai	3	0	96	0	156	335	503	93	2	1	0
126	jdm	0	0	6	1	0	0	185	15	1	1	0
127	phw	41	5	5343	600	37	667	25071	1978	1	1	0
186	oko	0	0	0	0	0	0	3992	0	0	1	0
201	steve	84	6	6106	1342	530	174	26944	16552	1	1	0

Dec 13 07:48 1988 DAILY COMMAND SUMMARY Page 1

COMMAND NAME	NUMBER CMDS	TOTAL KCOREMIN	TOTAL CPU-MI	TOTAL REAL-MIN	MEAN SIZE-K	MEAN CPU-MIN	HOG FACTOR	CHARS TRNSFD	BLOCKS READ
TOTALS	59681	29913.50	461.02	8580.25	64.89	0.01	0.01	0510136	370551
gmacs	35	4746.65	15.43	356.40	307.63	0.44	0.04	1320157	7896
nroff	123	3155.54	42.12	204.19	74.91	0.34	0.21	2806115	18247
vi	116	936.57	8.98	672.87	104.31	0.08	0.01	0494244	6303
troff	8	735.98	7.73	11.82	95.25	0.97	0.65	7253768	1145
sh	6515	709.78	37.56	7408.12	18.90	0.01	0.00	7347979	22411
login	218	251.09	12.11	1625.50	20.73	0.06	0.01	2865961	1795
expr	5256	243.91	9.87	13.80	24.71	0.00	0.72	38847	830
echo	9345	232.67	11.73	24.83	19.84	0.00	0.47	236902	2763
ls	766	193.99	3.69	18.92	52.51	0.00	0.20	2725177	3994
cut	2784	191.87	5.56	7.96	34.51	0.00	0.70	562239	1194
cat	2580	183.54	7.49	161.62	24.51	0.00	0.05	4227017	4949
ed	200	142.06	4.00	1417.55	35.50	0.02	0.00	7945845	4532
mv	1848	137.90	4.41	9.39	31.26	0.00	0.47	10986	7171
sort	249	125.86	2.46	11.76	51.17	0.01	0.21	595024	1907
grep	1249	110.90	4.59	18.20	24.18	0.00	0.25	4111626	5871
paste	1502	101.25	2.78	3.59	36.47	0.00	0.77	479718	802
cu	47	97.24	4.00	683.70	24.31	0.09	0.01	334588	548
tbl	45	86.16	1.24	68.47	69.40	0.03	0.02	1494318	1417
mail	714	3.45	2.27	69.24	36.83	0.00	0.03	265497	7367

Dec 13 07:48 1988 MONTHLY TOTAL COMMAND SUMMARY Page 1

COMMAND NAME	NUMBER CMDS	TOTAL KCOREMIN	TOTAL CPU-MIN	TOTAL REAL-MIN	MEAN SIZE-K	MEAN CPU-MIN	HOG FACTOR	CHARS TRNSFD	BLOCKS READ
TOTALS	337118	6961.97	941.45	78524.88	58.35	0.01	0.01	824898	16916

```
nroff      739   889.43  200.57   879.22   76.73  0.27   0.23   709995   6443
troff       69   847.30   70.40   172.92   94.42  1.02   0.41   680712   2413
vi         548   818.02   50.25  3392.06  108.82  0.09   0.04   320157   7896
gmacs       35   746.65   15.43   356.40  307.63  0.44   0.04  1320157   7896
sh       35325   725.94  215.62 95660.02   19.60  0.01   0.00   659315  34164
awk       5475   692.86   45.92    81.60   80.43  0.01   0.56   352767   1733
sed      24034   581.22   81.51   294.60   43.93  0.00   0.28   973855   7747
echo     66200   527.91   78.61   192.18   23.25  0.00   0.41   935104   8738
login     1510   404.83   60.74 14883.27   23.13  0.04   0.00   615527   8947
ls        3606   127.26   19.99   155.39   56.40  0.01   0.13   871481   1499
cut      15464    93.57   29.68    54.17   36.85  0.00   0.55   097338   6183
cat      14795    90.38   33.56   654.41   26.74  0.00   0.05   580572   2713
ed        1335    70.31   24.49  7791.43   35.53  0.02   0.00   881767   1275
sort      1125    64.93   13.95    68.33   53.41  0.01   0.20   486651   9869
grep      7636    47.27   29.73   121.21   23.79  0.00   0.25   284834   3281
make       145    40.36    8.87   346.90   77.81  0.06   0.03   094541   4630
expr     18192    27.82   23.83    39.35   26.34  0.00   0.61   151231   4024
paste     8269    22.95   15.39    24.59   39.17  0.00   0.63   684675   5179
mail      4608    17.30   14.85   344.84   36.86  0.00   0.04   996289   9655
```

```
Dec 13 07:48 1988 LAST LOGIN Page 1

00-00-00 pds      84-01-17 jhp        84-04-10 gss
83-01-07 59311    84-02-20 uucp       84-04-11 oko
83-06-17 vac      84-03-06 monadm     84-04-12 blb
84-04-12 dewh     84-04-13 9311mf     84-04-13 jdm
84-04-12 kel      84-04-13 9311nsv    84-04-13 jeff
84-04-12 rcc      84-04-13 ai         84-04-13 mboot
84-04-13 3700jms  84-04-13 fls440     84-04-13 ruth
84-04-13 3722cal  84-04-13 gemadm     84-04-13 steve
```

The report is divided into five sections. The first section prints out the accounting period (`from`/`to`) and lists statistics for each terminal port on the system. The second section lists the daily usage of the system by each user. The third and fourth sections give summaries of the commands used during the accounting period and the current month. The last section prints the date each user id was last used.

To look at any other day's report, you just tell `/usr/lib/cct/prdaily` the month and day (*mmdd*) of the report you want printed:

```
$ /usr/lib/acct/prdaily 1212        Print report for December 12
  . . .
$ /usr/lib/acct/prdaily 1127        Print report for November 27
  . . .
```

If you want to look back at the monthly accounting summaries, you can simply `cat` the files `/usr/adm/acct/fiscal/fiscrpt`*n*, where *n* is a number from 1 to 12 corresponding to the report for that month.

The `acctcom` Command

One command that is available to all users for printing the *current* day's accounting is the `acctcom` command. To see what it does, just try typing it in:

```
$ acctcom
COMMAND                        START     END       REAL     CPU     MEAN
NAME        USER    TTYNAME    TIME      TIME      (SECS)  (SECS) SIZE(K)
#accton     root    console    18:25:13  18:25:13   0.17    0.06    1.75
sh          adm     console    18:25:11  18:25:13   2.50    0.28    0.41
mv          adm     console    18:25:13  18:25:13   0.30    0.06    1.92
cp          adm     console    18:25:14  18:25:18   4.85    0.48    0.39
lpsched     lp      ?          18:37:27  18:37:27   0.24    0.02    4.00
init        root    console    18:39:54  18:39:54   0.32    0.06    2.75
ps          root    console    18:39:57  18:39:59   2.77    0.85    0.19
who         root    console    18:40:00  18:40:00   0.75    0.15    1.67
ls          root    console    18:40:01  18:40:03   2.57    0.20    0.98
su          root    console    18:49:38  18:49:39   1.10    0.18    0.50
stty        root    console    18:49:45  18:49:45   0.85    0.13    1.00
ls          pat     tty01      18:50:34  18:50:34   0.33    0.10    1.65
who         pat     tty01      18:50:35  18:50:35   0.80    0.17    0.97
vi          pat     tty01      18:50:37  18:50:38   1.66    0.19    0.87
ps          pat     tty01      18:50:40  18:50:41   1.64    0.44    0.60
sed         pat     tty01      18:50:43  18:50:43   0.41    0.10    1.80
tr          pat     tty01      18:50:46  18:50:47   1.02    0.07    2.36
cat         pat     tty01      18:50:48  18:50:48   0.57    0.04    4.13
who         pat     tty01      18:50:52  18:50:52   0.41    0.16    1.16
cpp         pat     tty01      18:51:05  18:51:08   3.54    0.96    0.20
comp        pat     tty01      18:51:08  18:51:19  11.56    1.29    0.10
cc          pat     tty01      18:51:04  18:51:20  16.17    0.23    0.63
make        pat     tty01      18:51:00  18:51:20  20.75    1.93    0.16
acctcom     root    console    18:51:09  18:51:26  17.25   14.44    0.02
ls          pat     tty01      18:52:12  18:52:13   1.07    0.31    0.53
```

The output is fairly self-explanatory.

♦ Administrating the uucp System ♦

The uucp system is the most widely used networking facility for UNIX systems. There are two reasons for this. First, it's the only standard networking system available for any release of UNIX. uucp is part of the standard UNIX system distribution and runs on any version of UNIX; there are even versions that run on MS-DOS. Second, it's the cheapest network you can have; all you need is a cable between two UNIX systems, and you can set up uucp. Also, if you want to interact with UNIX systems that are hundreds or thousands of miles away, all you need is a modem that can automatically dial the numbers of the systems you want to communicate with. (There are 1200 baud modems with auto-dial capability that cost less than $100.)

The uucp system is fairly simple to set up and maintain.

Setting Up uucp

The first thing you should do before trying to set up uucp is make sure all of the programs uucp needs exist. You can do this by checking the directory /usr/bin for the programs uucp, uux, uuname, and uulog. You should also check the directory /usr/lib/uucp for the programs uucico and uuxqt. If these programs or directories don't exist, you probably don't have the uucp software installed. What you should do is check to see if you received the uucp software with your UNIX system, and if you did whether it's on a tape or floppy disk somewhere.

The next thing you need are two user ids for uucp. One is for the ownership of all the uucp files and programs, and the other is for other systems to use to log into yours so they can send data. These user ids are usually uucp and nuucp, respectively. For this you need two lines in your /etc/passwd file like this:

```
uucp::5:5:UUCP owner:/usr/spool/uucp:
nuucp::10000:10000:UUCP login:/usr/spool/uucppublic:/usr/lib/uucp/uucico
```

Then you should use the passwd command to change the passwords for both user ids. Make sure the password for uucp isn't similar to the password for nuucp.

If you look at the /etc/passwd line for uucp, you will notice that it needs a HOME directory of /usr/spool/uucp. If this directory doesn't exist, create it and change the owner to uucp. Also note that the shell for nuucp is /usr/lib/uucp/uucico. This is the *copy in—copy out* program that performs the transfer of data for uucp. Any system calling yours expects this program to start up automatically when it logs in.

Next you need a few command lines in the crontab for uucp. The four programs, uudemon.poll, uudemon.hour, uudemon.admin, and uudemon.cleanup, perform administrative tasks for uucp on (typically) an hourly, daily, and weekly basis. These programs take care of almost all routine maintenance, including polling systems, deleting old requests, removing old files in the `uucp` directory structure, clearing old log files, and mailing the administrator (user id `uucp`) information on any actions taken.

```
1 * * * * /usr/lib/uucp/uudemon.poll > /dev/null
5 * * * * /usr/lib/uucp/uudemon.hour > /dev/null
45 5 * * * /usr/lib/uucp/uudemon.admin > /dev/null
55 5 * * 0 /usr/lib/uucp/uudemon.cleanup > /dev/null
```

Now your `uucp` system is ready to run. The only problem is that other systems can log into yours, but yours may not be able to log into theirs. You need to hook a modem with automatic-dialing capability to one of your ports. After doing this you need to make sure that the `getty` for that port is set up to allow outgoing calls as well as incoming ones. You can do this by looking at your `/etc/inittab` for that port. If there is a line that looks like

ttynum`:2:respawn:getty tty`*ttynum* ...

you should replace it with the following:

ttynum`:2:respawn:/usr/lib/uucp/uugetty -r -t 60 tty`*ttynum* ...

and run `init q`, which makes `init` read the changed `inittab`. Now that port can be used for both incoming and outgoing calls.

Well, you've got the modem set up; now you need to tell `uucp` about it. This is done via the `/usr/lib/uucp/Devices` file. This file has one line for each dial-out port. The lines have the format:

device line call-unit speed model

device is either the type of device on the port, such as `ACU` for an automatic-dial modem or the name of a directly connected system; *line* is the device in `dev` that corresponds to this device; *call-unit* allows you to specify a separate device for doing the calling, but with most modern modems you can just put in a – (in earlier days, special boxes called *automatic call units*, or ACUs, were attached to modems to do the dialing; these were accessed through a different device in `/dev`), *speed* is the speed of the line (typically 1200 or 2400 for modems, up to 19200 for hard-wired connections); and *model* is the model of modem on the port, or `direct` for hard-wired lines. So typical entries in this file look like:

```
ACU tty11 - 1200 hayes
ACU tty11 - 2400 hayes
local tty12 - 9600 direct
```

The `/usr/lib/uucp/Dialers` file contains control information for talking to a variety of modems. The *model* field of the `Devices` file must specify one of the entries in the `Dialers` file. Each line in the `Dialers` file describes one type of modem. If you don't see your modem type in the `Dialers` file, and it isn't Hayes compatible, you will have to add a new entry to the file. The mechanics of this are beyond the scope of this book. Refer to *UNIX System Administration* and the suggested readings for UUCP in Appendix A for more information.

The last step in setting up `uucp` is to tell it about the systems it's going to talk to. What you need to do is determine what UNIX systems you want to use `uucp` with, call the system administrators for those systems, and get the phone numbers, id's, and passwords for `uucp`. When you have gathered this information, put it in the file `/usr/lib/uucp/Systems`. This file contains information about each remote system that your system can call and send data to. Each line looks something like this:

name time device speed phone login-sequence

name
The name of the remote system.

time
The days of the week and time when the remote system should be called (e.g., `MoWeFr0800-1700` will allow calling on Monday, Wednesday, and Friday between 8 A.M. and 5 P.M.). The day portion may be a list containing `Su Mo Tu We Th Fr Sa` or `Wk` for any weekday or `Any` for any day. The time portion is a range of times (e.g., 0800-1230) in 24 hour format. If no time portion is specified, calls are allowed at any time.

device
This is the device from the `Devices` file.

speed
This is the speed of the connection to the remote system. It is usually `Any`, allowing `uucp` to choose a speed based on the information in the `Devices` file.

phone
This is the phone number to be used for calling the remote system.

login-sequence
The *login-sequence* is what `uucp` uses to establish a login on the remote system. It consists of pairs of words separated by blanks. Each pair describes what prompt `uucp` expects from the remote system (e.g., `login:`) and the response it should make to that prompt (e.g., `nuucp`). A typical *login-sequence* looks something like this:

```
login: nuucp password: nuucp123
```

You can also put a `login:--login:` in place of `login:`. This causes `uucp` to send a *RETURN* if it doesn't get a `login:` right away. This is useful when the calling system's modems run at one speed and the answering system's modems have a different initial speed. Usually, if a system has modems that support more than one speed, the modems will answer at one speed and then change speed when a *BREAK* or *RETURN* is entered, cycling through all the possible speeds. An entry like `login:--login:--login:` can be used to cycle the answering system's modem through three different speeds in the hope that one of those speeds will match the speed of the calling modem, which will then receive the string `login:`. You can also use portions of the words such as `gin:` and `word:` for `login:` and `password:`.

The `/usr/lib/uucp/Systems` and `/usr/lib/uucp/Devices` files will look something like this when you're done with them:

```
# cat /usr/lib/uucp/Systems
remote1 Any ACU Any 971-1770 gin:--gin: nuucp word: UUCP
remote2 Any ACU Any 971-1771 gin:--gin: nuucp word: UUCP
un1 Any0000-0800 ACU 1200 317-325-5601 gin:--gin: nuucp word: un1
local Any local Any - gin:--gin: nuucp word: uucp123
# cat /usr/lib/uucp/Devices
ACU tty11 - 2400 hayes
ACU tty11 - 1200 hayes
ACU tty11 - 300 hayes
local tty12 - 9600 direct
#
```

There are four entries for remote systems. The first two are systems that can be called any time, any day at 2400, 1200, or 300 baud. Note that the `ACU` entries are in decreasing order by speed. This is to make `uucp` to try the fastest speeds first when calling the remote systems. The system `un1` can be called only between the hours of midnight and eight A.M. (probably to save on long-distance phone bills) and only at 1200 baud. The system `local` is hard-wired to the port `tty12` at 9600 baud. Its `Systems` entry says that the device is `local`, which corresponds to the fourth line in `Devices`. This line tells `uucp` that the `local` line is `tty12`, the speed is 9600 baud, and the device is directly connected.

As an example of how this works, consider a user who sends mail to someone on `un1` in the afternoon. `mail` starts `uucp` to send the mail, and `uucp` starts `uucico` to perform the actual call and data transfer. `uucico` looks at the entry for `un1` and *doesn't* call `un1` because the system can't be called until after midnight. Every hour, however, `uudemon.hour` is started by the `cron`. It looks around for data that hasn't been transferred. It sees the mail message for `un1` and starts up `uucico` which goes through the above process to decide if it's time to send it. The first time `uucico` is started after midnight, it will call `un1` and send the mail. If `un1` is down or all of its phone lines are busy, `uucico` will continue to try to send the mail until eight o'clock. Each time `uucico` calls and fails, is waits a longer period before retrying the remote system. Usually, the period is first just under one hour, and on each failed try the period doubles until it reaches 23 hours.

Polling Other Systems

uucp can be set up to poll other systems on a regular basis. This can be done for several reasons:

- The remote system's modems don't have dial-out capability.

- The financial burden of contacting the remote system lies with the local one.

- The local system, for security reasons, must always call the remote system to be assured that it's not talking to a masquerading system.

- The local system's modem shares a voice line, and can't answer incoming calls.

The file `/usr/lib/uucp/Poll` contains information for all systems to poll. It contains lines of the form:

system<TAB>time1 time2 ...

where *system* is the name of the system to poll and *time1*, *time2*, ... are the hours that *system* should be polled:

```
remote1     0 8 16
```

This says that the system `remote1` should be polled at midnight, 8 a.m. and 4 p.m.

When the `/usr/lib/uucp/uudemon.poll` program runs it reads this file and queues a job for each system that should be polled at that time. When `/usr/lib/uucp/uudemon.hour` comes along, it starts up `uucico` for each system that has pending jobs, which includes, of course, the systems that are being polled this hour.

The following list summarizes the steps needed to set up `uucp`.

1. make sure `uucp` software is on your system.

2. add the user ids `uucp` and `nuucp` to `/etc/passwd`.

3. add lines that run `uucp`'s maintenance programs to `uucp`'s crontab.

4. make the `getty` for any ACU ports `uugetty`.

5. add a description of the ACU port to `/usr/lib/uucp/Devices`.

6. add remote system descriptions to `/usr/lib/uucp/Systems`.

That's all you need to know to get uucp running. If you want more information about uucp, you should read *UNIX System Administration*, *UNIX System Networking*, *UNIX System Security*, and the suggested readings for UUCP in Appendix A.

♦ The Line Printer Spooler ♦

The line printer spooler is a collection of programs that allows your users to share printers. They work by allowing users to *spool* files for printing. This means that instead of printing the file immediately, a request to print it is created, and the program that manages the printers handles these requests one at a time. When a user types in lp file.c, the request to print file.c is saved in the /usr/spool/lp directory structure, and a message is sent to the lpsched process, which is started up when the system goes into multiuser mode. lpsched gets this message, and if no files are already being printed, it spawns a process to print file.c. If the printer is busy, lpsched waits until all the requests created before the one to print file.c are handled, then it spawns a process to print file.c. lpsched can handle multiple printers, and multiple types of printers. We'll just look at the case of a single printer. Many of the following commands are located in /usr/lib, not /bin or /etc. The simplest thing to do is add /usr/lib to your PATH before performing any administration of the line printer spooler. We assume this has been done throughout this section.

The first thing you do to add a printer to your system is use the lpadmin command to tell the spooling software the type of printer you have and what I/O device it's hooked up to:

```
# lpadmin -pptr -v/dev/lp -mdumb
#
```

The -p option is followed by the printer's name, which you must choose. This is the name you will use to refer to the printer when dealing with it. The -v option is followed by the device the printer is attached to. Here it's attached to /dev/lp, the system's parallel port. The -m option is followed by the printer's type. Here we're assuming it's a dumb printer. The various interfaces for different printer types are stored in shell programs in the directory /usr/spool/lp/model. If you look at these, you may see one for your printer type; however, it's more likely that you won't find an entry, so you can use dumb for most 132-column parallel printers, mtx80 for most 80-column parallel printers, or serial for most serial printers (it assumes 9600 baud, eight bits, no parity).

If you get an error message from lpadmin that it "can't proceed - scheduler running," that means the printer scheduler lpsched is already running and needs to be turned off before you can perform any administration of the printer system. Simply run `lpshut` to shut off the scheduler.

After you've "installed" the printer with `lpadmin`, you have to get `lpsched` started. Since this program should be started whenever your system comes up, you can put a startup shell in `/etc/rc2.d`:

```
# cat /etc/rc2.d/Slpstartup
/usr/lib/lpsched
#
```

You must also tell the spooling system that it can accept print jobs for the new printer and enable the printer. You do this by running `accept` and `enable`:

```
# accept ptr
destination "ptr" now accepting requests
# enable ptr
printer "ptr" now enabled
#
```

If, for any reason, you need to temporarily shut off the printer, you can use `disable` to prevent files from being sent to the printer:

```
# disable ptr
printer "ptr" now disabled
#
```

You can use the `-c` option to `disable` to cancel the current job and disable the printer at the same time (e.g., to clear a paper jam). You can also use the `-r` option to give a reason to `disable` that is printed by `lpstat` if a user tries to find out about the status of a print job:

```
# disable -r"paper jam" ptr
printer "ptr" now disabled
# lpstat -pptr
printer ptr disabled since Dec 14 20:44 -
        paper jam
#
```

When the printer is ready to print again, you can run `enable` to restart it.

If a printer will be disconnected for an extended period of time, you should run `reject`. This will cause requests to print files on the printer to be rejected with an error message. You can also give a reason to `reject` with the `-r` option:

```
# reject -r"printer being repaired" ptr
destination "ptr" will no longer accept requests
# lp -pptr file.c
lp: can't accept requests for destination "ptr" -
        printer being repaired
#
```

This prevents files waiting to be printed from building up and informs the users that the printer is unavailable.

If you just need to cancel the current print job (suppose you goofed and sent a binary file to the printer), you can use the `cancel` command:

```
# cancel ptr
request "ptr-11" cancelled
#
```

The `lpadmin` command can be used to assign a *default* printer, i.e., the printer to which `lp` requests go when no -p option is used. The -d option is used with the printer name to be made the default printer:

```
# lp file.c
lp: no system default destination
# lpadmin -dptr
# lp file.c
request-id is ptr-12 (1 file)
#
```

If your printer isn't working, you can use the `lpstat` command to get information on the spooling system. The -t option will give you all the information `lpstat` knows:

```
# lpstat -t
scheduler is running
system default destination: ptr
device for ptr: /dev/lp
ptr accepting requests since Dec 14 20:56
printer ptr is disabled since Dec 14 21:18 -
        disabled by scheduler: can't open /dev/lp
#
```

Here, the printer was disabled automatically by the scheduler because it couldn't open /dev/lp. There are a couple of possibilities: the device file /dev/lp isn't there or has the wrong permissions (unlikely if the printer was working before) or the printer isn't on or hooked up (more likely). We'll assume the problem gets fixed:

```
# enable ptr
# lpstat -t
scheduler is running
system default destination: ptr
device for ptr: /dev/lp
ptr accepting requests since Dec 14 20:56
printer ptr is idle.  enabled since Dec 14 21:24 -
#
```

For a printer to operate properly, the following must all be true:

1. The printer must be installed with `lpadmin`.

2. The printer scheduler `lpsched` must be running.

3. The printer must be accepting jobs.

4. The printer must be enabled.

5. The printer must be properly hooked up and turned on.

A complete list of administrative commands, along with a short description of each command, is in Appendix D.

For More Information

There are many sources of information on the UNIX system; however, there is one reference that you cannot do without. This is the UNIX documentation for your particular version. It will give detailed descriptions on the syntax and various options for each of the commands. A complete set of UNIX documentation is available from Prentice Hall. This is the ten-volume set of standard System V, Release 3 produced by AT&T. The reference manuals (referred to as the "man pages" by UNIX users) are necessary for any serious use.

♦ Hayden Books UNIX System and C Libraries ♦

UNIX Shell Programming, S. G. Kochan and P. H. Wood, Howard W. Sams & Company, Indianapolis, IN, 1987.

> A complete introduction to Unix shell programming; it contains many practical programs that provide reinforcement for each new application.

UNIX Text Processing, D. Dougherty and T. O'Reilly, Howard W. Sams & Company, Indianapolis, IN, 1987.

> An in-depth reference covering all aspects of text processing in the UNIX environment.

Programming in C, Revised Edition, S. G. Kochan, Howard W. Sams & Company, Indianapolis, IN, 1988.

> A tutorial introduction to the C language; it contains many examples and teaches C in an organized fashion.

Topics in C Programming, S. G. Kochan and P. H. Wood, Howard W. Sams & Company, Indianapolis, IN, 1988.

> The sequel to *Programming in C*; describes in detail some of the most difficult concepts in C as well as the UNIX system interface, curses, make and debugging.

Advanced C: Tips and Techniques, P. Anderson and G. Anderson, Howard W. Sams & Company, Indianapolis, IN, 1988.

> In-depth look at debugging techniques, C's run-time environment, and memory object allocator. Loaded with useful examples.

Programming in ANSI C, S. G. Kochan, Howard W. Sams & Company, Indianapolis, IN, 1988.

> Comprehensive tutorial; assumes no previous exposure to the C language.

Portability And The C Language, R. Jaeschke, Howard W. Sams & Company, Indianapolis, IN, 1988.

> Thorough treatment of portability in C, for the well-versed C programmer.

UNIX System Security, P. H. Wood and S. G. Kochan, Howard W. Sams & Company, Indianapolis, IN, 1988.

> A practical guide to system security, with methods for making sure your UNIX system is as secure as you want it to be.

UNIX System Networking, P. H. Wood and S. G. Kochan (eds.), Howard W. Sams & Company, Indianapolis, IN, 1989.

> An in-depth look at the most popular UNIX networks. Each chapter is written by an expert on the subject.

UNIX System Administration, D. Fiedler and B. H. Hunter, Howard W. Sams & Company, Indianapolis, IN, 1988.

> A practical guide to system administration.

◆ UNIX Manuals ◆

UNIX System V Programmer's Guide, Prentice Hall, Englewood Cliffs, NJ, 1987.

UNIX System V Streams Primer, Prentice Hall, Englewood Cliffs, NJ, 1987.

UNIX System V Streams Programmer's Guide, Prentice Hall, Englewood Cliffs, NJ, 1987.

UNIX System V Network Programmer's Guide, Prentice Hall, Englewood Cliffs, NJ, 1987.

UNIX System V Programmer's Reference Manual, Prentice Hall, Englewood Cliffs, NJ, 1987.

UNIX System V User's Reference Manual, Prentice Hall, Englewood Cliffs, NJ, 1987.

UNIX System V User's Guide, Prentice Hall, Englewood Cliffs, NJ 1987.

UNIX System V Utilities Release Notes, Prentice Hall, Englewood Cliffs, NJ, 1987.

UNIX System V System Administrator's Guide, Prentice Hall, Englewood Cliffs, NJ, 1987.

UNIX System V System Administrator's Reference Manual, Prentice Hall, Englewood Cliffs, NJ, 1987.

◆ Suggested Readings ◆

The following lists periodicals, books, articles, and papers that are of interest to UNIX users. Papers marked with a † are printed in the Berkeley 4.3 *UNIX User's Supplementary Documents, UNIX Programmer's Supplementary Documents*, and *UNIX System Manager's Manual*, available from the USENIX Association, P.O. Box 2299, Berkeley, CA 94710.

UNIX Publications

UNIX Review, 500 Howard Street, San Francisco, CA 94105.

A monthly magazine devoted to UNIX; somewhat technical in nature.

UNIX World, 444 Castro Street, Mountain View, CA 94101.

Another monthly magazine devoted to UNIX; less technical than *UNIX Review*; lots of tutorial articles and market information.

UNIX Today!, 600 Community Drive, Manhasset, NY 11030.

A biweekly tabloid on UNIX; mostly news items and press releases.

;login, The USENIX Association, P.O. Box 2299, Berkeley, CA 94710.

> A bimonthly newsletter for USENIX members. You must join to receive it.

CommUNIXations, /usr/group, 4655 Old Ironsides Drive, Suite 200, Santa Clara, CA 95054.

> A bimonthly magazine for /usr/group members. You must join to receive it.

Unique, P.O. Box 220, Rescue, CA 95672.

> A monthly newsletter on the UNIX industry; mostly nontechnical articles on industry trends, company profiles, and product reviews.

General UNIX Topics

Design of the UNIX Operating System, Maurice Bach, Prentice Hall, Englewood Cliffs, NJ, 1986.

> Thorough description of the internal structure of UNIX.

UNIX System: Readings and Applications Vol. I, AT&T Bell Laboratories, Prentice Hall, Englewood Cliffs, NJ, 1987.

> Covers fundamentals such as real-time processing and microprocessor systems.

UNIX System: Readings and Applications Vol. II, AT&T Bell Laboratories, Prentice Hall, Englewood Cliffs, NJ, 1987.

> Covers graphics, security, networking and portability.

[†]"The UNIX Time Sharing System," D. M. Ritchie and K. Thompson.

> The original paper written by Ritchie and Thompson describing the UNIX system.

[†]"A Tutorial Introduction to the UNIX Text Editor," B. W. Kernighan.

> An introductory guide to ed.

[†]"Advanced Editing on UNIX," B. W. Kernighan.

> An advanced look at ed.

The Shell

Kornshell Command and Programming Language, Korn and Bolsky, Prentice Hall Englewood Cliffs, NJ, 1988.

[†]"An Introduction to the UNIX Shell," S. R. Bourne.

    A complete, albeit terse, description of the UNIX shell.

[†]"SED—A Non-interactive Text Editor," L. E. McMahon.

    A complete description of the `sed` editor.

The AWK Programming Language A.V. Aho, B. W. Kernighan, P. J. Weinberger, Addison-Wesley, Reading, MA 1988.

    A complete description of the `awk` language.

The UNIX C Shell Field Guide, G. Anderson and P. Anderson, Prentice Hall, Englewood Cliffs, NJ 07632, 1986.

    An in-depth reference to the C shell.

[†]"An introduction to the C shell," W. Joy.

    An Introduction to the C shell and many of its commonly used commands.

vi

[†]"An Introduction to Display Editing with VI," W. Joy.

    An introductory guide to `vi`.

[†]"Ex Reference Manual," W. Joy.

    A complete description of the `ex` text editor, which underlies `vi`.

Guide to Vi Visual Editing on the UNIX System, D. Sonnenschein, Prentice Hall Englewood Cliffs, NJ 07632, 1987.

Learning the Vi Editor, Lamb, O'Reilly & Associates, Inc., Cambridge, MA 02140, 1987.

    One of the Nutshell series of handbooks.

Document Processing

[†]"A TROFF Tutorial," B. W. Kernighan.

A quick introduction to the `troff` typesetting program.

[†]"NROFF/TROFF User's Manual," J. F. Ossanna.

A complete description of the `nroff` and `troff` programs.

[†]"TBL—A Program to Format Tables," M. E. Lesk.

A description of the `tbl` preprocessor for `troff`.

[†]"A System for Typesetting Mathematics," B. W. Kernighan, L. L. Cherry.

A description of the `eqn` preprocessor for `troff`.

Programming

The C Programming Language, B. W. Kernighan and D. M. Ritchie, Prentice Hall, Englewood Cliffs, NJ,1978.

The standard reference for the C language.

Advanced UNIX Programming, M. J. Rochkind, Prentice Hall, Englewood Cliffs, NJ 07632, 1985.

How to write efficient, portable programs at the UNIX system call level.

The UNIX Programming Environment, B. W. Kernighan and R. Pike, Prentice Hall, Englewood Cliffs, NJ 07632, 1984.

The UNIX philosophy.

Managing Projects with Make, Talbott, O'Reilly & Associates, Inc, Cambridge, MA 02140, 1987.

One of the Nutshell series of handbooks.

[†]"Make—A Program for Maintaining Computer Programs," S. I. Feldman.

An overview of `make`.

Security

"A Loss of Innocence," P. H. Wood, "Tales of the Damned," K. Smith, "Assessing the Costs," V. Gligor and C. S. Chandersekaran, and "Interview with Roger Schell," T. Berson, *UNIX Review*, Vol. 6, No. 2 (February 1988), pp. 37-69.

Four articles on various aspects of UNIX security.

[†]"On The Security of UNIX," D. M. Ritchie.

An overview of UNIX security.

[†]"Password Security: A Case History," R. H. Morris and K. Thompson.

Many reasons for choosing good passwords.

"The UNIX System: UNIX Operating System Security," F. T. Grampp and R. H. Morris, *UNIX System: Readings and Applications Vol. II*, AT&T Bell Laboratories, Prentice Hall, Englewood Cliffs, NJ, 1987.

An overview of UNIX security.

"The UNIX System: File Security and the UNIX System Crypt Command," J. A. Reeds and P. J. Weinberger, *UNIX System: Readings and Applications Vol. II*, AT&T Bell Laboratories, Prentice Hall, Englewood Cliffs, NJ, 1987.

A description of how the `crypt` command was cracked.

R. Farrow, "Further Cures for Business Ills, Part 2a," *UNIX World*, Vol. III, No. 4 (April 1986), pp. 65-71.

An article on good security practices.

R. Farrow, "Further Cures for Business Ills, Part 2b," *UNIX World*, Vol. III, No. 5 (May 1986), pp. 65-70.

An article on some of the better known security holes in UNIX.

A. Filipski and J. Hanko, "Making UNIX Secure," *Byte*, Vol. II, No. 4 (April 1986), pp. 113-128.

An article on making UNIX more secure.

Networking and UUCP

UNIX Communications, B. Anderson, B. Costales, H. Henderson, Howard W. Sams & Company, Indianapolis, IN, 1987.

Step-by-step instructions on using UNIX facilities for electronic mail, USENET, UUCP, and more.

Using Uucp and Usenet, Grace Todino, O'Reilly & Associates, Inc, Cambridge, MA 02140, 1986.

One of the Nutshell series of handbooks.

Managing Uucp and Usenet, Grace Todino, O'Reilly & Associates, Inc, Cambridge, MA 02140, 1986.

One of he Nutshell series of handbooks.

[†]"A Dial-Up Network of UNIX Systems," D. A. Nowitz, M. E. Lesk.

An early description of the UUCP system.

[†]"Mail Reference Manual," K. Shoens.

A description of the Berkeley `mail` command, the model for AT&T's `mailx` command.

Overview of Commands

Often-used UNIX commands are listed here. All commands are fully described in the *UNIX User's Reference Manual* and *UNIX System Administrator's Reference Manual*.[†] Due to hardware constraints, not all the commands listed here will work on all the supported hardware configurations.

(Portions of this overview were adapted from the document "UNIX— Overview and Synopsis of Facilities," by T. A. Dolatta, R. C. Haight, and A. G. Petruccelli.)

♦ Basic Software ♦

Included are the operating system with utilities, an assembler, and a compiler for the programming language C—enough software to regenerate, maintain, and modify UNIX itself, and to write and run new applications.

Operating System

☐ UNIX   This is the basic resident code, also known as the kernel, on which everything else depends. It executes the system calls, maintains the file system, and manages the system's resources; it contains device drivers, I/O buffers, and other system information. A general description of UNIX design philosophy and system facilities appeared in an article in the *Communications of the ACM*. A more extensive survey is in *The Bell System Technical Journal* for July-August 1978 and Maurice Bach's book *The Design of the UNIX*

---

† And the *UNIX Programmer's Reference Manual* if you have UNIX System V, Release 2 or later.

Operating System (see Appendix A for details). Further capabilities include:

- Automatically-supported reentrant code.
- Separation of instruction and data spaces (machine dependent).
- Timer-interrupt sampling and interprocess monitoring for debugging and measurement.
- Shared libraries

☐ Devices All I/O is logically synchronous. Normally, automatic buffering by the system makes the physical record structure invisible and exploits the hardware's ability to do overlapped I/O. Unbuffered physical record I/O is available for unusual applications. Software drivers are provided for many devices; others can be easily written.

User Access Control

☐ login Signs on a new user:

- Adapts to characteristics of terminal.
- Verifies password and establishes user's individual and group (project) identity.
- Establishes working directory.
- Publishes message of the day.
- Announces presence of mail.
- Lists unseen news items.
- Executes an optional user-specified profile.
- Starts command interpreter (shell) or other user-specified program.

☐ passwd Changes a password:

- User can change own password.
- Passwords are kept encrypted for security.

☐ su Allows a user to assume the permissions and privileges of another user or root (super-user) provided that the proper password is supplied.

☐ `newgrp` Changes working group (project id). This provides access with protection for groups of related users.

☐ `stty` Sets up options for control of a terminal:

- Erase and line kill characters.
- Speed.
- Parity
- Mapping of upper-case characters to lower case.
- Carriage-return plus line-feed versus newline.
- Interpretation of tab characters.
- Delays for tab, newline, and carriage-return characters.
- Raw versus edited input.

☐ `tabs` Sets terminal's tab stops. Knows several "standard" formats.

Manipulation of Files and Directories

☐ `ed` Interactive line-oriented context editor. Random access to all lines of a file. It can:

- Find lines by number or pattern (regular expressions). Patterns can include: specified characters, "don't care" characters, choices among characters, (specified numbers of) repetitions of these constructs, beginning of line, end of line.
- Add, delete, change, copy, or move lines.
- Permute contents of a line.
- Replace one or more instances of a pattern within a line.
- Combine or split lines.
- Combine or split files.
- Do any of the above operations on every line (in a given range) that matches a pattern.
- Escape to the shell (UNIX command language) during editing.

☐ vi   Screen-oriented display editor for video terminals When using vi, changes made to the file are reflected by what is displayed on the terminal screen. Note: this command is available in Berkeley UNIX and System V, Release 2 and later releases of UNIX.

☐ sed   A stream (one pass) editor with facilities similar to those of ed.

☐ cat   Concatenates one or more files onto standard output. Mostly used for unadorned printing, for inserting data into a "pipe," and for buffering output that comes in dribs and drabs.

☐ pg   Prints files one screenful at a time. Note: this command is available in System V, Release 2 and later releases of UNIX.

☐ pr   Prints files with title, date, and page number on every page:

   • Multicolumn output.

   • Parallel column merge of several files.

☐ split   Splits a large file into more manageable pieces.

☐ csplit   Like split, with the splitting controlled by context.

☐ sum   Computes the check sum of a file.

☐ dd   Physical file format translator, for exchanging data with non-UNIX systems, especially OS/360, VS1, MVS, etc.

☐ cp   Copies one file to another or many files to a directory. Works on any file regardless of its contents.

☐ ln   Links another name (alias) to an existing file.

☐ mv   Moves one or more files. Usually used for renaming files or directories.

☐ rm   Removes one or more files. If any names are linked to the file, only the name being removed goes away.

☐ chmod   Changes access permissions on a file(s). Executable by the owner of the file(s) or by the super-user.

☐ chown   Changes owner of a file(s).

☐ mkdir   Makes one or more new directories.

☐ rmdir   Removes one or more (empty) directories.

☐ cd   Changes working (i.e., current) directory.

☐ find   Searches the directory hierarchy for, and performs specified commands on, every file that meets given criteria:

- File name matches a given pattern.
- Modified date in given range.
- Date of last use in given range.
- Given permissions.
- Given owner.
- Given special file characteristics.
- Any logical combination of the above.
- Any directory can be the starting "node."

☐ tar   Tape file archiver: tar saves and restores files and directory structures on magnetic tape.

☐ cpio   Copies a subtree of the file system (directories, links, and all) to another place in the file system. Can also copy a subtree onto a tape and later recreate it from tape. Often used with the find command.

☐ SCCS   SCCS (Source Code Control System) is a collection of UNIX commands (some interactive) for controlling changes to files of text (typically the source code of programs or the text of documents). It provides facilities for:

- Storing, updating, and retrieving any version of any source or text file.
- Controlling updating privileges.
- Identifying both source and object (or load) modules by version number.
- Recording who made each change, when it was made, and why.

Execution of Programs

☐ sh
The shell, or command language interpreter, understands a set of constructs that constitute a full programming language; it allows a user or a command procedure to:

- Supply arguments to and run any executable program.

- Redirect standard input, standard output, and standard error files.

- Pipes: simultaneous execution with output of one process connected to the input of another.

- Compose compound commands using:

  if...then...else
  case switches
  while loops
  for loops over lists
  break, continue, and exit
  parentheses for grouping.

- Initiate background processes.

- Perform shell procedures (i.e., command scripts with substitutable arguments).

- Construct argument lists from all file names matching specified patterns.

- Take user-specified action on traps and interrupts.

- Specify a search path for finding commands.

- Upon login, automatically create a user-specifiable environment.

- Optionally announces presence of mail as it arrives.

- Provide variables and parameters with default settings.

☐ rsh
Restricted shell; restricts a user to a subset of UNIX commands.The system administrator may construct different levels of restriction.

☐ shl
Shell layer manager: shl allows a user to interact with more than one shell from a single terminal. Note: This command is available in System V, Release 2 and later releases of UNIX.

☐ `test`   Tests argument values in shell conditional constructs:

- String comparison.
- File nature and accessibility.
- Boolean combinations of the above.

☐ `expr`   String computations for calculating command arguments:

- Integer arithmetic
- Pattern matching
- Like `test` above, `expr` can be used for conditional side-effect.

☐ `echo`   Prints its arguments on the standard output. Useful for diagnostics or prompts in shell procedures or for inserting data into a "pipe."

☐ `sleep`   Suspends execution for a specified time.

☐ `wait`   Waits for termination of a specific or all processes that are running in the background.

☐ `nohup`   Runs a command immune to interruption from "hanging up" the terminal.

☐ `nice`   Runs a command at low (or high) priority.

☐ `kill`   Terminates named process(es).

☐ `at`   Runs commands at specified times.

☐ `batch`   Queues commands to be run when system load level permits.

☐ `cron`   Runs commands on a regularly scheduled basis.

- Actions are arbitrary shell procedures or executable programs.
- Times are conjunctions of month, day of month, day of week, hour, and minute. Ranges are specifiable for each.

☐ `crontab` Command to allow user access to the `cron`. Note: this command is available in System V, Release 2 and later releases of UNIX.

☐ tee   Passes data between processes (like a "pipe") but also diverts copies into one or more files.

☐ help   Explains error messages from certain other programs.

Information Commands

☐ man   Prints UNIX manual entries at the terminal.

☐ ls   Lists the names of one, several, or all files in one or more directories:

- Alphabetic or chronological sorting, up or down.
- Optional information: size, owner, group, date last modified, date last accessed, permissions.

☐ file   Tries to determine what kind of information is in a file by consulting the file system index and by reading the file itself.

☐ date   Print current date and time. Has considerable knowledge of calendrical and horologic peculiarities; can be used to set UNIX's idea of date and time. (As yet, cannot cope with Daylight Savings Time in the Southern Hemisphere.)

☐ df   Reports amount of free space in file system.

☐ du   Prints a summary of total space occupied by all files in a hierarchy.

☐ tty   Prints the "name" of your terminal (i.e., the name of the port to which your terminal is connected).

☐ who   Tells who is logged onto the system:

- Lists logged-in users, their ports, and time they logged in.
- Optional history of all logins and logouts.
- Tells you who you are logged in as.

☐ ps   Reports on active processes:

- Lists your own or everybody's processes.

- Tells what commands are being executed at the moment.

- Optional status information; state and scheduling information, priority, attached terminal, what the process is waiting for, its size, etc.

☐ acctcom   Reports a chronological history of all processes that have terminated. Information includes:

- User and system times and sizes.

- Start and end real times.

- Owner and terminal line associated with process.

- System exit status.

☐ pwd   Prints name of your working (i.e., current) directory.

Interuser Communication

☐ mailx   Mails a message to one or more users. Also used to read and dispose of incoming mail. The presence of mail is announced by login.

☐ news   Prints out current general information and announcement files.

☐ calendar An automaic reminder service.

☐ write   Establishes direct, interactive terminal-to-terminal communication with another user.

☐ wall   Broadcasts a message to all users who are logged in.

☐ mesg   Inhibits or permits receipt of messages from write and wall.

Intermachine Communication

☐ uucp   Sends files back and forth between UNIX machines.

☐ send   Collects files together to be sent as a "job" to an IBM host.

☐ cu   Dials a phone number and attempts to make an interactive connection with another machine.

☐ ct   Dials the phone number of a modem that is attached to a terminal and spawns a `login` process to that terminal.

☐ RFS   Remote File Sharing. A software package for sharing files and resources across a network. It allows users transparent access to remote resources. Standard with System V, Release 3.

☐ NFS   Network File System. A software package for sharing files across a network. It allows users transparent access to remote files. Standard with most Berkeley and many System V, Release 3 UNIX systems.

Program Development Package

A kit of fundamental programming tools. Some of these are used as integral parts of the higher-level languages described in the next section.

☐ ar   Maintains library archives, especially useful with `ld`. Combines several files into one for housekeeping efficiency:

- Creates new archive.
- Updates archive by date.
- Replaces or deletes files.
- Prints table of contents.
- Retrieves from archive.

☐ Libraries Basic run-time libraries. They are used freely by all system software:

- Number conversions.
- Time conversions.
- Mathematical functions: *sin, cos, log, exp, atan, sqrt, gamma.*
- Random number generator.
- An elaborate library for formatted I/O.
- Password encryption.

☐ sdb   Symbolic debugger for C and FORTRAN 77 programs:

- Interactive debugging of C code.
- Knows sbout structures and arrays.
- Postmortem dumping.

- Examination of arbitrary files, with no limit on size.
- Interactive breakpoint debugging; the debugger is a separate process.
- Stack trace for C programs.
- Output formats: 1-, 2-, or 4-byte integers in octal, decimal, or hex single and double floating point character and string disassembled machine instructions.
- Patching.
- Searching for integer, character, or floating patterns.

☐ ctrace C program debugger. `ctrace` prints a statement by statement trace of the execution of a C program. Note: this program is available with System V, Release 2 and later releases of UNIX.

☐ od Dumps any file:

- Output options include: octal or decimal by words, octal by bytes, ASCII, operation codes, hexadecimal, or any combination thereof.
- Range of dumping is controllable.

☐ ld Linkage editor. Combines relocatable object files. Inserts required routines from specified libraries; resulting code:

- Can be made sharable.
- Can be made to have separate instruction and data spaces.

☐ nm Prints the *namelist* (symbol table) of an object program. Provides control over the style and order of names that are printed.

☐ size Reports the main memory requirements of one or more object files.

☐ strip Removes the relocation and symbol table information from an object file to save file space.

☐ prof Constructs a profile of time spent in each routine from data gathered by time-sampling the execution of a program; gives subroutine call frequencies and average times for C programs.

☐ make Controls creation of large programs. Uses a control file specifying source file dependencies to make new version; uses time last changed to deduce minimum amount of work necessary. Knows about SCCS, `cc`, `yacc`, `lex`, etc.

Utilities

☐ cxref   Makes cross-reference listings of a set of C source files. The listing contains all symbols in each file seperately or, optionally, in combination. An asterisk appears before a symbol's declaration.

☐ sort   Merges and/or sorts ASCII files line-by-line:

- In ascending or descending order.
- Lexicographically or on numeric key.
- On multiple keys located by delimiters or by position.
- Can fold upper-case characters together with lower-case into dictionary order.

☐ uniq   Deletes successive duplicate lines in a file:

- Prints lines that were originally unique, duplicated, or both.
- Can give redundancy count for each line.

☐ tr   Does character translation according to an arbitrary code:

- Can "squeeze out" repetitions of selected characters.
- Can delete selected characters.

☐ diff   Reports line changes, additions, and deletions necessary to bring two files into agreement; can produce an editor script to convert one file into another.

☐ comm   Identifies common lines in two sorted files. Output in up to three columns shows lines present in first file only, present in second file only, and/or present in both.

☐ cmp   Compares two files and reports disagreeing bytes.

☐ grep   Prints all lines in one or more files that match a pattern of the kind used by ed (the editor):

- Can print all lines that fail to match.
- Can print count of "hits."

☐ wc   Counts lines and "words" (strings separated by blanks or tab characters) in a file.

☐ time   Runs a command and reports timing information about it.

♦ Programing Languages ♦

The Programming Language C

☐ cc   Compiles and/or link-edits programs in the C language. The UNIX operating system, almost all of its subsystems, and C itself are written in C:

- General-purpose language designed for structured programming.

- Data types:
  - character
  - short
  - integer
  - long integer
  - floating point
  - double
  - pointers to all types
  - functions returning all types
  - arrays of any type
  - structures containing various types

- Provides machine-independent control of all machine facilities, including to-memory operations and pointer arithmetic.

- Macro-preprocessor for parameterized code and for the inclusion of other files.

- All procedures recursive, with parameters passed by value.

- Run-time library gives access to all system facilities .

☐ pcc   Portable version of cc for a variety of computers.

☐ cb   C beautifier: gives a C program that well-groomed, structured, indented look.

FORTRAN

☐ f77   A full compiler for ANSI Standard FORTRAN 77:

- Compatible with C and supporting tools at object level.

- Optional source compatibility with FORTRAN 66.

- Free format source.

- Optional subscript-range checking, detection of uninitialized variables.

- All widths of arithmetic: 2- and 4-byte integer; 4- and 8-byte real; 8- and 16-byte complex.

Other Algorithmic Languages

☐ awk   Pattern scanning and processing language. Searches input for patterns and performs actions on each line of input that satisfies the pattern:

- Patterns include regular expressions, arithmetic and lexicographic conditions, Boolean combinations, and ranges of these.

- Data treated as string or numeric as appropriate.

- Can break input into fields; fields are variables.

- Variables and arrays (with nonnumeric subscripts).

- Full set of arithmetic operators and control flow.

- Multiple output streams to files and pipes.

- Output can be formatted as desired.

- Multiline capabilities.

☐ dc   Interactive programmable desk calculator. Has named storage locations, as well as conventional stack for holding integers and programs:

- Arbitrary-precision decimal arithmetic.

- Appropriate treatment of decimal fractions.

- Arbitrary input and output radices, in particular binary, octal, decimal, and hexadecimal.

- Postfix ("Reverse Polish") operators: +, -, *, /, remainder, power, square root, load, store, duplicate, clear print, enter program text, execute.

☐ bc   A C-like interactive interface to the desk calculator dc:

- All the capabilities of dc with a high-level syntax.

- Arrays and recursive functions.

- Immediate evaluation of expressions and evaluation of functions upon call.

- Arbitrary-precision elementary functions: *exp, sin, cos, atan*.

Macro-Processors and Compiler-Compilers

☐ m4   A general-purpose macro-processor:

- Stream oriented, recognizes macros anywhere in text.

- Integer arithmetic.

- String and substring capabilities.

- Condition testing, file manipulation, arguments.

☐ cpp   The C language preprocessor. cpp has the same features as the m4 macro-processor above.

☐ yacc   An LALR(1)-based compiler-writing system. During execution of resulting parsers, arbitrary C functions can be called to do code generation or take semantic actions:

- BNF syntax specifications.

- Precedence relations.

- Accepts formally ambiguous grammars with BNF resolution rules.

☐ lex   lex helps write programs whose control flow is directed by instances of regular expressions in the input stream. It is well suited for editor-script type transformations and for segmented input in preparation for a parsing routine.

◆ Text Processing ◆

DOCUMENTER'S WORKBENCH

Note: As of UNIX System V, Release 2, the programs described in this section are not supplied with the standard distribution of the UNIX system; they are now available in a separate software package known as the DOCUMENTER'S WORKBENCH.

High-level formatting macros have been developed to ease the preperation of documents with `nroff` and `troff`, as well as to exploit their more complex formating capabilities.

☐ `nroff`   Advanced formatter for terminals. Capable of many elaborate feats:

- Justification of either or both margins.

- Automatic hyphenation.

- Generalized page headers and footers, automatic page numbering, with even-odd page differentiation capability, etc.

- Hanging indents and one-line indents.

- Absolute and relative parameter settings.

- Optional legal-style numbering of output lines.

- Nested or chained input files.

- Complete page format control, keyed to dynamically planted "traps" at specified lines.

- Several separately definable formatting environments (e.g., one for regular text, one for footnotes, and one for"floating" tables and displays).

- Macros with substitutable arguments.

- Conditional execution of macros.

- Conditional insertion or deletion of text.

- String variables that can be invoked in midline.

- Computation and printing of numerical quantities.

- String-width computations for unusually difficult layout problems

- Positions and distances expressible in inches, centimeters, ems, ens, line spaces, points, picas, machine units, and arithmetic combinations thereof.

- Dynamic (relative or absolute) positioning.

- Horizontal and vertical line drawing.

- Multicolumn output on terminals capable of reverse line-feed or through the post processor `col`.

☐ `troff`   This formatter generates output for a phototypesetter or other suitable graphics device. Its output is independent of the final printing device. Postprocessors are available to translate the `troff` output into a stream of device-specific codes that produce the correct representation. Devices presently supported by postprocessors are the Autologic APS-5 phototypesetter (`daps`), the Imagen Imprint-10 laser printer (`di10`), and the Tektronix 4014 graphics terminal (`tc`). The old version of `troff`, renamed `otroff`, produces output for the Wang CAT phototypesetter.

`troff` provides facilities that are upward-compatible with `nroff`, but with the following additions:

- Unlimited vocabulary of fonts (any ten simultaneously) in up to 100 different point sizes.

- Character-width and string-width computations for unusually difficult layout problems.

- Overstrikes and built-up brackets.

- Dynamic (relative or absolute) point size selection, globally or at the character level.

- Terminal output for rough sampling of the product.

This entire book was typeset by `troff`, *assisted by* `tbl`, `eqn` *and MacDraw.*

☐ `pic`   A `troff` preprocessor for drawing pictures. Translates in-line pictures from a simple language into phototypesetter commands. The basic objects are box, line, arrow, circle, ellipse, arc, spline, and text. For example:

```
.PS
circle"book"
arrow
box"pic"
arrow
box"troff"
arrow
ellipse"typesetter"
.PE
```

produces

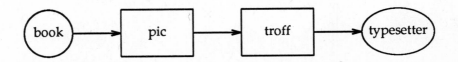

□ grap   A `pic` preprocessor for drawing charts and graphs. Translates in-
                line graphs and data points from a simple language into pic draw-
                ing commands. Basic commands exist to add labels, tick marks,
                define alternate coordinates and transformations, and include data
                from files. For example:

```
.G1
label bottom "Year"
label left "Units" "(Thousands)"
1988  10
1989  20
1990  30
1991  45
1992  48
.G2
```

produces

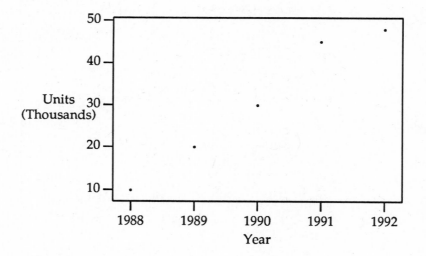

□ cip   An interactive drawing system for the AT&T TELETYPE® 630 ter-
                minal. The output of `cip` is compatible with the input to `pic`,
                allowing pictures to be created by `cip` and later incorporated into
                documents processed by `troff`. Note: `cip` is *not* part of the
                DOCUMENTER'S WORKBENCH; it is part of a software package
                distributed by AT&T for the AT&T Teletype 630 terminal.

□ eqn   A mathematical preprocessor for `troff`. Translates in-line or displayed formulae from a very east-to-type form into detailed typesetting instructions. For example:

```
.EQ
sigma sup 2 = 1 over N sum from j=1 to N ( x sub j - x bar ) sup 2
.EN
```

produces:

$$\sigma^2 = \frac{1}{N} \sum_{j=1}^{N} (x_j - \overline{x})^2$$

- Automatic calculation of point size changes for subscripts, superscripts, sub-subscripts, etc.
- Full vocabulary of Greek letters.
- Automatic calculation of the size of large brackets.
- Vertical "piling" of formulae for matrices, conditional alternatives, etc.
- Integrals, sums, etc., with arbitrarily complex limits.
- Diacriticals: dots, double dots, hats, bars, etc.
- Easily learned by nonprogrammers and mathematical typists.
- Formulae can appear within tables to be formatted by `tbl` (see below).

□ neqn   A mathematical preprocessor for `nroff` with the same facilities as `eqn`, except for the limitations imposed by the graphic capabilities of the terminal being used. Prepares formulae for display on various Diablo-mechanism terminals, etc.

□ MM   A standardized manuscript layout macro package for use with `nroff` and `troff`. Provides a flexible, user-oriented intreface to these two formatters; designed to be:

- Robust in face of user errors.
- Adaptable to a wide range of output styles.
- Can be extended by users familiar with the formatter.

- Compatible with both `nroff` and `troff`. Some of its features are:
- Page numbers and draft dates.
- Cover sheets and title pages.
- Automatically numbered or "lettered" headings.
- Automatically numbered or "lettered" lists.
- Automatically numbered figure and table captions.
- Automatically numbered and positioned footnotes.
- Single- or double-column text.
- Paragraphing, displays, and indentation.
- Automatic table of contents.

□ MV   A `troff` macro package that makes it easy to typeset professional-looking projection foils and slides.

□ tbl   A preprocessor for `nroff` and `troff` that translates simple descriptions of table layouts and contents into detailed formatting instructions:

- Computes appropriate column widths.
- Handles left- and right-justified columns, centered columns, and decimal-point aligned columns.
- Places column titles; spans these titles, as appropriate. For example:

```
.TS
center doublebox;
cfB s s s.
Composition of Foods
_
.T&
cfI || cfI s s
c || c s s
c || c | c | c.
Food Percent by Weight
    _
    Protein    Fat Carbo-
          hydrate
=
.T&
```

```
1 || n | n | n.
Apples      .4 .5 13.0
Halibut    18.4  5.2    ...
Lima beans 7.5    .8 22.0
Milk        3.3   4.0   5.0
Mushrooms   3.5   .4 6.0
Rye bread   9.0   .6 52.7
.TE
```

produces:

Composition of Foods			
Food	*Percent by Weight*		
	Protein	Fat	Carbo-hydrate
Apples	.4	.5	13.0
Halibut	18.4	5.2	...
Lima beans	7.5	.8	22.0
Milk	3.3	4.0	5.0
Mushrooms	3.5	.4	6.0
Rye bread	9.0	.6	52.7

Other Text-Processing Tools

☐ spell Finds spelling errors by looking up all words from a document in a large spelling list. Knows about prefixes and suffixes and can cope with such rotten spellings as "roted."

☐ ptx Generates a permuted index, like the one in the *UNIX System User's Manual.*

☐ graph Given the coordinates of the points to be plotted, draws the corresponding graph; has many options for scaling, axes, grids, labeling, etc.

☐ tplot Makes the output of graph suitable for plotting on a Diablo-mechanism terminal.

☐ 300,450 Exploits the hardware facilities of GSI 300, DASI 450, and other Diablo-mechanism terminals:

- Implements reverse line-feeds and forward and reverse fractional-line motions.

- Allows any combination of 10- or 12-pitch printing with 6 or 8 lines/inch spacing.

- Approximates Greek letters and other special characters by overstriking in plot mode.

☐ hp   Like 300, but for the Hewlett-Packard 2640 family of terminals.

☐ col   Reformats files with reverse line-feeds so that they can be correctly printed on terminals that cannot reverse line-feed.

◆ System Administration ◆

Normal Day-to-Day Administration and Maintenance

☐ sysadm Menu-based administration program for installing software, adding and removing users, backing up and restoring files, managing disks and file systems, and setting up the system.

☐ mount   Attaches a device containing a file system to the tree of directories. Protects against nonsense arrangements.

☐ umount Removes the file system contained on a device from the tree of directories. Protects against removing a busy device.

☐ mkfs   Makes a new file system on a device.

☐ mknod   Makes a file system entry for a special file. Specail files are physical devices, virtual devices, physical memory, etc.

☐ volcopy File system backup/recovery system for disk/disk or disk/tape. Protective labeling of disks and apes is included.

☐ dcopy   Produces copy of file systems reorganized for optimal access time.

☐ fsck   Used to check the consistency of file sysems and directories and make interactive repairs:

- Print statistics: number of files, space used, free space.

- Report duplicate use of space.

- Retrieve lost space.

- Report inaccessible files.

- Check consistency of directories.

- Reorganize free disk space for maximum operating efficiency.

☐ `sync`   Forces all outstanding I/O on the system to completion. Used to shut down the system gracefully.

☐ `config`   Tailors device-dependent system code to a specific hardware configuration. As distributed, UNIX can be brought up directly on any supported computer equipped with an acceptable tape drive and disk, sufficient amount of main memory, a console terminal, and a clock.

☐ `crash`   Prints out tables and structures in the operating system. May be used on a running system, but more useful for examining operating system core dumps after a "crash."

System Monitoring Facilities

☐ Accounting

The process accounting package covers connect time accounting, command usage, command frequency, disk utilization, and line usage. All of these are summarized by user and by command on a daily, monthly, and fiscal basis. The system lends itself to local needs and modification.

☐ Error Logging

The Unix operating system incorporates continuous hardware error detection and reporting.

☐ System Activity Report

The System Activity Report (SAR) package is a body of programs for sampling the behavior of the operating system. The sampling consists of several time counters, I/O activity counters, context-switching counters, system-call counters, and file-access counters. Reports can be generated on a daily basis or as desired.

☐ Profiler

The Profiler is another group of commands for studying the activity of the operating system. It reports the percentage of time that the operating system spends on user tasks, on system functions, and in being idle.

Complete Command Summary

All of the following commands are available on UNIX System V, Release 3. All commands marked with DWB are part of the DOCUMENTER'S WORKBENCH and are not distributed with System V, Release 3 (although old versions of these commands are distributed with System V); DWB is usually available from UNIX vendors as an add-on package. Commands in the last section of this appendix (Berkeley UNIX Commands) are distributed by the University of California, Berkeley, and are available on many versions of System V.

◆ Directory Commands ◆

cd	change working directory
chgrp	change group of a file or directory
chmod	change mode of a file or directoy
chown	change owner of a file or a directory
cpio	copy directory structures in and out
dircmp	compare directory contents
du	summarize disk usage
find	walk a directory tree
ls	list contents of directories
mkdir	make directory
pwd	working directory name
rm	remove files
rmdir	remove directory
tar	tape archiver for directory structures

◆ File Commands ◆

cat	concatenate and print files
chgrp	change group of a file or directory
chmod	change mode of a file or directoy
chown	change owner of a file or a directory
cp	copy files
csplit	context split
cut	cut out selected columns from each line of a file
dd	convert and copy a file between ASCII and EBCDIC
egrep	search a file for a pattern (variant of grep)
fgrep	search a file for a pattern (variant of grep)
file	determine file type
find	walk a directory tree
fsplit	split f77, ratfor, or efl files
grep	search a file for a pattern
hpio	HP 2645A terminal tape file archiver
join	relational database operator
ln	link files
ls	list contents of directories
mv	move files
newform	change the format of a text file
nl	line numbering filter
od	dump file in octal, decimal, or hexadecimal
pack	compress files
paste	merge same lines of several files or subsequent lines of one file
pcat	print files compressed with pack
pg	file scanning program for screen terminals
pr	format files for line printer listings
rm	remove files
split	split a file into pieces
sum	print checksum and block count of a file
tail	print the last part of a file
touch	update access and modification times of a file
tr	translate characters
umask	set file-creation permissions mask
uniq	report repeated lines in a file
unpack	expand file compressed with pack

◆ Editors ◆

bfs	big file scanner
ed	text editor
edit	Berkeley text editor for casual users

`ex`	Berkeley text editor (superset of `ed`)
`red`	restricted version of `ed`
`sed`	noninteractive stream editor
`vi`	Berkeley screen editor

◆ File Comparison ◆

`bdiff`	`diff` for big files
`cmp`	compare two files
`comm`	select or reject lines common to two sorted files
`dd`	convert and copy a file between ASCII and EBCDIC
`diff`	print differences between files
`diff3`	three file `diff`
`diffmk`	`diff` preprocessor for `nroff`/`troff` (DWB)
`dircmp`	compare directory contents
`sccsdiff`	compare two versions of an SCCS file
`sdiff`	side-by-side `diff`
`uniq`	report repeated lines in a file

◆ Information, Please ◆

`acctcom`	search and print process accounting file(s)
`date`	print or set the date
`du`	summarize disk usage
`glossary`	give definitions of common UNIX terms and commands
`help`	give information on common UNIX terms and commands
`id`	print user and group id's and names
`locate`	identify UNIX command using keywords
`logname`	print login name
`ls`	list contents of directories
`man`	print entries in the *UNIX System User's Manual*
`mesg`	permit or deny `writes` to your terminal
`news`	print news items
`ps`	report process status
`pwd`	working directory name
`sag`	system activity graph
`sar`	system activity reporter
`starter`	give information on UNIX for beginning users
`stty`	set the options for a terminal
`time`	time execution of a command

`timex`	better version of `time`
`tty`	get the terminal's name in `/dev`
`uname`	print UNIX system name
`usage`	give usage information for UNIX commands
`uulog`	print log of `uucp` actions
`uuname`	print names of remote systems known to `uucp`
`uustat`	`uucp` status inquiry and job control
`who`	print who is on the system

♦ Shell Programming ♦

`basename`	extract file name from path
`cut`	cut out selected columns from each line of a file
`dirname`	exract directory name path
`echo`	print arguments
`egrep`	search a file for a pattern (variant of `grep`)
`env`	set environment for command execution
`expr`	evaluate arguments as an expression
`false`	provide false value
`fgrep`	search a file for a pattern (variant of `grep`)
`getopt`	parse command options
`getopts`	parse command options
`grep`	search a file for a pattern
`line`	read one line
`logname`	print login name
`paste`	merge same lines of several files or subsequent lines of one file
`rsh`	restricted shell
`sed`	noninteractive stream editor
`sh`	shell, the standard command interpreter
`shl`	shell layer manager
`sleep`	suspend execution for an interval
`sort`	sort and/or merge files
`tail`	print the last part of a file
`tee`	send intermediae pipeline output to file
`test`	condition evaluation for shell programs
`tr`	translate characters
`true`	provide truth value
`wait`	await completion of process
`wc`	character, word, and line count
`xargs`	construct argument list(s) and execute command

◆ Office Automation ◆

`bc`	arbitrary-precision arithmetic language
`cal`	print calendar
`calendar`	reminder service
`date`	print or set the date
`dc`	desk calculator
`mail`	send mail to users or read mail
`mailx`	Berkeley version of `mail`
`mesg`	permit or deny `writes` to your terminal
`rmail`	restricted version of `mail`
`sort`	sort and/or merge files
`spell`	find spelling errors
`units`	conversion program for weights and measures
`write`	write to another user

Text Processing

`checkmm`	checks documents for proper use of MM macros (DWB)
`col`	filter reverse line-feeds
`daps`	postprocessor for Autologic APS-5 phototypesetter (DWB)
`deroff`	remove `nroff/troff`, `tbl`, and `eqn` constructs (DWB)
`di10`	postprocessor for Imagen Imprint-10 laser printer (DWB)
`diffmk`	`diff` preprocessor for `nroff/troff` (DWB)
`eqn`	format mathematical text for `troff` (DWB)
`grap`	`pic` preprocessor for drawing graphs
`greek`	terminal filter for `nroff`
`hp`	handle special `nroff` functions for Hewlett-Packard terminals
`hyphen`	find hyphenated words (DWB)
`macref`	print cross-reference listing of macro files (DWB)
`man`	print entries in the *UNIX User's Manual*
`mm`	print/check documents formatted with the MM macros (DWB)
`mmt`	typeset documents (DWB)
`mvt`	typeset view graphs and slides (DWB)
`ndx`	create a subject-page index for a document
`neqn`	format mathematical text for `nroff` (DWB)
`nroff`	text formatter (DWB)
`pic`	figure drawing preprocessor for `troff` (DWB)
`ptx`	permuted index generator for `nroff/troff`
`subj`	generate a list of subjects from a document
`tbl`	format tables for `nroff/troff` (DWB)
`tc`	`troff` terminal filter for Tekronix 4014 terminal(DWB)
`troff`	text formatting for phototypesetters (DWB)

◆ Program Development ◆

Programming Languages

cpp	the C language preprocessor
as	assembler
awk	pattern scanning and processing language
bc	arbitrary-precision arithmetic language
cc	C compiler
f77	FORTRAN 77 compiler
lex	generate programs for simple lexical tasks
m4	macro processor
yacc	yet another compiler-compiler

Program Development Tools

machid[†]	provide truth value about your processor type
ar	archive and library maintainer for portable archives
cb	C program beautifier
ccoff	convert a COFF file to local format
cflow	generate C flow graph
conv	convert archive and object files to different machine formats
convert	convert archive files to common formats
cprs	compress object file
ctrace	C program debugger
cxref	generate C program cross-reference
dis	disassembler
dump	dump selected parts of an object file
fsplit	split f77 files
gencc	create front-end to the cc command
ld	link editor
lint	a C program checker
list	produce C source listing from object file
lorder	print ordering relation for an object library
make	maintain, update, and regenerate groups of programs
mcs	manipulate comment section of an object file
mkshlib	create a shared library
nm	print name list
omf	convert AT&T common object file format to Xenix object format module
prof	display profile data for C programs

---

† The commands distributed with the standard AT&T release of the UNIX system are i286, i386, pdp11, u3b, u3b2, u3b5,, and vax. They provide true or false values depending upon which machine you're using. If you're using a machine other than the seven above, your system may provide a similar command (e.g., sun or hp).

regcmp	regular expression compile
sdb	symbolic debugger
size	print sizes of object files
strip	strip symbol table and relocation bits from object module
tsort	topological sort for use with `lorder` in creating object libraries

SCCS

admin	create and administer SCCS files
cdc	change the delta commentary of an SCCS delta
comb	combine SCCS deltas
dd	convert and copy a file between ASCII and EBCDIC
delta	make a delta (change) o an SCCS file
get	get a version of an SCCS file
help	ask for help
prs	print an SCCS file
rmdel	remove a delta from an SCCS file
sact	print current SCCS file editing activity
sccsdiff	compare two versions of an SCCS file
unget	undo a previous get of an SCCS file
val	validate SCCS file
vc	control version of SCCS file
what	identify SCCS files

♦ Security ♦

chgrp	change group of a file or directory
chmod	change mode of a file or directory
chown	change owner of a file or directory
crypt	encrypt/decrypt files
id	print user and group id's and names
makekey	generate encryption key
newgrp	change to a new group
passwd	change password
red	restricted version of ed
rsh	restricted shell
su	become super-user or another user
umask	set file-creation permissions mask

◆ Communications ◆

ct	spawn getty to a remote terminal
cu	call another UNIX system
uucp	UNIX-to-UNIX copy
uulog	print log of uucp actions
uuname	print names of remote systems known to uucp
uupick	get files from /usr/spool/uucpublic
uustat	uucp status inquiry and job control
uuto	public UNIX-to-UNIX file copy
uux	UNIX-to-UNIX remote command execution

◆ Process Control ◆

at	execute commands at a later time
batch	execute commands when system load is low
crontab	user access to cron
kill	terminate a process
nice	run a command at low priority
nohup	run a command immune to hangups and quits
ps	report process status

◆ Graphics ◆

gdev†	graphical device routines and filters
gutil†	graphical utilities
stat†	statistical commands useful with graphical commands
toc†	graphical table of contents routines
ged	graphical editor for TEKTRONIX 401X series terminals
graph	draw a graph
graphics	access graphical and numerical commands
spline	interpolate smooth curve
tplot	graphics filters for printing terminals

† These commands are too numerous to mention. Refer to the *UNIX System User's Manual* for more information.

♦ Line Printer Commands ♦

`asa`	interpret ASA carraige control characters
`cancel`	cancel request to an LP line printer
`disable`	disable LP printers
`enable`	enable LP printers
`lp`	send request to an LP line printer
`lpstat`	print LP status information
`nl`	line numbering filter
`pr`	format files for line printer listings

♦ Terminal Commands ♦

`300`	handle special functions of DASI 300 terminal
`300s`	handle special functions of DASI 300s terminal
`4014`	paginator for the Tektronix 4014 terminal
`450`	handle special functions of the DASI 450 terminal
`col`	filter reverse line-feeds
`ged`	graphical editor for Tektronix 401X series terminals
`greek`	terminal filter for `nroff`
`hp`	handle special `nroff` functions for Hewlett-Packard terminals
`hpio`	HP 2645A terminal tape file archiver
`pg`	file scanning program for screen terminals
`stty`	set the options for a terminal port
`tabs`	set tabs on a terminal
`tc`	`troff` terminal filter for Tektronix 4014 terminal (DWB)
`tplot`	graphics filter for printing terminals
`tput`	shell program access to `terminfo` database
`tty`	get the terminal's name in `/dev`

AT&T 5620 Support Programs

`cip`	interactive drawing program for 5620
`ismpx`	return windowing terminal state
`jterm`	reset layer of windowing terminal
`jwin`	print size of layer
`layers`	start up 5620 windowing system
`relogin`	rename login entry to show current layer
`wtinit`	download object file to 5620 terminal
`xtd`	extract and print window driver link structure
`xts`	extract and print window driver statistics
`xtt`	extract and print window packet traces

♦ Miscellaneous ♦

banner	make posters
factor	factor a number
ipcrm	remove a message queue, semaphore set, or shared memory id
ipcs	report interprocess communication facilities status
join	relational database operator
login	sign on
units	conversion program for weights and measures

♦ Berkeley UNIX Commands ♦

clear	clear terminal screen
csh	C shell
head	print first lines of a file (opposite of tail)
lf	horizontal ls
more	print files one screen at a time
see	list file showing nonprinting characters
vi[†]	Berkeley screen editor

---

† Also included in AT&T's UNIX System V as of Release 2.

Administrative Commands

All of the following commands are available on UNIX System V, Release 3.

◆ Information, Please ◆

dname	print domain and network names (RFS)
/etc/ff	list file names and statistics for a file system
/etc/fsstat	report file system status
/etc/fstyp	report file system type
fusage	report I/O usage on local and remote file systems (RFS)
/etc/fuser	identify processes using a file or file structure
/etc/whodo	see who is doing what
df	report number of free disk blocks and i-nodes
du	summarize disk usage
lpstat	print LP status information
nsquery	list available resources (RFS)
ps	report process status
rmntstat	display mounted resource information (RFS)
sar	system activity reporter
time	time execution of a command
timex	better version of time
uulog	print log of uucp actions
uustat	uucp status inquiry and job control
who	print who is on the system

◆ Startup/Shutdown ◆

/etc/bcheckrc	system initialization shell script
/etc/brc	system initialization shell script
/etc/config	configure a UNIX system
/etc/init	process control initialization
/etc/killall	kill all active processes
/etc/mount	mount file system
/etc/rc0	system shutdown shell script
/etc/rc2	system initialization shell script
/etc/setmnt	establish mount table
/etc/shutdown	shutdown system
/etc/telinit	process control initialization
/etc/umount	unmount file system
/etc/wall	write to all users
date	print or set the date
setup	initialize system for first user

◆ File Systems ◆

/etc/checkall	fast file system checking procedure
/etc/chroot	change root directory for a command
/etc/ckbupscd	check file system backup schedule
/etc/clri	clear i-node
/etc/dcopy	copy file systems for optimal access time
/etc/devnm	print file system device associated with a file
/etc/diskadd	partition disks
/etc/ff	list file names and statistics for a file system
/etc/finc	fast incremental backup
/etc/frec	recover files from a backup tape
/etc/fsck	file system consistency check
/etc/fsdb	file system debugger
/etc/fsstat	report file system status
/etc/fstyp	report file system type
/etc/fuser	identify processes using a file or file structure
/etc/labelit	label file system
/etc/link	exercise link system calls
/etc/mkfs	construct a file system
/etc/mknod	build special file
/etc/mkpart	maintain disk partitioning data
/etc/mount	mount file system
/etc/mountall	mount all file systems in /etc/fstab

/etc/mvdir	move a directory
/etc/ncheck	generate path names from i-numbers
/etc/setmnt	establish mount table
/etc/swap	manage swap areas
/etc/umount	unmount file system
/etc/umountall	unmount all file systems
/etc/unlink	exercise unlink system calls
/etc/volcopy	copy file systems with label checking
df	report number of free disk blocks and i-nodes
diskusg	same as acctdusg
du	summarize disk usage
format	format floppy disks
sadp	disk access profiler
sync	complete pending I/O on file systems
tar	tape archiver for directory structures

♦ Security ♦

/etc/grpck	/etc/group file consistency checker
/etc/pwck	/etc/passwd file consistency checker
chgrp	change group of a file or directory
chmod	change mode of a file or directory
chown	change owner of a file or directory
passwd	change password
su	become super-user or another user
umask	set file-creation permissions mask

♦ Accounting ♦

/usr/lib/acct/acctcms	summarize per-process accounting records
/usr/lib/acct/acctcon1	connect-time accounting (pass 1)
/usr/lib/acct/acctcon2	connect-time accounting (pass 2)
/usr/lib/acct/acctdisk	merge disk usage report with other accounting information
/usr/lib/acct/acctdusg	report disk usage by userid
/usr/lib/acct/acctmerg	merge accounting files
/usr/lib/acct/accton	turn per-process accounting on or off
/usr/lib/acct/acctprc1	process accounting (pass1)
/usr/lib/acct/acctprc2	process accounting (pass2)
/usr/lib/acct/acctwtmp	put comments into /etc/wtmp

`/usr/lib/acct/chargefee`	charge user for something
`/usr/lib/acct/ckpacct`	make sure `/usr/adm/pacct` doesn't get too big
`/usr/lib/acct/dodisk`	performs disk accounting functions
`/usr/lib/acct/fwtmp`	format and print connect accounting records
`/usr/lib/acct/lastlogin`	update log of last time each user logged in
`/usr/lib/acct/monacct`	run monthly accounting summary programs
`/usr/lib/acct/nulladm`	create accounting file with correct permissions
`/usr/lib/acct/prctmp`	format and print `/usr/adm/ acct/nite/ctmp` created by `acctcon1`
`/usr/lib/acct/prdaily`	format and print daily accounting reports
`/usr/lib/acct/prtacct`	format and print an accounting file in `tacct` format (produced by `acctcon2`, `acctprc2`, and `acctmerg`)
`/usr/lib/acct/runacct`	run daily accounting summary programs
`/usr/lib/acct/shutacct`	turn accounting off
`/usr/lib/acct/startup`	turn accounting on
`/usr/lib/acct/turnacct`	smart interface to `accton`
`/usr/lib/acct/wtmpfix`	check consistency of and fix connect accounting records
`acctcom`	search and print process accounting file(s)

◆ Line Printer (LP) ◆

`/etc/stprint`	synchronous terminal control for printers
`/usr/lib/accept`	allow LP requests
`/usr/lib/lpadmin`	configure the LP spooling system
`/usr/lib/lpmove`	move LP requests
`/usr/lib/lpsched`	LP scheduler
`/usr/lib/lpshut`	stop the LP request scheduler
`/usr/lib/reject`	prevent LP requests
`disable`	diasble LP printers
`enable`	enable LP printers
`lpstat`	print LP status information

◆ Networking ◆

`adv`	advertise a resource for remote access (RFS)
`dname`	print domain and network names (RFS)
`funmount`	force unmount of an advertised resource (RFS)

fusage	report I/O usage on local and remote file systems (RFS)
idload	build user and group translation tables (RFS)
nlsadmin	administrate network listener processes
nsquery	list available resources (RFS)
rfadmin	administrate remote file sharing domains (RFS)
rfpasswd	change remote file sharing host password (RFS)
rfstart	start remote file sharing (RFS)
rfstop	stop remote file sharing (RFS)
rfuadmin	handle unexpected remote file sharing events (RFS)
rfudaemon	listen for unexpected remote file sharing events (RFS)
rmntstat	display mounted resource information (RFS)
/etc/rmount	retry remote resource mounts (RFS)
/etc/rmountall	mount all remote resources (RFS)
/etc/rumountall	unmount all remote resources (RFS)
strace	print STREAMS trace messages
strclean	clean up STREAMS error logger directory
strerr	log STREAMS error messages
unadv	unadvertise a resource for remote access (RFS)
/usr/lib/uucp/uucheck	check the uucp directories and files
/usr/lib/uucp/uucico	file transfer program
/usr/lib/uucp/uucleanup	uucp spool directory cleanup
/usr/lib/uucp/uugetty	bidirectional getty for use with uucico
/usr/lib/uucp/uusched	schedule work for spooled files
/usr/lib/uucp/uusub	monitor uucp network
/usr/lib/uucp/Uutry	try to contact remote system with debugging on
/usr/lib/uucp/uuxqt	execute remote command requests
uulog	print log of uucp actions
uustat	uucp status inquiry and job control

♦ Operating System ♦

/etc/config	configure a UNIX system
/etc/crash	examine system core images
/etc/mkunix	configure and make a bootable kernel
/etc/prfdc	collect data from operating system profiler
/etc/prfpr	format data from prffdc and prfsnap
/etc/prfld	initialize operating system profiler
/etc/prfsnap	give snapshot of operating system profiler
/etc/prfstat	enable/disable operating system profiler
/etc/sysdef	extract system definition information from operating system file

`/usr/lib/sa/sa1`	variant of `sadc` for automatic data collection
`/usr/lib/sa/sa2`	variant of `sar` for automatic reporting of output from `sa1`
`/usr/lib/sa/sadc`	system activity data collection program
`sag`	system activity graph
`sar`	system activity reporter
`/etc/uadmin`	low level administrative functions

♦ Command Installation ♦

`captoinfo`	convert a `termcap` description into a `terminfo` description
`cpset`	install object files in `bin` directories
`/etc/install`	install commands

♦ Miscellaneous ♦

`/etc/config`	configure a UNIX system
`/etc/cron`	clock daemon
`/etc/getty`	set up line discipline for logging in
`helpadm`	make changes to the Help Facility data base
`infocmp`	compare or print two `terminfo` descriptions
`sysadm`	general purpose administrative program
`tic`	`terminfo` compiler
`tpfix`	pad object file
`/etc/wall`	write to all users

Index

Topics in C Programming

Stephen G. Kochan and Patrick H. Wood

Here is the most advanced and comprehensive coverage of the maturing C market. This sequel to *Programming in C* describes in detail some of the most difficult concepts in the C language—structures and pointers. It also explores the standard C library and standard I/O library, dynamic memory allocation, linked lists, tree structures, and dispatch tables.

Experienced C programmers can examine the UNIX System Interface through discussions on controlling processes, pipes, and terminal I/O. *Topics in C Programming* also explains how to write terminal-independent programs, how to debug C programs and analyze their performance, and how to use "make" for automatic generation of a programming system.

Topics covered include:

■ Structures and Pointers
■ The Standard C Library
■ The Standard I/O Library
■ UNIX System Interface
■ Writing Terminal-Independent Programs with "curses" Library
■ Debug and Performance Analysis of C Programs
■ Generating Programs with "make"

528 Pages, 7½ x 9¾, Softbound
ISBN: 0-672-46290-7
No. 46290, $24.95

UNIX Networking

Stephen Kochan & Patrick Wood, Editors

The newest title in the Hayden Books UNIX Library, this is a comprehensive overview of the major aspects of networking in the UNIX operating systems. Computer professionals and students with a basic understanding of the technical aspects of programming and networking will benefit from the contributions of these UNIX experts.

Programming considerations, system security, and the respective advantages of various networks are discussed in detail as it presents the major UNIX system architectures. Written by a team of experts on UNIX, this is an excellent source for information on any networking system for UNIX computer applications.

Topics covered include:

■ Introduction and Overview; Kochan and Wood
■ uucp (UNIX to UNIX CoPy); Brian Redman
■ TCP/IP (transmission control protocol/internet protocol); Douglas Comer
■ NFS & RPC: Lou Delzompo
■ Streams and TLI; Douglas Harris
■ RFS (a UNIX Networking Standard); Douglas Harris
■ Networking X; Adrian Nye
■ Networking NeWS; Owen Densmore
■ OS/2 to UNIX LAN: Martin Dunsmuir

600 Pages, 7½ x 9¾, Softbound
ISBN: 0-672-48440-4
No. 48440, $29.95

UNIX® Shell Programming, Revised Edition

Stephen G. Kochan & Patrick H. Wood

For non-programmers who need to use shell programming to automate computer tasks, UNIX programmers, and system administrators, this book provides a comprehensive overview of shell programming concepts.

Revised to reflect System V Release 3 changes and organized in a step-by-step fashion, the book explains how to use the shell and its functions, with numerous practical programs to illustrate the concepts.

Topics covered include:

■ A Quick Review of the Basics
■ What is the Shell?
■ Tools of the Trade–Programming Tools
■ And Away We Go–Getting Started with Commands
■ Can I Quote You on That?–Interpreting Quote Characters
■ Passing Arguments–Arguments from Command Lines
■ Decisions, Decisions–If Statements
■ 'Round and 'Round She Goes–Program Loops
■ Reading Data--The Read Command
■ Your Environment–Using Your Own Shell
■ More on Parameters
■ Loose Ends–Miscellaneous Commands and Features
■ Rolo Revisited–An Enhanced Rolo Program
■ Introducing the Korn Shell

460 Pages, 7½ x 9¾, Softbound
ISBN: 0-672-48448-4
No. 48448, $26.95

UNIX® System Security

Wood and Kochan

This practical guide to system security describes and provides programs for administrating passwords, security auditing, checking file permissions, securing terminals, DES data encryption, and setting up a restricted environment. Sources for the programs described are included.

If you're a UNIX user, administrator, or potential UNIX buyer, this excellent reference contains everything you need to know to make your system secure and keep it that way.

Topics covered include:

■ A Perspective on Security
■ Security for Users
■ Security for Administrators
■ Network Security
■ Appendices
    References, Security Commands and Functions, Permissions, Security Auditing Program, File Permission Program, Password Administration Program, Password Expiration Program, Terminal Security Program, SUID/SGID Shell Execution Program, Restricted Environment Program, DES Encryption Program, and SUID Patent

300 Pages, 7¼ x 10, Hardbound
ISBN: 0-8104-6267-2
No. 46267, $34.95

UNIX® Text Processing
Dougherty and O'Reilly

This practical, in-depth reference presents a range of useful UNIX tools that facilitate such word processing functions as format design, printing, and editing. It introduces the tools and illustrates how they can work together to create large writing projects such as technical manuals, reports, and proposals.

With the examples in this text you can put your knowledge to work immediately. It provides examples of integrating the text processing tools of the UNIX environment in document preparation. It also mentions other useful UNIX capabilities and suggests directions for future study.

Topics covered include:

■ What's in the UNIX Toolbox for Writers
■ Fundamental Concepts
■ Coding and Formatting a Document
■ Essential UNIX Commands
■ Producing Tables and Mathematical Equations
■ Shell Scripts
■ Advanced NROFF/TROFF Operations
■ Custom Macros for Document Formatting
■ Building Documentation Tools
■ Integrated UNIX

680 Pages, 7½ x 9¾, Softbound
ISBN: 0-672-46291-5
No. 46291, $26.95

Exploring the UNIX® System
Second Edition
Kochan and Wood

Updated and revised to reflect the latest changes to System V, Release 3, this is an excellent choice for the computer novice who needs a clear basic introduction to the UNIX operating system. The book covers everything needed to become operational—how operating systems work; how the UNIX file system is organized and how to identify files; how to create, copy, rename, and remove files; and much more.

Topics covered include:

■ What is an Operating System?
■ The UNIX File System
■ Getting Started
■ Using the UNIX System
■ The Old Shell Game
■ Screen Editing with vi
■ UNIX in the Office
■ Program Development
■ Security
■ Communications
■ Administrating Your System
■ Appendices: For More Information, Overview of Commands, Complete Command Summary, Administrative Commands, Comparison of sh and csh, Adding New Users

450 Pages, 7½ x 9¾, Softbound
ISBN: 0-672-48447-1
No. 48447, $26.95

UNIX® System Administration
Fiedler and Hunter

This is an essential guide for everyone who runs a UNIX operating system—UNIX owners, operators, and administrators. It contains the tricks and shortcuts to making your system run easier.

The book begins with a system overview and then proceeds through setting up file systems, adding and removing users from the system, and improving system security. Troubleshooting charts and ready-to-run programs are included.

Topics covered include:

■ The System Administrator's Overview of UNIX
■ Bringing Up the System
■ Checking the File System
■ Where Everything Is and How to Find It
■ Mounting and Unmounting File Systems
■ Shutting Down the System
■ Adding and Removing Users for the System
■ Backups
■ Security
■ Terminals
■ Printers on the UNIX System
■ Modems and an Even Bigger World
■ Shell Programming
■ Assorted Administration Tips
■ Appendices Include: Where to Learn More, Talking to the Outside World, A Typical UUCP Connection

336 Pages, 7 x 9¾, Softbound
ISBN: 0-8104-6289-3
No. 46289, $24.95

UNIX® Communications
Anderson, Costales, and Henderson, The Waite Group

For UNIX users who need to communicate with other users and other systems, this book takes up where the standard UNIX documentation leaves off, demystifying a sometimes bewildering array of programs, options, and settings. The authors show you step by step how to use, control, and program UNIX communications tools, give examples of their use, and show how they all fit together.

Whether you are a novice or expert UNIX user or programmer, you'll welcome the detailed coverage of UNIX mail, networking, and file transfer tools.

Topics covered include:

■ Review of the UNIX Operating System
■ Electronic Mail: The Basics of *mailx* and *mail*
■ Intermediate and Advanced Mail
■ Conferencing with *write* and *talk*
■ USENET, the UNIX Bulletin Board System
■ Reading and Posting News
■ Newswriting and Net Etiquette
■ Using UUCP Programs to Send Files

576 Pages, 7½ x 9¾, Softbound
ISBN: 0-672-22511-5
No. 22511, $26.95

**Visit your local book retailer or call
800-428-SAMS.**

UNIX® System V Bible
Prata and Martin, The Waite Group

You'll never have to open the UNIX manual again! This is a comprehensive reference to UNIX commands and utilities, focusing on the basic and advanced command groups found in standard UNIX System V manuals.

Commands are listed alphabetically and explained in down-to-earth language. Each entry states the purpose of a command, what it does, and how it is used. A graduated set of example programs goes far beyond the UNIX manuals, showing you each command in several different situations.

Features of this unique resource include:

■ Detailed Table of Contents for Quick Reference
■ Cross-Referencing of Commands and Features
■ Friendly Format for Beginning and Advanced Users
■ Coverage of All Major UNIX Features
■ Guidance to UNIX Command Idiosyncracies

528 Pages, 7½ x 9¾, Softbound
ISBN: 0-672-22562-X
No. 22562, $24.95

Inside XENIX®
Christopher L. Morgan, The Waite Group

Written for programmers, students, and administrators, *Inside XENIX* presents the bit level of XENIX, while teaching the major issues that must be understood to write first-rate programs, drivers, and filters. Using a course level approach and 62 illustrations, the book provides programmers with a systematic study of the XENIX kernel and operating system.

The heart of XENIX, the kernel, is explored in detail and a terminal device driver is created. The reader will see how to bring up XENIX with different devices, from printers to LANs, receiver interrupts, blocking, flushing, and how to compile and test a new custom kernel.

Topics covered include:

■ Organization of XENIX
■ Programming Tools in XENIX
■ Filters
■ System Variables
■ Screen and Keyboard
■ Files and Directories
■ Process, Control
■ Device Drivers
■ Advanced Tools for Programmers

336 Pages, 7½ x 9¾, Softbound
ISBN: 0-672-22445-3
No. 22445, $24.95

Advanced UNIX® —A Programmer's Guide
Stephen Prata, The Waite Group

This advanced guidebook goes beyond the basics of UNIX and spells out the details of the system's key components and various programming mechanisms. It shows how to use simple and complex commands, including the Bourne shell, shell scripts, loops, and system calls; how to create UNIX graphics; how to allocate and structure data in memory; and how to maximize the C-UNIX interface.

Topics covered include:

■ UNIX Overview
■ Problem-Solving Approaches in UNIX
■ Working with the Bourne Shell
■ Shell Scripts: Looping and Making Choices
■ Shell Script Examples
■ System Calls and the C Library
■ The UNIX-C Interface
■ Working with UNIX C Files and Graphics
■ UNIX Program Development: cc, make, and Applications
■ Appendices: UNIX Tools, A Survey of the C Shell, Binary Numbers and Others, ASCII Table, UNIX System Calls, UNIX Library Functions (System V)

496 Pages, 7½ x 9¾, Softbound
ISBN: 0-672-22403-8
No. 22403, $24.95

**Visit your local book retailer or call
800-428-SAMS.**